NEW TECHNIQUES FOR
CHURCH FUND RAISING

NEW TECHNIQUES FOR CHURCH FUND RAISING

A Ten-step Plan to Increase Your Pledges and Strengthen Your Church

OTHNIEL A. PENDLETON, Jr.

Foreword by the Rt. Rev. W. Appleton Lawrence
Bishop of the Diocese of Western Massachusetts
The Protestant Episcopal Church

1955

McGRAW-HILL BOOK COMPANY, INC.

New York   Toronto   London

THE MAPLE PRESS COMPANY, YORK, PA.

To FLORDORA,
Mother of five,
Missionary at heart,
Fund raiser in her own right,
Whose meticulous concern
Has made possible this book.

O God, of whose bounties we have so freely received,
  make us finely aware and richly responsible.
Save us from growing a protective shell about ourselves
  or allowing our hearts to harden and our sympathies to contract.
Remind us that Christianity teaches us to care,
  that caring is the greatest thing,
  that caring matters most.
Because we love much constrain us to give much. Amen.

Robert J. McCracken
THE RIVERSIDE CHURCH
NEW YORK

FOREWORD

"**If you really mean business,** make your call person-to-person." "Niel" Pendleton puts this slogan of the Telephone Company to work for the glory of God rather than for the profit of man.

There is no magic to raising money, but there are some methods that work with a higher average of successful results than others because they follow the known laws of human behavior. No method is "sure fire"—but out of many years of wide experience, "Niel" Pendleton has here set forth a technique (which he and many others have helped to develop) that works with amazingly uniform success.

Thirty-one churches in the Diocese of Western Massachusetts have followed the plan outlined in this book and have increased their pledging from $248,168 to $405,060, an average increase of 63 per cent.

In this book "Niel" Pendleton records the results of his experience. He gives you facts as to what has actually happened, tells you simply what others have done, and reminds you that what others have done, you, too, can do.

Then, with remarkable clarity he tells you, step by step, how you can do it. There are no secrets to the process—except that you cannot jump any of the steps and expect to get the desired results. You have to begin at the beginning and follow through to the end. But if you do this, you will find that you have not only raised a sum of money well above any figure you have previously raised, but you will also have raised the vision of the people. By making them set up a "dream budget," you will have enlisted the interest of a large number of parishioners previously on the fringe. By enlisting their help and making them participants in the plan, they will naturally give more willingly and more generously. You will also have deepened their faith, by proving to them that where God guides, He will also provide. And finally, you will have lifted the whole spiritual temperature of the people and parish by changing their attitude toward giving from a painful experience into a satisfying and responsible sense of stewardship.

The plan that is set forth takes giving out of the "hit-or-miss" category, where the amount of the gift is apt to be dependent upon our temporary financial situation or our current bank balance, into the area where we come to know that our giving is perhaps the most accurate visible reflection of the measure of our faith. Too many of us are content to "play" at Christianity. We relate our giving to what we have been giving previously, rather than on the basis of our capacity to give. This plan will help you and many others to reevaluate not only the program and purpose of your Church but also the meaning and purpose of your life.

In this book you will find another of those paradoxes so common in the Christian life. You will start out to raise more money to strengthen your Church, but if you will follow the plan through from beginning to end, you will find that, in the process of raising more money, what you have really done is to strengthen your faith.

W. APPLETON LAWRENCE
Bishop of the
Diocese of Western Massachusetts

PREFACE

Within these pages will be found a new plan to raise greater funds for your church. The plan, new to churches in current budget raising, has been proved for many years by use in capital-fund campaigns for hospitals, colleges, and churches. This system, originally developed by the YMCA and since refined by the great fund-raising organizations of America, has now been adapted for Every Member Canvasses in churches everywhere. Detailed know-how for the ten essential steps is presented, illustrated with scores of case histories. The names of over one thousand churches which have proved the worth of this program are listed. Here is human interest with inspiration. The plan, having worked in so many churches, because it seeks to glorify Jesus Christ, will, if you desire it, work in your church.

This is a workbook, designed to be used. Many of the forms will be mimeographed. Check lists and calendars will be marked. The pages of the Canvass Kit, at the end of the book, are to be torn out and used according to directions. Only as this book is so used does it bring the greatest returns.

This manual is planned to answer the need of four groups: the church which, working alone, is searching for a workbook containing all the helps needed for a successful effort; a council of churches which desires to go beyond the United Church Canvass; a denomination which is seeking a manual to aid its churches in a greater stewardship emphasis; theological schools looking for a text in the field of church financing.

O. A. PENDLETON

ACKNOWLEDGMENTS

It would be impossible for a book such as this to be the work of one person. What is here presented is the result of many years of thinking and experimentation by pioneer and contemporary fund raisers in America, to which has been added the experience of hundreds of churches.

I am indebted to the Field Counseling staff, past and present, of the Council on Missionary Cooperation, American Baptist Convention, for their sharing of ideas, supplying of information, and fellowship of "kindred minds"—Norman Booth, M. E. Bratcher, Arthur L. Farrell, Richard J. Hanson, William E. Hayler, Marple M. Lewis, Herbert E. MacCombie, Clifford P. MacDonald, Roy I. Madsen, Charles R. Osborn, J. Russell Raker, John A. Ramsay, Frank Robeson, Paul Shelford, Richard W. Sorenson, John Roy Wolfe, and Miss Grace E. Abrahams.

Dr. Ralph M. Johnson, the General Director of the Council, has given valuable counsel. He has been more than generous in his willingness to supply information and help.

Loyde Aukerman's contribution has been outstanding. Jack Krause brought a layman's approach to a minister's problem. His enthusiastic selling did much to commit the American Baptists to the program out of which this book arose. Isaac Higginbotham's support made possible the first sector project in Boston. Newton E. Woodbury has been a good teammate in presenting these plans to church gatherings. Kenneth L. Cober was one of the first to see the adaptability of this program to the United Church Canvass.

To Dr. Luther Wesley Smith goes great credit for his vision and his courageous enthusiasm. George Moll has urged me on in many quiet ways.

Several have served as readers of this manuscript. Dr. Everett C. Herrick, Louis W. Robey, Rev. H. Campbell Eatough, and Rev. Otto E. Loverude have given welcome advice and correction. Ernest Cushing was tireless in his detailed criticism and suggestions. He will recognize many of his ideas. To Mrs. Miriam Faulcon Phillips, my former secretary, I owe much.

The staff members of Marts and Lundy, Inc., have been gracious and liberal in giving help through several years. I especially think of James H. Duchine, Harold C. Dudley, Charles A. Herschleb, and Austin V. McClain. For the privilege of attending several summer staff conferences, I am indebted to Arnaud C. Marts, George E. Lundy, and Louis W. Robey.

My greatest debt is to Louis W. Robey. He is a fund raiser par excellence, a kindly critic, a discerning counselor. But most of all he has been a friend. She to whom this book is justly dedicated insists that this honor belongs to Dr. Robey.

Over a thousand ministers and laymen have given me facts, figures, and fun. They have been willing listeners and believing workers. I am especially thankful for those who answered letters, filled out forms, shared their stories, and in many ways aided this book. Perhaps I am most indebted to those who supplied me with the many good illustrations I have been unable to use.

Sixteen clergymen composed the stewardship prayers. Their time and thought and good wishes, graciously contributed, have enriched the book. I am happy that my first pastor, Dr. William S. Abernethy, could offer one of these prayers.

O. A. PENDLETON

CONTENTS

NEW TECHNIQUES FOR
CHURCH FUND RAISING

CHAPTER A: *What Others Have Done, You Can Do*

*"The new plan of the Every Member Canvass has brought
new life into our Diocese. For the first time, our
people are conscious that the Church is a big operation,
not just a five-and-dime business. Our people are now
concerned not only with dollars and cents, but with
Christ working in and through us."*
       ROBERT W. BOYER, BUSINESS MANAGER
    EPISCOPAL DIOCESE OF WESTERN MASSACHUSETTS

You can raise more money for your church.

You can do so now, within the next ten weeks.

You can, because others like you and your church have been doing so
since 1951.

Because these other people desired not budgets but programs, not
money but lives, they saw their churches awaken. Attendance increased,
new leaders were discovered, converts were won, buildings were remodeled, and a new spiritual concern developed.

WHY SHOULD OUR CHURCHES RAISE MORE MONEY?

Because the spiritual bases of America need strengthening. Our civiliza-
tion is beginning to realize that tailored clothing, air-conditioned homes,
faster automobiles, and nuclear weapons do not build a great nation.
This realization renews the church's opportunity to proclaim that in-
tegrity, morality, service to man, and devotion to God are bases upon
which true greatness can arise. The world has not fully understood this
message, for the voice of the church has been weak. The church has
faltered, not through lack of idealism, but through want of strength.

Because our churches need strengthening. Gold cannot purchase
spiritual insight, conviction, and courage for the pulpit. But gold will aid
the presentation—and reception—of the sermon. Money will aid the

1

minister when it is spent on further education, on books and travel, on attendance at conferences, and on building a staff to aid the minister in serving his people. Money will also help in the receiving of the message. For dollars spent on attractive buildings and furnishings, on finer music and stronger weekday programs, and on radio and television presentations will command a larger audience.

Many of our churches lack lay leadership. Their appeal has been too weak to challenge strong men. Too often their idea of a challenging job has been that of ushering at the morning service. An aggressive financial program, while it is making possible the building of a more adequate program for the future, will, in the meantime

> Attract and develop leadership
> Provide invigorating fellowship
> Call forth more complete devotion from those who supervise such an effort

Members will be strengthened as they learn to give, for devotion is generally in proportion to giving. Heavy investment in the Kingdom of God will lead to heightened concern.

Because we have in our church giving failed to keep pace with our increase in income. Average personal income increased 217 per cent per capita from 1939 to 1953. In the same period the per capita giving to fifteen representative denominations increased but 184 per cent.[1] Americans give about 2 per cent of gross personal income to philanthropy, of which one-half goes to churches.[2] If we would indeed serve God, we cannot be content with 1 per cent of the national dollar—less than one-half the amount spent on tobacco and less than one-fifth that spent on alcoholic beverages. The seriousness of the world situation impels the church to demand a much greater portion of each dollar.

There is a man who sits in the back pew of every church. He has a good income. His children are married. His house is paid for, and he buys a new car every year or two. He takes three weeks summer vacation at a lakeside cottage or traveling from motel to motel. His name is Mr. Fifty-Cents-a-Week, for that is what he gives to his church. Now this highly respected man is neither mean nor stingy. He does what he thinks is right, based somewhat upon what his minister preaches. A few times every year he hears his minister say what a wonderful congregation this is. He hears that the church budget is balanced and that there is wondrous harmony in the church. Being one of the congregation, Mr. Fifty-Cents-a-

---

[1] See Appendix A.

[2] F. E. Andrews, "Philanthropic Giving," Russell Sage Foundation, New York, 1950, pp. 71, 73.

Week infers that some of the praise is intended for him. This member's trouble is ignorance. He needs fewer comforting sermons and more enlightenment as to his individual responsibilities to Christ's Kingdom. This man is legion. He and his problem are one of the reasons for this book.

WHAT FOUR TYPICAL CHURCHES HAVE DONE

Over one thousand churches across America have been helping Mr. Fifty-Cents, and strengthening themselves, by following an intensive new financial plan.

The Old First Congregational Church in Springfield, Massachusetts, increased its giving in one year from $40,000 to $60,000. In Hanson, Massachusetts, receipts of the little Baptist Church rose from $2,200 to $4,700. Up in East Barre, Vermont, the Congregational church pledged $8,000, after receiving $2,500 the previous year. The oldest Baptist Church in America, First of Providence, increased its funds from $12,400 to $18,000.

The new dollars received are but a bookkeeping entry. What really matters is what happened to these churches. During the year of this large increase at Old First Church, worship attendance increased 20 per cent and Sunday School attendance broke all records. A revitalized youth program was made possible. Leaders were discovered, and throughout the entire church there arose a new spirit of enthusiasm.

The Baptist Church in Hanson fulfilled its dream of many years by becoming self-supporting. The pastor's salary was raised $900 plus pension and travel expenses. Janitorial service was provided, and a bus was hired for the Sunday School. These accomplishments stirred the people to even greater effort. They began a building program, raised $3,000 extra, and with volunteer labor constructed a new wing. Meanwhile membership increased from 78 to 110, a Boy Scout troop and an Explorers Club were organized, a Men's Fellowship and a Woman's Missionary Society were founded.

The Providence church, in danger of closing its doors because of lack of funds, faced a seemingly unanswerable situation in 1952. A thoroughgoing enlistment saved the historic church and brought courage to the congregation. In East Barre the whole town began talking church as a result of the campaign.

These four churches are typical of hundreds of others which have worked together to bring phenomenal results to their income. Fourteen churches in the Los Angeles area averaged 55 per cent increase. Indianapolis saw twenty churches add 54 per cent to their pledges. Newark, Buffalo, Sioux Falls, and Denver were among the cities where groups of churches united to bring about increases ranging from 14 to 69 per cent in one year. From September, 1951, to December, 1954, the American Baptist Convention conducted fifty-one "sector projects" in church financing, benefiting 820 churches with an increase of $4.3 million. Seven of these projects, all but one in New England, have been interdenominational, demonstrating that Congregational, Episcopal, Evangelical and Reformed, Methodist, and Presbyterian churches can increase their budgets as greatly as can the Baptists.

Scores of churches, working singly, have used the same techniques and made significant advances. In Etna, New Hampshire, a church increased its giving from $832 to $2,324. Tremont Temple, Boston, added $25,000 in new pledges. In Washington, D.C., the National Memorial Baptist Church raised pledges $50,000. The First Baptist Church of Steubenville, Ohio, completely discouraged in 1952, had met for twenty-five years in a partially finished building. The pastor's salary was $1,800, and the congregation had shriveled to as few as one worshipper. Under their new pastor this church put on a vigorous enlistment. The budget jumped in one year from $3,000 to $10,500, a building campaign for $55,000 was launched, and forty-five new members were won.

Churches engaged in major building or renovation projects have also experienced marked gains. Note four Baptist churches in Massachusetts:

	New building costs	Increase in pledging for current budgets
Arlington, First—Rev. N. W. Wood	$125,000	40% (*in 18-month period*)
North Adams—Rev. R. K. Adams (*major renovation*)	70,000	27
Wakefield—Rev. H. G. Payne	120,000	113
Wollaston—Rev. H. O. Tatum	86,000	35

All these churches, working singly or in groups, won their advances by following the plan outlined in this book.

Spiritual benefits have equaled or exceeded the financial results. Virtually every church testifies to larger attendance and greater zeal. Many churches win new members. Increasing its pledges by $11,000, the First Baptist Church of Beverly, Massachusetts, made other notable progress— engaged an assistant pastor, enlarged the choir, increased attendance, improved the building. A prominent attorney stated that the greatest benefit of all to this church was the discovery of three new leaders who had agreed to direct the next year's campaign. There has been "a deepening and strengthening of our own spiritual drive," declared canvass chairman William West of Columbia Street Baptist Church in Bangor, Maine. "We have added to our church program," stated a member of St. Barnabas

Episcopal Church in Springfield, "$9,000 cash, plus one million dollars in spirit."

You can raise more money for your church.

You can do so now, within the next ten weeks.

You can, because others like you and your church have been doing so for the past several years.

Moreover, this financial gain will be secondary to the spiritual awakening in your church!

"Lord, Thy goodness to me is constant, boundless. Save
me from the heresy of acting as if it can all be sealed up
in my narrow life—without any overflow! That would be boast-
fulness on my part, slander toward Thee, robbery of my fellow
men."

> *Franklin Clark Fry*
> PRESIDENT
> THE UNITED LUTHERAN CHURCH IN
> AMERICA

CHAPTER B: *Ten Steps to Victory*

*"I would recommend heartily the financial and spiritual
benefits of a thoroughly conducted Every Member Canvass.
. . . It was the largest and most successful undertaking
in the history of our church."*

REV. C. OSCAR JOHNSON
THIRD BAPTIST CHURCH
ST. LOUIS, MISSOURI

There is no easy way to raise money. Yet raising money is not a hard job, either, if certain fundamentals are followed. For a church enlistment to produce the kind of results we have been talking about, there is needed:

A vision
Enthusiasm
A plan

If you have the vision to attempt great things for God—if you will supply enthusiasm enough to sweep away all objections and arouse a like ardor in others—this book will give you the plan to follow.

A VISION

To do a more effective work for Jesus Christ in the church, the community, and around the world—this is the vision needed. No progress can come out of complacency with last year's record. A divine discontent is imperative. We need to ask ourselves: How significant a Christian force is it possible for our church to become in the community and around the globe? What forward program might our church build—if budgets were no problem? If we had all the money we desired, could we spend it wisely, transforming it immediately into worthy services?

6

ENTHUSIASM

Since there are several new features in this plan, it will tend to arouse questions and perhaps opposition from some persons. Many church members will prefer to continue at last year's pace, especially in their giving. But these people are reasonable—and emotional. People will listen if you present your ideas enthusiastically. Men assent more quickly to an idea presented with vigor and conviction.

Every step of this enlistment program involves selling. The minister must "sell" his idea to his finance board. They, in turn, must "sell" their idea to the congregation. The various steps, many of which involve much work, must be "sold" one by one. Without a contagious enthusiasm, the entire project may collapse. A holy zeal, undaunted by hesitancy and opposition, will carry the program to a glorious end.

You will need only two sales points:

1. We *can* have a greater program for Christ next year. If our people sincerely wish to do more for the Master, we can do so.
2. *Others,* not unlike us, using this financial plan have reached new heights. What others have done, we can do.

There will be objections to overcome. Objections due to misunderstanding are taken care of by patient repetition of the truth. Objections arising from fear of what others might think are best handled by interviews with these "others." Often such persons turn out to be your staunchest allies. Sometimes the objection is groundless, indicating a stubborn resistance to any change. Thus an opposing vestryman in one church spoke out: "I move we table the whole thing. We ought to fix the roof." It was pointed out to him that the roof had been fixed five years earlier. Overriding his opposition, the church went on in the program to a significant increase.

Study this plan until you can get enthusiastic over it. Then present it enthusiastically to others. Appendixes E and F of this book list hundreds of churches which have proved the soundness of the plan. A retelling of the experience of one of these churches in your state, together with your enthusiastic "selling," will influence your leaders to vote to enter the plan.

A PLAN

The plan here presented works equally well in a church that has a large or small congregation, that is in a city or in the country, that is well organized or not. It is a flexible scheme. One of the reasons it will work in *your church* is that it is designed to use *your laymen.* The plan gives a complete framework upon which minister and laymen will add bricks and trim, erecting a structure adapted to your individual needs. There is nothing experimental about the plan. Built upon experience, these techniques will bring results if you use them.

The plan followed by the churches mentioned in Chapter A uses five elemental ideas:

A program of *advance* will be presented to the people.

The giving potential of the church will be determined not by last year's giving but by an intelligent estimate of the potential of each member.

Colorful and pictorial publicity will be prepared.

Workers will be thoroughly trained with the use of the latest available tools.

Every home will be called upon.

These ideas take form in a series of ten steps, outlined below. Succeeding chapters explain the steps in detail, telling each chairman what he is to do, and how, and when. Following the ten steps will mean more money for your church—and more service for the Kingdom of God. (See Fig. B-1.)

STEP ONE: *Building Your Organization*

Your organization must be composed of the strongest possible men. Your General chairman particularly must be a leader. He will be assisted by a committee of five others, each of whom will be assigned a definite responsibility in the campaign. If one man fails, he will slow up, and perhaps defeat, the entire effort.

STEP TWO: *Following the Calendar*

The calendar must be set up while the organization is being built. It will show the General Committee

What each one is to do

When each is to do it

How the task of each dovetails with the tasks of others

How victory will be possible as each step is done on time

STEP THREE: *Programming for Tomorrow*

Unless there is a program of *advance*, there will be little incentive for increased giving. The church must dream about tomorrow, giving op-

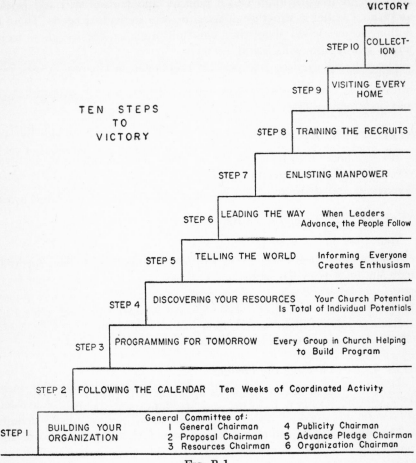

TEN STEPS
TO
VICTORY

VICTORY

STEP 10 | COLLECT-ION

STEP 9 | VISITING EVERY HOME

STEP 8 | TRAINING THE RECRUITS

STEP 7 | ENLISTING MANPOWER

STEP 6 | LEADING THE WAY   When Leaders Advance, the People Follow

STEP 5 | TELLING THE WORLD   Informing Everyone Creates Enthusiasm

STEP 4 | DISCOVERING YOUR RESOURCES   Your Church Potential Is Total of Individual Potentials

STEP 3 | PROGRAMMING FOR TOMORROW   Every Group in Church Helping to Build Program

STEP 2 | FOLLOWING THE CALENDAR   Ten Weeks of Coordinated Activity

STEP 1 | BUILDING YOUR ORGANIZATION | General Committee of:
1 General Chairman   4 Publicity Chairman
2 Proposal Chairman   5 Advance Pledge Chairman
3 Resources Chairman   6 Organization Chairman

Fig. B-1

portunity to as many members as possible to share their ideas for a greater program in the local church and throughout the world.

STEP FOUR: *Discovering Your Resources*

Your proposed budget for next year is to be based, not upon present giving, not upon fanciful hopes, but upon the actual potential of your people. The question to be faced is: "How much money *could* your church raise?" This step will determine in advance what is an attainable goal for next year.

STEP FIVE: *Telling the World*

No matter how good your program, people will not support it until they understand it, believe in it, desire it. The aim of the Publicity Committee is to arouse as much enthusiasm in every member of the congregation as there is in the General Committee.

STEP SIX: Leading the Way

Unless the leaders lead, the people will not follow. If your program is sensible and worthy, your leaders will be the first to give their allegiance and their money. Their commitment in turn influences others.

STEP SEVEN: Enlisting Manpower

If every home is to be called upon, a large team of volunteers must be recruited well in advance of the visitation. They must be organized into companies and divisions.

STEP EIGHT: Training the Recruits

Your plan to increase pledging will be most successful only as the visitors who go into every home are thoroughly trained and provided with the most effective tools.

STEP NINE: Calling in Every Home

Each member will be called upon in his own home, where the most effective presentation can be made. No home will be omitted.

STEP TEN: Collecting the Pledges

The collection of pledges depends upon the help given to the pledgers. A plan is worked out to keep the members informed and interested.

The omission or radical change of any one of these ten steps will lessen your victory. There are not six steps, or eight steps, or nine to victory. There are TEN steps to Victory.

The plan has been tested. It needs only you.

"We have been waiting years for a program like this."
>   Rev. Robert H. Cummings
>   Grace Episcopal Church
>   Chicopee, Massachusetts

"If you believe you can, you will do it."
>   Rev. John Wallace
>   Congregational Church
>   Springfield, Massachusetts
>   (Now of Wellesley Hills
>   Congregational Church
>   Wellesley, Massachusetts)

"Our Father: May all that we have be ever at Thy service.
May we take our seeds of silver, the grain of our gold, and not merely
bury them by spending them on secular things; may we, rather, *plant* them
in spiritual furrows, that they may bring forth the harvest—thirty-,
fifty-, and a hundredfold.
"Add a purpose to our purses, a passion to our possessions
and properties, that thus we may be children of the King and builders
of the Kingdom. Through Jesus Christ, our Lord. Amen."

Louis H. Evans
BOARD OF NATIONAL MISSIONS OF THE
PRESBYTERIAN CHURCH IN THE
UNITED STATES OF AMERICA

STEP 1: *Building Your Organization*

"*My church, especially the leaders, was very much opposed to the project at first. I prayed for a chairman, and a man with ability came forward to offer his services. This has acted almost like an evangelistic campaign in my church, and I thank God for all that has gone into it.*"

> MRS. F. A. MACDONALD, PASTOR
> HARVEY STREET COMMUNITY CHURCH
> SPRINGFIELD, MASSACHUSETTS

IMPORTANCE OF STRONG LAY LEADERSHIP

I have heard two different remarks from ministers at the end of campaigns: "I never worked so hard before," and, "I never had it so easy before." The difference lies in the choosing of strong lay leadership. The selection of proper leadership for the enlistment means not only a great timesaver for the pastor and a more wonderful experience for everyone, but the difference between success and near-success. Because of the illness of Rev. Arthayer Sanborn, it seemed as though the Woonsocket (Rhode Island) Baptist Church could not take part in the 1952 enlistment. But five laymen, headed by Chairman Byron Young, led the church to a 40 per cent increase. "It proved to me," declared the pastor, "that laymen can really do a big job in the church."

Churches temporarily without ministers can also follow this program. The First Congregational Church of South Hadley, Massachusetts, under the drive of Chairman Richard Johnson added $4,400 to their income. Aggressive laymen in the Grace Episcopal Church of North Attleboro, Massachusetts, without a rector's guidance, increased pledging 50 per cent.

Some will ask: Should we use any women in these positions of leadership? Churches can count upon their women for a multitude of services, but here is a work big enough and exciting enough to absorb the attention of half a dozen of your most capable men. Give these leadership posts to men rather than women. Men will challenge other men to pledge large

12

gifts easier than women will. Women tend to think of church financing in terms of silver teas and rummage sales rather than pledges of five or ten dollars a week. Use men if at all possible. Your guiding rule, however, should be: Use the best leaders in your church, regardless of sex.

THE GENERAL CHAIRMAN

Every church, regardless of size, has the same basic Every Member Enlistment organization. Building your organization begins with naming your General chairman. Experience shows that it is not wise to leave the appointment of this all-important man to some board or committee. The trustees should give the minister authority to name him. He might well be selected twelve weeks or more before the canvass. He *must* be secured at least eight weeks before.

"My general chairman, Charles Weller, was a whiz," Pastor Harold Metzner told me after his enlistment at Trinity Union Methodist Church in Providence. "I didn't do anything. He carried it all. He checked up on me rather than I on him. He did things I thought couldn't be done." Weller, an aggressive young member of a firm that manufactures shoe buckles, insisted on thoroughness. "We considered no one a dud," he said. "Not one person was missed." Results: $4,845 from 113 families pledging for the first time. The total church increase was well over $10,000.

The outstanding leader in the church should be chosen for this position of General chairman. Such a man is almost certain to be a busy man. Therefore it will be necessary for the minister to call on him in his home and sell him on the importance of his taking this job. The chairman should be a genuine executive who holds the respect of the entire church. He must know how to choose able assistants and direct them efficiently. He must be able and willing to give many hours to the task. His loyalty to his church must be unquestioned. If he is a person of financial means, he will find it easier to attract the support of other persons of means. He need not be a good public speaker, since most of his work will be behind the scenes. Should he, however, possess speaking ability in addition to the above qualifications, you would have a giant indeed.

Some of the functions of this pivotal person are as follows:

To select assistants, including the General Committee
To allocate duties and to supervise their performance
    By stressing the close use of this manual
    By insisting on following the calendar
To give needed counsel and encouragement
To receive reports and keep records
To follow through to completion

The wise General chairman will parcel out all jobs. He is to multiply his own effectiveness by using many persons, knowing that the more workers he has, the greater the enthusiasm for the campaign. His primary task, then, is to see that all work is assigned and that it is properly done by his assistants. This manual has no chapter for the General chairman. He will inform himself of the duties of each of his committeemen (as outlined in the next six chapters) and will supervise their performance. He will coordinate the work of each through use of the Master Calendar. His first task—to be completed the same week he is named—is to secure the other five members of his General Committee.

The minister's duties do not end with his naming of the General chairman. He will give advice on personnel, help iron out difficulties, support the program from pulpit and press, and act as general morale builder.

Use the following to help your thinking:

Whom could we use for General chairman?

First choice: M . . . .

Second choice: M . . . .

Third choice: M . . . .

THE GENERAL COMMITTEE

The first task of the chairman is to name, with suggestions from the minister, the members of the General Committee: Proposal chairman, Resources chairman, Publicity chairman, Advance Pledge chairman, and Organization chairman. One or two other church leaders may be asked to serve as reservists to take over any job in an emergency.

These persons will supervise the entire canvass. Their leadership should be such that everyone will have confidence in their recommendations. They need to understand the program and to believe in it fervently. They will clear dates, aid in enlisting personnel, and give counsel to the General chairman should any problems arise. Each will have a specific duty and may name a subcommittee. You may wish each member of the General Committee to have a copy of this book. Three copies of the plan should be available for each church—one for the minister, one for the General chairman, and one to be torn apart and divided among the rest of the committee.

The first meeting of the General Committee is all-important and should be held early in the second week of the campaign. A suggested agenda (Form N) for this first meeting is shown in Fig. 1-1.

AGENDA
General Committee Meeting
MONDAY, WEEK 2

Presiding: GENERAL CHAIRMAN

Prayer for the Success of the Canvass

MINISTER

(*5 min.*) Our Hopes for Next Year   MINISTER
The Needs and Opportunities Facing Us

(*25 min.*) General Plan of Procedure

GENERAL CHAIRMAN

The Ten Steps
The Number of Committees
The Function of Committees
Proposal
Resources
Publicity
Advance Pledge
Organization

(*10 min.*) Highlights of the Time Schedule

PUBLICITY CHAIRMAN

(*5 min.*) Number of Visitors Needed

ORGANIZATION CHAIRMAN

(*5 min.*) How Visitors Are Enlisted and Trained

ORGANIZATION CHAIRMAN

(*5 min.*) Materials Needed for Campaign

PUBLICITY CHAIRMAN

(*5 min.*) Importance of Following the Plan and
Keeping on Schedule GENERAL CHAIRMAN
Prayer and Adjournment

FIG. 1-1

THE PROPOSAL CHAIRMAN

The duty of the Proposal chairman is to direct the thinking of many persons in formulating a challenging church program for next year. It is important that he have a committee which includes representatives from many church organizations or interests—the trustees, elders, vestry, deacons, board of education, Sunday School, and men's, women's, and youth organizations. In this way the ideas of many groups are brought into the planning. The duty of this committee is to *discover the needs and opportunities of the church, both in its local program and its world-wide ministry.*

Whom could we use for Proposal chairman:

First choice: M . . . .

Second choice: M . . . .

Third choice: M . . . .

THE RESOURCES CHAIRMAN

The Resources chairman, with the aid of his subcommittee, will determine how far the church might expect to go in realizing its ideal budget. This committee is to discover prospective workers and to determine the giving ability of the church through estimating the ability of each member. The chairman must be one who is fearless of criticism and who likes to work with figures.

Whom could we use for Resources chairman?

First choice: M . . . .

Second choice: M . . . .

Third choice: M . . . .

THE PUBLICITY CHAIRMAN

It is the duty of the Publicity chairman to see that full information is passed along to all church members. Some campaigns fail to reach their objectives because the proper effort is not made to spread information, out of which grows enthusiasm. In addition to writing publicity, this chairman will act as office manager, making certain that all supplies, forms, and letters are prepared beforehand. He must be adept at directing the clerical work of many volunteers. He should be a stickler for details.

Whom could we use for Publicity chairman?

> First choice: M . . . .
>
> Second choice: M . . . .
>
> Third choice: M . . . .

THE ADVANCE PLEDGE CHAIRMAN

The Advance Pledge chairman should be one who is in a position to make one of your highest subscriptions. He must be able to approach other substantial givers and all church leaders. It is his responsibility to discover the names of those who are able to give in larger amounts and to enlist others to help him in calling upon these leaders in advance of the general visitation.

Whom could we use for Advance Pledge chairman?

> First choice: M . . . .
>
> Second choice: M . . . . :
>
> Third choice: M . . . .

THE ORGANIZATION CHAIRMAN

The task of the Organization chairman is to build the corps of visitors needed to ensure that each home is called upon. He must train the visitors in the art of conducting a sales interview that will result in the finest possible pledge. He must receive reports from the visitors, making sure that every prospect is seen. This is a big job, and the Organization chairman must be chosen with care. One who is not meticulous in pinpointing all unmade calls can easily lose 10 per cent in possible income for next year's budget. One who is careless about recruiting enough visitors and insisting on their attending training sessions and report meetings can be responsible for an even greater loss. The General chairman will need to check the work of the Organization chairman closer than that of anyone else on the committee.

Whom could we use for Organization chairman?

> First choice: M . . . .
>
> Second choice: M . . . .
>
> Third choice: M . . . .

Six persons are now responsible for your enlistment:

General chairman: M . . . .

Proposal chairman: M . . . .

Resources chairman: M. . . . .

Publicity chairman: M . . . .

Advance Pledge chairman: M . . . . . .

Organization chairman: M . . . .

There are TEN steps to Victory. Step ONE is building your organization.

"Almighty God, who so loved the world that Thou has
given thy Son Jesus Christ to be the way, the truth
and life. Grant us such love and gratitude to thee
that we may dedicate all that we are and have to thy
joyful service, through Jesus Christ, our Lord."

Henry Knox Sherrill
PRESIDING BISHOP
THE PROTESTANT EPISCOPAL CHURCH

STEP 2: *Following the Calendar*

THE IMPORTANCE OF THE CALENDAR

There are two rules for each member of the General Committee:

1. Follow the plan in every detail.
2. Check your calendar day by day.

The ten-step plan has evolved out of the experience of hundreds of churches. To implement the plan there is presented a detailed calendar, "the Master Time Schedule," which should be rigidly observed. With so many committees working at the same time, it is imperative that everyone check the timetable frequently. The calendar will serve as

A *coordinator,* dovetailing the activities of each committee and preventing overlapping

A *taskmaster* to prevent one committee from falling behind and delaying other committees

A *guide* to prevent frustration resulting from wondering what to do next

A *timesaver,* enabling all chairmen to assign parts of their responsibility to many individuals

The entire program will take a minimum of ten weeks. This does not mean that every day will be filled. It does mean that time is allowed for cultivation of prospects and for building and training a corps of workers.

Some chairmen state that six months is needed, feeling that the earlier they can get their congregations thinking about next year's progress and the earlier the leaders begin enrolling their visitors, the smoother will be the final weeks of the effort. The calendar here suggested, however, will suffice for most churches.

The first two weeks of the schedule are in some respects the most important. Everyone realizes that the final weeks will be crowded. Not everyone understands that a strong start makes for a strong finish. The selection of an able team the first week, and their preliminary organization the second week, not only lays the groundwork upon which all else is built but also sets habits of punctuality that will be invaluable later on.

"Keep up with the calendar" should be repeated so often that it becomes a slogan for the enlistment.

The use of the calendar allows the General chairman greater freedom, since he may foresee what responsibilities may be delegated to other persons and groups. He can pay less attention to the subchairmen once they understand the schedule and see how their tasks dovetail with all others.

The calendar relieves the General chairman of the need for pleading with or scolding the members of his organization. Should he discover that some individual or committee is working too slowly, he has but to point out in the schedule how tardiness of one may cause tardiness of all. It is therefore the program, rather than the chairman, that prods.

Why is it sometimes difficult to enlist men for jobs in the church? Often it is because of the vagueness of the assignment. The man is given a task without any goals, with little promise of help, with few or no tools. No one wants to "flub" a job. Fear of doing so makes many prospects say: "No." But if we supply definite know-how—with tools and a schedule— the would-be leader will see the forest as well as the trees, and the meadow beyond the forest. The calendar here presented will remove the frustration that is common to all of us when wondering "what comes next?"

Now and then one or two vigorous laymen will take hold of this program and virtually unaided push the whole church through all the steps. They have a glorious time, too. But it is not the best way to work the plan, nor do many men have so much time to devote. The timetable is designed to use the services of many volunteers. Particularly will the Publicity chairman wish to delegate his duties. He can do much of his work alone, but, by looking ahead in the calendar, he can act as office manager, seeing that others take care of the actual detail work. Proper use of the schedule not only will save hours and headaches for each of the subchairmen but also will create enthusiasm within the corps of volunteers for the entire program.

During the first week of the enlistment, the General chairman will determine the canvass calendar by correlating the Master Time Schedule with all church engagements. All conflicts will be adjusted. Once this calendar has been set up, a sheet of Guiding Principles and Important Dates (see Form A in the Canvass Kit at the back of the book) should be mimeographed. As each leader or visitor accepts his responsibility, the General chairman will hand him a copy of this outline.

If the General chairman takes care every two weeks to fill in the check lists at the end of this chapter, he will readily learn whether the enlistment is going on schedule.

TWO SALIENT DATES IN YOUR CALENDAR

Your campaign calendar will be built around two dates. Unless the importance of both these dates is kept clearly in mind, there will be confusion and delay.

The *pivotal* date is the Congregational Dinner Meeting, on Wednesday, Week 5. All activity in the first half of the program leads up to this date. All activity in the second half arises from this date.

The Congregational Dinner Meeting serves a twofold purpose:

1. The church here gives the General Committee authority to go ahead with the *program of advance* as worked out by the Proposal Committee (see next chapter). Although the Finance Committee needs no authority to raise money (since that is the reason for its existence), it does seek the approval of the church for the specific program and goal. The question put to this meeting is: "Will the church approve our Proposal, calling for a goal of so many dollars?" Then should some member exclaim when he first sees the high goal: "What a preposterous sum! What right do those men have to propose such an amount?" the answer is: "The church, in business session the other night, voted its approval. We wish that you had accepted our invitation to attend."

Some churches are so constituted that the official board or the vestry needs no authority to undertake an advanced program. It is still very important, however, to hold this meeting, for the following reason:

2. The church here gives the General Committee opportunity to promote the *program of advance*. Here many of the members first learn what is being planned. Here they can ask their questions. Each one of your committee has an interest in the Congregational Dinner Meeting and should take an active part in the program.

The moment the church approves the enlistment goal, the campaign is in high gear.

The *climax* date is Dedication Day, Sunday, Week 9, when the public campaign opens. The advance pledging is completed. Now the great body of church members will vote by their pledges whether the Proposal is to become Reality.

The eight weeks leading up to Dedication Day may be likened to the submerged part of an iceberg. They are the foundation weeks—invisible to most observers—yet without which there can be no superstructure.

There are TEN steps to Victory. Step TWO is following the calendar.

"Our Father, God, we thank Thee for the talents and substance which Thou hast committed to our keeping. Would Thou give us clear minds and right hearts that we may be worthy stewards, using Thy gifts for the welfare of all mankind. We pray in the name of Jesus Christ, our Lord and Saviour."

Roy G. Ross,
GENERAL SECRETARY
NATIONAL COUNCIL OF THE CHURCHES OF CHRIST

SCHEDULE FOR SETTING UP AN EVERY MEMBER ENLISTMENT

The following schedule is a greatly condensed version of the Master Calendar. Use it as a preview of the enlistment. Do not use it as a substitution for the detailed calendar.

WEEK 1 *CALENDAR IS DRAWN UP*
WEEKS 1– 2 *GENERAL COMMITTEE IS NAMED*
WEEKS 3– 5 *GOAL IS DETERMINED AND APPROVED*
WEEKS 4– 7 *PUBLICITY IS PREPARED*
WEEKS 4– 8 *WORKERS ARE ENLISTED AND TRAINED*
WEEKS 7– 8 *ADVANCE PLEDGERS ARE APPROACHED*
WEEKS 9–10 *EVERY HOME IS VISITED*
WEEKS 10–11 *INCOMPLETE CALLS ARE COMPLETED*
WEEKS 10–11 *RESULTS ARE TABULATED*
WEEKS 10–11 *COLLECTION SYSTEM IS SET UP*

CHECK LISTS FOR GENERAL CHAIRMAN

If the General chairman will refer to the following check lists at two-week intervals, it will help him keep his various committees up to date:

General chairman should begin checking this list on MONDAY, Week 1, immediately upon appointment.

CHECK LIST 1

Important Steps for Next Two Weeks

(Check as soon as completed)

A. GENERAL COMMITTEE
1. Name full committee at once
   a. Proposal chairman _____
   b. Resources chairman _____
   c. Publicity chairman _____
   d. Advance Pledge chairman _____
   e. Organization chairman _____
2. Notify committee of first meeting, to be held Monday, Week 2 _____
3. Hold first General Committee meeting _____
   a. Outline ten steps _____
   b. Explain duties of committee members _____
   c. Determine the calendar _____
   d. Discuss materials needed _____
   e. Agree on number of workers needed _____
   f. Urge members to name subcommittees _____

B. PUBLICITY COMMITTEE
1. Begin appraisal list, Wednesday, Week 2 (deadline for completion: Thursday, Week 3) _____
2. Make arrangements with printer _____
   Order Proposal envelopes _____

C. SUPPLIES
Since Publicity chairman will be busy preparing appraisal lists, General chairman may order all canvass supplies and weekly collection envelopes
   Immediate need for ordering
      Master Lists _____
      Weekly offering envelopes _____
      Proposal blanks and envelopes _____

Later need for
   Training film   ———
   Missionary film   ———
   Sunday calendars   ———
   Posters   ———
   Stewardship leaflets   ———
   Missionary leaflets   ———
   Workers' handbooks   ———
   Report envelopes   ———
   Turnover charts   ———

General chairman should check this list on THURSDAY, Week 2.

CHECK LIST 2

Where Do You Stand Today?   (*Check here*)

A. Is your full General Committee named?   _____

    1. Proposal chairman is M_____

       Address:

       Telephone:

    2. Resources chairman is M_____

       Address:

       Telephone:

    3. Publicity chairman is M_____

       Address:

       Telephone:

    4. Advance Pledge chairman is M_____

       Address:

       Telephone:

    5. Organization chairman is M_____

       Address:

       Telephone:

B. Has first meeting of General Committee been held?   _____

C. Have canvass materials and new weekly pledge envelopes been ordered?   _____

D. Has Publicity chairman begun preparation of fifty mimeographed appraisal lists?   _____

E. Has Publicity chairman made arrangements with printer?   _____

F. Has Proposal Committee been named?
Has first meeting date been set?   _____

Important Steps for Next Two Weeks   (*Check as soon as completed*)

A. PUBLICITY COMMITTEE
   1. Secure professional photographer for Sunday, Week 3 or Week 4 (deadline)   ———
   2. Mimeograph fifty sets of appraisal lists by Thursday, Week 3   ———
   3. Mail Letter A on Tuesday, Week 3   ———
   4. Mail Letter B on Wednesday, Week 3   ———
   5. Have pictures taken and receive prints on Monday, Week 4   ———
   6. Begin Master List   ———
   7. Prepare leadership cards   ———
   8. Mail Letter F on Thursday, Week 4   ———

B. RESOURCES COMMITTEE
   1. Send letters to fifty or sixty to be sure thirty attend   ———
   2. Committee meets, Sunday, Week 4   ———
   3. Average appraisals, Monday, Week 4   ———
   4. Review Committee meets, Tuesday, Week 4   ———

C. PROPOSAL COMMITTEE
   1. Receive suggestions from every group   ———
   2. Complete preliminary draft of Proposal, Wednesday, Week 4   ———

D. ORGANIZATION CHAIRMAN
   1. Secure all division leaders by Monday, Week 4   ———
   2. Secure all captains by Monday, Week 5   ———

General chairman should check this list on THURSDAY, Week 4.

CHECK LIST 3

Where Do You Stand Today?   (*Check here*)

A. PUBLICITY COMMITTEE
  1. Have you received pictures?   _____
  2. Have you cropped them and taken them to
     printer?   _____
  3. Are leadership cards being prepared?   _____
  4. Is Master List being prepared?   _____
  5. Has Letter F been mailed?   _____

B. RESOURCES COMMITTEE
  1. Have all appraisals been averaged?   _____
  2. Have all appraisals been revised?   _____

C. PROPOSAL COMMITTEE
  Is preliminary Proposal complete?   _____

D. ORGANIZATION
  1. Have all division leaders been secured?   _____
  2. Have all captains been secured?   _____

Important Steps for Next Two Weeks   (*Check as soon
                                              as completed*)

A. PUBLICITY COMMITTEE
  1. Mail Letter F, Thursday, Week 4   _____
  2. Mail Letter C, Friday, Week 4   _____
  3. Use telephone squad, Saturday, Week 4   _____
  4. Deliver approved Proposal copy to printer,
     Thursday, Week 5   _____
  5. Direct mail crew in addressing Proposal en-
     velopes   _____
  6. Alert mail crew to prepare for mailing Pro-
     posals to advance pledgers   _____

B. PROPOSAL COMMITTEE
  1. Meet with Resources chairman   _____
  2. Present Proposal to Church Council   _____
  3. Congregational Dinner Meeting   _____

C. ORGANIZATION CHAIRMAN
  1. Captains meet to select visitors, Monday,
     Week 5   _____
  2. Deadline for securing visitors, Thursday,
     Week 6   _____

D. ADVANCE PLEDGES
  1. Pastor and General chairman sign pledges   ———
  2. Meeting of Advance Pledge Committee   ———
  3. General chairman calls on each member of General Committee for pledge   ———
  4. Advance Pledge chairman calls on each member of Advance Pledge Committee for pledge   ———

General chairman should check this list on THURSDAY, Week 6.

CHECK LIST 4

Where Do You Stand Today?   (*Check here*)

A. PUBLICITY COMMITTEE
1. Is Master List made up?   ————
2. Have you received all canvass supplies? ————
3. Have all Proposal envelopes been addressed and stamped with sufficient postage? ————

B. ORGANIZATION CHAIRMAN
1. Did captains meet to select visitors? ————
2. Have all visitors been secured? ————
3. Have you any reserve visitors? ————

C. ADVANCE PLEDGE COMMITTEE
1. Have pastor and General chairman pledged? ————
2. Was first Advance Pledge Committee meeting held? ————
3. Have all of General Committee pledged? ————
4. Have all of Advance Pledge Committee pledged? ————
5. What is total amount pledged to date? $————

Important Steps for Next Two Weeks   (*Check as soon as completed*)

A. PUBLICITY COMMITTEE
1. Mail Proposal and Letter D to advance pledge prospects, Saturday, Week 6 ————
2. Type advance pledge cards first ————
3. Type remainder of pledge cards ————
4. Mail Letter E, Tuesday, Week 7 ————
5. Mail Letter G, Wednesday, Week 7 ————
6. Mail Proposals, with Letter H or J, to rest of members, Saturday, Week 7 ————
7. Meeting place arranged for First Workers' Training Conference ————
   Notify caterer (if any meal) ————
   Have room decorated with posters ————
   Set up equipment—projector, etc. ————
8. Mail Letters K and L, Wednesday, Week 8 ————

B. ORGANIZATION CHAIRMAN
1. Deadline for securing all visitors, Thursday, Week 6 ————
2. Division leaders sign pledges by Saturday, Week 6 ————

3. Division leaders call on captains for pledges by Saturday, Week 7   ———

4. Leaders telephone all workers, Saturday, Week 7   ———

5. Captains begin solicitation of visitors, Monday, Week 8   ———

6. Leaders telephone all workers, Thursday, Week 8   ———

C. ADVANCE PLEDGES
   1. Hold second Advance Pledge Committee meeting, Sunday, Week 7   ———
   2. Begin advance pledge solicitation   ———
   3. Hold first advance pledge report meeting, Friday, Week 7   ———

D. RESOURCES CHAIRMAN
   1. Check appraisal figure on each advance pledge card, Saturday, Week 6   ———
   2. Check appraisal figures on remainder of pledge cards, Wednesday, Week 7   ———

General chairman should check this list on **THURSDAY**, Week 8.

CHECK LIST 5

Where Do You Stand Today?   (*Check here*)

A. PUBLICITY COMMITTEE
  1. Have proposals been mailed to everyone?   ____
  2. Have Letters E, G, H, J, K, and L been mailed?   ____
  3. Are all pledge cards typed and have appraisals been checked?   ____

B. ORGANIZATION CHAIRMAN
  1. Have all division leaders and captains signed pledges?   ____
  2. Have all visitors signed pledges?   ____
  3. Have leaders called all workers about instruction dinners?   ____

C. ADVANCE PLEDGES
  1. Is advance pledging complete?   ____
  2. How many calls are yet to be made?   ____
  3. What is total amount pledged? $____

Important Steps for Final Two Weeks   (*Check as soon as completed*)

A. PUBLICITY COMMITTEE
  1. Telephone squad calls entire congregation, Saturday, Week 8   ____
  2. Mail Letters K and L, Wednesday, Week 8   ____

B. ORGANIZATION CHAIRMAN
  1. Check on results of Second Workers' Training Conference
     a. How many visitors were present?   ____
     b. How many were absent?   ____
     c. Are captains training all absentees in their homes Saturday, Week 8?   ____
     d. How many workers signed pledges?   ____
     e. How many workers did not sign pledges?   ____
     f. Are captains getting these pledges signed Saturday, Week 8?   ____
  2. VISITATION
     a. How many visitors were absent Dedication Day?   ____
     b. Were their cards reassigned?   ____

3. REPORT MEETINGS

What was total amount of pledges announced

   a. At Dedication Day service? $_____

   b. At first report meeting? $_____

   c. At second report meeting? $_____

   d. At third report meeting? $_____

   e. At fourth report meeting? $_____

   f. At Victory report meeting? $_____

C. FOLLOW-UP

1. Meeting of General Committee to evaluate canvass   _____
2. Meeting of General Committee to plan follow-up   _____
3. Meeting of General Committee to plan collection program   _____
4. Mail Letter M, Friday, Week 10   _____

MASTER TIME SCHEDULE

Detailed information for all canvass activities is found in the chairmen's chapters of this book.

Insert the proper date in the upper right-hand corner of each calendar square.

	SUNDAY	MONDAY	TUESDAY	WEDNESDAY	THURSDAY	FRIDAY	SATURDAY
WEEK 1		MINISTER SELECTS GENERAL CHAIRMAN USE CHECK LIST 1	MINISTER AND CHAIRMAN APPROVE CALENDAR		GENERAL CHAIRMAN SELECTS COMMITTEE CHAIRMEN	FORMS B & C MIMEOGRAPHED	
WEEK 2	MINISTER GIVES NAME OF GENERAL CHAIRMAN AND STATEMENT ON ENLARGED PROGRAM FORM B DISTRIBUTED	FIRST MEETING OF GENERAL COMMITTEE COCHAIRMEN SELECT COMMITTEES	ORDER CANVASS MATERIALS	PUBLICITY CHAIRMAN PREPARES APPRAISAL LIST SEE FORM D	MAKE ARRANGEMENTS FOR PRINTING PROPOSAL USE CHECK LIST 2	PUBLICITY CHAIRMAN SECURES PROFESSIONAL PHOTOGRAPHER FOR SUNDAY, WEEK 4	
WEEK 3	FIRST MEETING OF PROPOSAL COMMITTEE	MIMEOGRAPH 50 COPIES OF APPRAISAL LIST	SELECT DIVISION LEADERS MINISTER MAILS LETTER A	GENERAL CHAIRMAN MAILS LETTER B		SECOND MEETING OF PROPOSAL COMMITTEE	
WEEK 4	PHOTOGRAPHS TAKEN FOR USE IN PRINTED PROPOSAL RESOURCES COMMITTEE MEETS	RESOURCES CHAIRMAN TABULATES AVERAGES SELECT CAPTAINS	REVIEW COMMITTEE MEETS TO STUDY APPRAISAL	THIRD MEETING OF PROPOSAL COMMITTEE PUBLICITY CHAIRMAN PREPARES LEADERSHIP CARDS	BEGIN MASTER LIST GENERAL CHAIRMAN MAILS LETTER F USE CHECK LIST 3	TELEPHONE SQUAD MEETS MAIL LETTER C	PUBLICITY COMMITTEE TELEPHONES MEMBERS ABOUT CONGREGATIONAL DINNER.
WEEK 5	JOINT MEETING OF PROPOSAL COMMITTEE & RESOURCES CHAIRMEN PREPARE FORM G	PROPOSAL AND RESOURCES CHAIRMEN MEET WITH CHURCH COUNCIL / CAPTAINS MEET TO SELECT WORKERS.		CONGREGATIONAL DINNER MEETING	DELIVER COPY FOR PRINTED PROPOSAL TO PRINTER, USING FORMS G AND H	DEADLINE FOR SECURING ADVANCE PLEDGE COMMITTEE	MINISTER AND GENERAL CHAIRMAN SIGN PLEDGES

WEEK 6	MINISTER BEGINS USING STEWARDSHIP EMPHASIS IN SERVICES / ADVANCE PLEDGE COMMITTEE MEETS	GENERAL CHAIRMAN CALLS ON ALL MEMBERS OF GENERAL COMMITTEE FOR THEIR PLEDGES	ADVANCE PLEDGE CHAIRMAN CALLS ON ALL HIS COMMITTEE FOR THEIR PLEDGES.		DEADLINE FOR SECURING VISITORS / USE CHECK LIST 4	PICK UP PROPOSALS AND PLEDGE CARDS BEGIN TYPING PLEDGE CARDS	PROPOSALS MAILED TO ADVANCE PLEDGE PROSPECTS WITH LETTER D
WEEK 7	ADVANCE PLEDGE COMMITTEE MEETS FOR INSTRUCTION AND SELECTION OF CARDS	ADVANCE PLEDGE SOLICITATION BEGINS	MAIL LETTER E	MAIL LETTER G		FIRST ADVANCE PLEDGE REPORT	MAIL LETTERS H AND J AND PRINTED PROPOSALS TO ALL PROSPECTS
WEEK 8	FIRST WORKERS' TRAINING CONFERENCE	BEGIN SOLICITATION OF WORKERS		MAIL LETTERS K AND L	USE CHECK LIST 5	SECOND WORKERS' TRAINING CONFERENCE / ADVANCE PLEDGE FINAL REPORT	PUBLICITY COMMITTEE BUILDS UP ATTENDANCE FOR DEDICATION SUNDAY / FILL IN MASTER LIST
WEEK 9	11:00 SPECIAL SERMON AND DEDICATION SERVICE 12:30 WORKERS' LUNCH FIRST REPORT MEETING			SECOND REPORT MEETING		THIRD REPORT MEETING	
WEEK 10	FOURTH REPORT MEETING			VICTORY REPORT MEETING / GENERAL COMMITTEE MEETS TO EVALUATE CANVASS AND PLAN FOLLOW-UP		MAIL LETTER M PLAN COLLECTION PROGRAM	

FIG. 2-1

STEP 3: *Programming for Tomorrow**

*"Audacious faith is needed to do the job right. It
needs real audacity to attempt the impossible, and to
most people having to do with the finances of churches
the boosting of the income seems to be an impossible thing."*
                    REV. CHARLES O. WRIGHT (deceased)
                    FIRST BAPTIST CHURCH
                    WHITE PLAINS, NEW YORK

The church of Jesus Christ does not exist to operate a budget. The church has been ordained to provide a program of evangelism, fellowship, service, and missions. This task is primary, and here each church must begin. Money must always be thought of in terms of what it can do to glorify God and to bless the giver.

In most churches the board of trustees or the finance committee prepares the proposed budget for the coming year. Since trustees are expected to conserve, protect, and cut down expenses, they tend to develop a conservative attitude. They generally think in terms of last year's budget, and so it is difficult to introduce new projects into the church. The emphasis is taken away from services and placed upon dollars.

Our churches need to do more dreaming. How much faster could we win the world to Christ if we had better tools and more missionaries? How many more children and youth could we reach if we had larger staffs and better facilities? Are we doing enough for older folks? Do our church schools have modern teaching aids to help convey their messages? Do our church offices use up-to-date equipment to lighten their loads? We need, at least once a year, to think of improving our program—of giving greater service to Jesus Christ—rather than of continuing last year's activities and last year's budget.

* Many of the ideas embodied in this step were developed by the Council on Missionary Cooperation of the American Baptist Convention. Early manuals, setting forth these ideas, were written by Loyde Aukerman, Jack Krause, and the author.

The forward step taken by the First–United Baptist Church in Lowell, Massachusetts, began with the pastor. One day Otto Loverude sat in his office dreaming of how his church could become more effective. Analysis showed that the church had in his ten-year pastorate increased giving to local expenses by 148 per cent, compared with an average increase of 70 per cent for 300 other churches in the state. Contributions to missions increased 370 per cent, compared with the state average of 91 per cent. "It might have seemed," he wrote, "that we should have been content, but we knew that our people had only begun to realize their responsibility as stewards of God." For the entire day the minister dreamed, at the same time praying for courage to present his challenging program. By evening he had resolved to place before his finance committee a proposed budget of $50,000, calling for $10,000 for missions (an increase of 50 per cent), $20,000 for local expenses (up 10 per cent), and $20,000 for building improvement (a 100 per cent increase). Several weeks later, after much prayer and work, the church reported that pledging for missionary work was up 37 per cent, for local expenses up 32 per cent, and for the improvement fund up 74 per cent. Perhaps the most amazing result was that this church of 836 members listed 1,116 persons as givers of record!

DISCOVERING NEEDS AND OPPORTUNITIES

To promote new services and inject new ideas into your church program, let the Finance Committee delay the drawing up of the actual budget until *after* the enlistment is ended. *Before* anyone is asked to subscribe, draw up a PROPOSAL—an outline of what the church *should* do next year if it had the funds. The proper group to plan the Proposal is a wide representation from all phases of the church life—deacons or elders, the property committee, the choir, the Sunday School and youth groups, the men's and women's organizations, and the missionary committee.

This Proposal Committee will search out *needs* and *opportunities* in the church, community, and world. It will not limit its thinking to last year's budget but will constantly ask: "What should we do for Christ next year if we had all the money we needed?" The words of the New Testament must be ever before this committee: "Ye have not because ye ask not." It will be the task of another committee to determine *how much* the church could raise. The Proposal Committee will not face this question until it has finished dreaming.

Hundreds of churches across the country have had their sights lifted by using a check list prepared by the American Baptist Council on Missionary Cooperation. Entitled, "Thinking about Our Church," it is designed to allow church leaders to evaluate their present program and to check those activities they might wish to undertake next year (see Appendix A).

Another aid in raising sights is the filmstrip, "Through the Looking Glass," designed to prompt church leaders to desire a more aggressive program. The filmstrip should be shown several days or weeks before the check list is used. Both aids may be obtained from the American Baptist Convention or from the Joint Department of Stewardship, the National Council of Churches.

TWO PROBLEMS

Church finance committees have tended to neglect two responsibilities. The first is the mattter of salaries, which need to be restudied in relationship to 1939, when the inflation spiral began.

The cost of living since 1939 had risen 92 per cent by 1954.[1] The average United States personal income (exclusive of corporation earnings) from 1939 to 1953 increased 217 per cent ($539 to $1,709).[2]

The net income of professional men has risen sharply[3]:

	Physicians	Dentists	Lawyers
1940	$ 4,441	$3,314	$4,507
1951	13,432	7,820	8,730
Per cent increase	202	136	94

The net income of farm operators climbed from $4,261,000,000 in 1939 to $12,500,000,000 in 1953, an increase of 193 per cent.[4]

The average annual earnings of all employees in the manufacturing industry went from $1,269 in 1939 to $3,428 in 1952, up 170 per cent. In 1953 they were yet higher. Average weekly earnings in mid-1954 were $71.69.[5]

How much have pastors' salaries risen since 1939? The average Episcopalian rector's salary has gone from about $2,800 to $4,219, an increase of 50 per cent.[6] The median salary in this denomination in 1952 was $3,933, including value of parsonage. In the American Baptist Convention the median salary in 1951 was $3,486, including value of parsonage, an increase of 39 per cent since 1945.[7] Ministers in the Massachusetts Congregational Christian Conference have gone from an average of $2,299 in 1939 to $3,520 in 1952, up 53 per cent.

Thus, while the cost of living has climbed 92 per cent, and personal

[1] *Survey of Current Business,* U.S. Department of Commerce, August, 1954, p. S-5.
[2] *Ibid.,* August, 1954.
[3] *Ibid.,* July, 1952, p. 7.
[4] "Agricultural Outlook Chart," 1954, U.S. Department of Agriculture, p. 14.
[5] "National Income," 1951, U.S. Department of Commerce, p. 184; *Monthly Labor Review,* U.S. Department of Labor, August, 1954.
[6] *Protection Points,* November, 1952, Church Pension Fund, New York.
[7] *Crusader,* Summer, 1952, American Baptist Convention, New York.

income 217 per cent, the clergyman's salary has gone up only about 50 per cent.[8]

In light of the foregoing, should not churches be paying salaries at least twice what they paid in 1939? Here is one of the most pressing needs that the Proposal Committee can take care of.

The minister of one church in western Pennsylvania was a former painter. When the committee wondered what salary to propose in their new budget, sector director Herbert E. MacCombie suggested they pay the minister the same that he would be receiving if he were still a painter. The union informed them that the local prevailing wage was $100 a week. This pastor of a church of 170 members thereby became the fourth highest paid minister in his metropolitan area.

The clergyman's salary is down primarily because he has not insisted—and often not even hinted—on increases as have labor unions, business and professional men, farmers, and other groups.

Many churches unwittingly take advantage of their minister's reluctance to ask anything for himself. As one of my elder friends laughingly said after a lifetime in the pastorate: "I never asked for an increase in salary—and I never got one!" Most churches raise salaries *after* their clergyman has resigned and they experience difficulty finding a man who will accept the call on the former salary base. Often the minister can take his problem to an influential member, who will in turn become his champion. Or he can present his needs to the finance committee or the board of trustees or elders.

Money is not filthy lucre. It can, and should, be transformed lives—our energy converted into a medium of exchange. Dollars are as sacred as hours or as prayer. Let not the minister disdain to speak of it—for his own use, to make him less fretful over paying past-due bills, and for the advancement of Christ's Kingdom at home and abroad.

The second area neglected by many finance committees is the church's benevolent and missionary program.

[8] Benson Y. Landis has made other studies of this subject. In the 1953 *Yearbook of American Churches* (pp. 287–293) he concludes that in terms of dollar devaluation since 1939 most ministers have had a decrease in "real" salary. In the January 9, 1954, issue of *Information Service* he quotes from the United States Census, 1950, the following median incomes:

Mail carriers	$3,465
Bus drivers	3,116
Bakers	2,917
Longshoremen	2,501
Clergymen	2,412

Both these publications are periodicals of the National Council of Churches. See "Why Not a Living Wage for Ministers?" *Reader's Digest*, November, 1954. Reprints have been available.

We Christians believe that Jesus Christ is the true hope of the world, that there can be no permanent world peace without the peace of Christ in every heart. Yet how we spend our money does not back up our beliefs. In 1953, Americans paid for defense $312.00 per person, including all children, while for foreign missions, which may be called the church's overseas defense program, we gave $1.45 per Protestant church member—excluding children. (For our total missionary and benevolence program, we contributed $8.57 per member annually.)

The Proposal Committee in every church has a unique opportunity to help change this picture. My work with hundreds of churches has clearly revealed two facts:

1. Missionary giving is frozen in many churches because finance committees do not ask for an increase.
2. If a church uses the ten-step Every Member Enlistment, and *if it asks for an increase in missions, it will get it.*

Our sector experience has been that churches get the increase in both local expenses and missions that the Proposal Committee suggests.

"If you want to raise a million dollars for your church, give more to missions," stated Dr. Winfield Edson, former president of the American Baptist Convention. Twice since 1946 his church (First Baptist of Long Beach, California) interrupted its million-dollar building program to raise large sums—more than $100,000 the first time—for extra-special missionary projects. "These years since 1946 have shown a remarkable growth, spiritually and financially," declared Dr. Edson. "We have discovered that if a church wishes to raise more money for itself, it should first give more to missions." Hundreds of other churches have demonstrated this truth.

"The Church of Christ is today a world-wide fellowship;
yet there are countless people to whom He is unknown. How
much do you care about this? Does your congregation live
for itself, or for the world around it and beyond it? . . .
We affirm our faith in Jesus Christ as the hope of the world,
and desire to share that faith with all men. May God forgive
us that by our sin we have often hidden this hope from the
world."

A MESSAGE FROM THE SECOND ASSEMBLY
OF THE WORLD COUNCIL OF CHURCHES
EVANSTON, ILLINOIS, AUGUST, 1954

THE FIRST DRAFT OF THE PROPOSAL

The various members of the Proposal Committee begin their work by conferring with the groups they represent for suggestions for next year's program. They will stress that planning is to be based upon *needs* and *opportunities* of the church regardless of costs. Each society or organization will list suggestions upon Form B (in the Canvass Kit), marking whether it considers each item to be "optional," "preferred," or "must."

"Optional" items represent ideal appropriations if the church had all the money it needed.

"Preferred" items are those which provide an aggressive, forward-moving ministry.

"Must" items are absolutely essential to the life of the church.

One pastor called these the three "U's"—Utopia, U-oughta, and U-gotta.

There are many variations in using this fascinating step. St. Stephen's Episcopal Church in Westboro, Massachusetts, won wide "audience participation" by distributing a mimeographed sheet to each worshipper one Sunday morning. Each was requested to mark and return his "ballot." Tremont Temple in Boston used the same technique. The First Baptist Church of Pittsfield, Massachusetts, ran the following notice in the church calendar for several weeks prior to the Proposal Committee meeting:

"Please indicate any budget item or improvement in church program or facilities which you would like to see incorporated into next year's plans. Indicate whether you consider it a "must," something we "ought" to do, or a "would-like" item.

	SUGGESTION			
Estimated cost		Must	Ought	Would like

While pastor of the Washington Street Baptist Church in Lynn, Massachusetts, the Rev. Robert Baggs sent a letter to each member stating that each had been appointed an honorary member of the church finance committee. Included in the letter was a mimeographed form listing some items and services and providing space for new ideas. No amounts were included, and no total figures, since it was desired that each one do his own estimating. Each was also to check the Optional, Preferred, or Must column for the various items.

"The educational value to our people was most heartening," commented Pastor Baggs later. "Untold members could not send the estimates back because they did not have the slightest idea of the cost of different items. They began to ask questions, and they were amazed to learn that lighting, heating, and maintenance were so low or so high. Some of them, good loyal souls, did not have the slightest idea whether an item in the budget should be $10 or $1,000. I can truly say it awakened many folk, and that was its value."

After each organization puts its ideas on Form B, it is returned to the Proposal Committee. It then looks something like Fig. 3-1.

Name of Group: HOUSE COMMITTEE		Date: September 28		
Services to be performed	Estimated cost	Check one of the following		
		Optional	Preferred	Must
New oil burner	$900			x
Linoleum for nursery	250			x
New bulletin board			x	
Etc.				

(*Courtesy of American Baptist Convention*)

Fig. 3-1

The Proposal Committee now gathers together all the Forms B which have been submitted and makes a composite proposal, using Form C (Canvass Kit). After the committee has estimated the cost of each item, it decides whether each one is to be classified as Optional, Preferred, or Must. There is now a fourth column to be filled in on Form C entitled Proposed Budget. This is a summary column which will include only those services which the committee feels are practical for the coming year. This column, when completed, will include *some* of the services in column 1, *most* of the services in column 2, and *all* the services in column 3. Column 4 thus becomes the cost of the program the Proposal Committee recommends. Form C will now look like Fig. 3-2.

Services to be performed	(1) Optional	(2) Preferred	(3) Must	(4) Proposed budget
FOR WORSHIP AND SERVICE				
Choir director		$2,000		$2,000
Music supplies			$250	250
Rebuild organ		3,000		
New mimeograph machine	$800			
New filing cabinets		400		300

(*Courtesy of American Baptist Convention*)

Fig. 3-2

Now check your composite proposal against the suggested budget in Appendix A to make sure you have omitted nothing.

CORRELATION OF THE PROPOSAL AND RESOURCES COMMITTEES

Once the Resources Committee has determined the financial potential of the church (see Step 4), the next step is a meeting of the Proposal

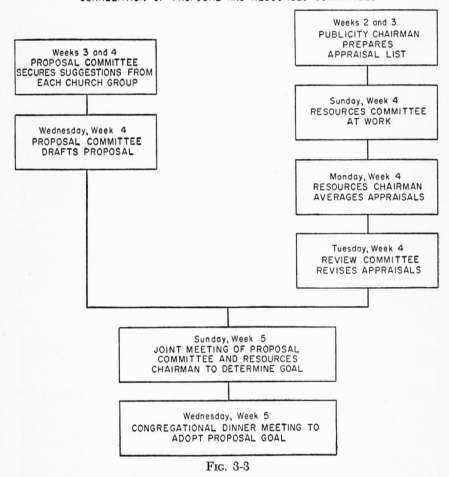

CORRELATION OF PROPOSAL AND RESOURCES COMMITTEES

Fig. 3-3

Committee and the Resources chairman to compare figures. The accompanying chart (Fig. 3-3) correlates the work of these two committees.

When the Proposal and Resources chairmen compare results, there will be need for an adjustment of figures. If the proposed budget calls for more money than the potential income figure arrived at by the Resources Committee, the budget must be lowered. If it calls for a much smaller amount, a few more items should be added to the proposed budget to bring the two figures closer together. The Resources Committee is the court of final appeal. The Proposal Committee dares not ask for more than the former committee indicates can be raised. If the canvass goal is set too high, it will discourage both the workers and the prospects. Setting the goal slightly under the amount it is expected can be raised will not prevent the church from oversubscribing its proposal.

MEETING WITH CHURCH COUNCIL

After the Proposal and Resources chairmen have agreed upon a canvass goal, the General Committee presents the Proposal to the advisory board or church council. At this session the committee begins selling the program. The General chairman reports all the steps which have been taken to date. The Proposal Committee presents the needs of the church as outlined in the Proposal, telling how this program was arrived at, what it will do for the church and the world, and what it will cost. The Resources chairman tells why he thinks the sum total can be raised. He explains the appraisal procedure, telling how "average" goals were arrived at for each prospect and how this information will help individuals to determine their fair share in the program. Questions and discussion are encouraged.

Since many church leaders have given so much thought to the Proposal, the church council is almost sure to adopt the proposed plan without changes. Whatever proposal is adopted by this advisory group should be presented for further discussion and adoption at a meeting of the entire congregation.

THE CONGREGATIONAL MEETING

The meeting of the congregation to hear the recommendation of the General Committee should not be one of the regular business meetings of the church. To get as many as possible to attend, it is good procedure to hold a complimentary church dinner. An agenda for this meeting is given in the Canvass Kit (Form P). As in the meeting with the advisory board, it is wise to have several members of the committee speak.

The purpose of the Congregational Meeting is twofold:

To obtain authority
To begin promoting the program

Here the church votes approval of the canvass goal. Here the members begin to sell themselves on the value of the program of advance as they discuss the various items.

This meeting offers the first opportunity to test whether the program is likely to secure financial support. Great care should be given in answering all questions. There is a direct relationship between the amount of money which can be raised and the interest expressed at this meeting in comments and questions. It is important to know what the people are thinking. Do not be afraid of criticism. Any negative note at this point will be effectively answered by one or more of those members who have given thought to building the Proposal.

Do not be tempted to raise the goal because of enthusiastic comments. An equal amount of confidence may not be expressed toward a larger goal. Retaining the original goal will not prevent a church from exceeding it.

The calendar calls for the Congregational Meeting on Wednesday of Week 5. The Congregational Church in West Medford, Massachusetts, however, held a very successful dinner meeting on a Sunday. Following a Roll Call Communion Sunday service, over three hundred persons sat down to a complimentary dinner and a program conducted by the Rev. Gordon Washburn and the General Committee.

Immediately after the Congregational Meeting, the Proposal chairman gives to the Publicity chairman copy for printing the Proposal. Your campaign is now well under way.

There are TEN steps to Victory. Step THREE is programming for tomorrow.

"Our Father, Thou who hast given unsparingly unto us
through Jesus Christ, Thy Son, we praise Thee for the joy
of giving. Grant that we may give from hearts ever-expanding
to include all who are in the circle of Thy love. Through
Thy mercy, multiply the gifts we give, translating them into
Christian personalities that shall make Thy goodness and
sacrificial love real to all men everywhere. Amen."
                        Reuben E. Nelson
                        GENERAL SECRETARY
                        AMERICAN BAPTIST CONVENTION

IMPORTANT DATES FOR THE PROPOSAL CHAIRMAN

THURSDAY *Week 1* Proposal chairman agrees to serve. Confer with pastor about announcement to congregation next Sunday asking for Proposal suggestions. Jointly with pastor, begin selecting committee members from representative organizations, asking each to be present for first meeting, Sunday, Week 3. Arrange for mimeographing of Form B (Canvass Kit) for use at this meeting.

SUNDAY *Week 2* Form B is distributed to every society and organization.

MONDAY *Week 2* Attend first meeting of General Committee, reporting progress on securing committee members.

TUESDAY *Week 2* Check with Publicity chairman about photographs for Proposal.

FRIDAY *Week 2* Deadline for securing Proposal Committee members.

SUNDAY *Week 3* Minister requests congregation to make suggestions for next year's program.

Proposal Committee's first meeting. Chairman outlines plans for the intensive Every Member Canvass. Everything begins with a challenging proposed budget. Instruct each member to find out from his group what they would like to accomplish for Christ next year if more money were available. Make sure each representative has copies of Form B. Explain how they are to be filled in. Chairman or pastor should be available to speak before each group. Forms are to be returned, if possible, at next meeting, Friday, Week 3.

WEDNESDAY *Week 3* Several copies of Form C (Canvass Kit) are prepared.

FRIDAY *Week 3* Second meeting of Proposal Committee. Call for presentation and discussion of items on all the Forms B. Transfer the suggestions to Form C, placing the estimated cost in the proper column (Optional, Preferred, or Must). Column 4 should be left blank until the next meeting. Announce that each suggested item is to be listed on Form C under the five following categories: (1) church home, (2) pastoral ministry, (3) worship and service, (4) Christian education, (5) missions and benevolences. Use a separate sheet of Form C for each of these five divisions.

SUNDAY *Week 4* Remind minister to request Proposal suggestions from the congregation. Deadline for submission is the following Wednesday.

WEDNESDAY *Week 4* Third meeting of Proposal Committee. Call for final report on remaining Forms B. Committee adds any necessary items omitted thus far, paying particular attention to present year's budget. After all suggestions are transferred to Form C, committee begins to decide which should go into column 4, which becomes the first draft of proposed budget. The total figure thus arrived at may be changed after a joint meeting with Resources chairman. Proposal Committee should review each item, testing it with three questions: Is it practical? Does it meet a need? Is the need easily recognizable?

Review Proposal to determine proportion suggested for benevolences and missions. Is the per cent increase *for others* at least as great as the per cent increase *for ourselves?*

SUNDAY *Week 5* Joint meeting of Resources chairman and Proposal Committee. Resources chairman states figure his Review Committee arrived at. If the preliminary total of Proposal Committee is larger than the figure presented by the Resources Committee, it must be reduced. This can be done by eliminating "optional" and "preferred" items from the budget until the totals of resources and Proposal correspond. If the preliminary total of the Proposal is smaller, additional items should be added to the budget. The Proposal must be completed this night, since it will be presented tomorrow for approval by church council.

Prepare Form G (Canvass Kit) for printer.

MONDAY *Week 5* Appear before church council, seeking its approval of Proposal. Explain all new budget items, stating how and why they were included. Encourage questions, since you are now beginning to sell this program to the church leaders.

WEDNESDAY *Week 5* Congregational Meeting. At this important session, you are seeking (1) to get official endorsement of the Proposal and (2) to sell those present on the value of the increased program. Be prepared to make the strongest presentation possible, feeling free to use visual aids and help from other voices. Strive to create enthusiasm, but guard against further additions to the Proposal, since these would jeopardize reaching the goal as determined by the Resources Committee.

After close of the meeting, go over copy of Proposal with Publicity chairman who will deliver it to printer in morning. Check spelling of all names and addition of all figures. Use Form G completely filled out.

SUNDAY *Week 6* Assist at first meeting of Advance Pledge Committee. Speak on the needs and the opportunities of the church which call for a high goal.

SUNDAY *Week 8* Attend First Workers' Training Conference. Assist in explaining why various new items are in the Proposal.

FRIDAY *Week 8* Attend Second Workers' Training Conference.

SUNDAY *Week 9* Dedication Sunday. Attend worship service, workers' luncheon, and First Report Meeting.

WEDNESDAY *Week 9* Second Report Meeting.

FRIDAY *Week 9* Third Report Meeting.

SUNDAY *Week 10* Fourth Report Meeting.

WEDNESDAY *Week 10* Victory Report Meeting. General Committee evaluates canvass and plans follow-up.

TIME SCHEDULE
PROPOSAL CHAIRMAN

For detailed information consult the "Important Dates" for the Proposal Chairman" in this chapter.

Insert the proper date in the upper right-hand corner of each calendar square.

	SUNDAY	MONDAY	TUESDAY	WEDNESDAY	THURSDAY	FRIDAY	SATURDAY
WEEK 1							
WEEK 2	FORM B DISTRIBUTED TO EVERY CHURCH GROUP	FIRST MEETING OF GENERAL COMMITTEE / PROPOSAL CHAIRMAN SELECTS COMMITTEE	PROPOSAL CHAIRMAN CHECKS WITH PUBLICITY CHAIRMAN ABOUT PROPOSAL PHOTOGRAPHS		PROPOSAL CHAIRMAN AGREES TO SERVE	DEADLINE FOR SECURING PROPOSAL COMMITTEE	
WEEK 3	MINISTER REQUESTS PROPOSAL SUGGESTIONS FROM CONGREGATION / FIRST MEETING OF PROPOSAL COMMITTEE			PROPOSAL COMMITTEE BEGINS SECURING GROUP PROPOSALS / FORM C IS PREPARED		SECOND MEETING OF PROPOSAL COMMITTEE	
WEEK 4				THIRD MEETING OF PROPOSAL COMMITTEE			
WEEK 5	JOINT MEETING OF PROPOSAL AND RESOURCES CHAIRMEN / PROPOSAL CHAIRMAN PREPARES FORM G	PROPOSAL AND RESOURCES CHAIRMEN MEET WITH CHURCH COUNCIL		CONGREGATIONAL DINNER MEETING TO ADOPT PROPOSED BUDGET AS CANVASS GOAL	COPY FOR PROPOSAL DELIVERED TO PRINTER		

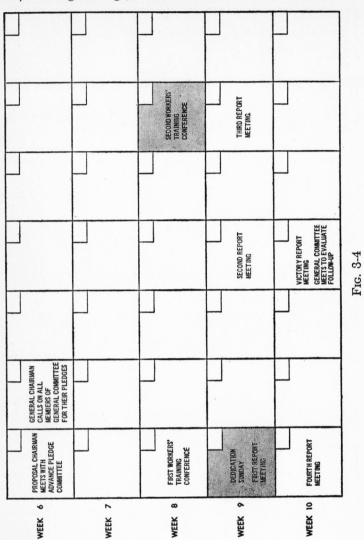

WEEK 6 — PROPOSAL CHAIRMAN MEETS WITH ADVANCE PLEDGE COMMITTEE — GENERAL CHAIRMAN CALLS ON ALL MEMBERS OF GENERAL COMMITTEE FOR THEIR PLEDGES

WEEK 7

WEEK 8 — FIRST WORKERS' TRAINING CONFERENCE — SECOND WORKERS' TRAINING CONFERENCE

WEEK 9 — DEDICATION SUNDAY FIRST REPORT MEETING — SECOND REPORT MEETING — THIRD REPORT MEETING

WEEK 10 — FOURTH REPORT MEETING — VICTORY REPORT MEETING GENERAL COMMITTEE MEETS TO EVALUATE FOLLOW-UP

FIG. 3-4

STEP 4: *Discovering Your Resources*

*"We found out we could do some things
we thought we could not do."*
>REV. GLEN D. GLAZIER
>ST. JAMES METHODIST CHURCH
>SPRINGFIELD, MASSACHUSETTS

"Convert the purse and you win the man."
>REV. DANIEL C. TUTTLE
>OLD MYSTIC BAPTIST CHURCH
>OLD MYSTIC, CONNECTICUT

HOW MUCH MONEY CAN YOUR CHURCH RAISE NEXT YEAR?

Before reading further, write your estimate here: For local expenses and benevolences (exclusive of capital funds)—$_____.

What did you base your estimate upon?

Last year's experience? But how do you know your people gave last year all that they could or should? Was last year's performance satisfying to God?

A tithe? The Old Testament certainly teaches this, and the New Testament seems to commend it. But not many Christians reach it, and very few churches can claim it for all their membership. Test it for yourself. Multiply your total membership by $1,709 which was the average per capita income in the United States in 1953. How close were your receipts to one-tenth of this figure? Some day it is to be hoped that all Christians will give at least a tithe, but the modern church is far beneath that goal today.

A total of $70—$100—$150 per member? That depends on many circumstances, such as the general financial level of your congregation, their past habits of giving, and whether you are engaged in a major building project.

50

Although each church is different, the answer is the same for all:

Your church can raise the total of what each member can and will give.

If your church is small but has several members of affluence, it *could* raise more than a much larger church that has no one of more than average income. The question then becomes a very individual one for each congregation. And it is a question which only the church members themselves can answer.

The task of the Resources Committee is to find this answer. But while they are finding the sum total that the church can raise, they will also discover other useful information. There are, then, four reasons for the work of this committee.

1. To discover names of persons who can help in the visitation. This will answer the objection: "We cannot find enough workers to call on every home."

2. To discover the total figure that your church can be expected to raise for next year's budget. This figure will prevent the Proposal Committee from asking for too high a budget or from staying too close to the present budget.

3. To provide an answer to the visitor when he wonders what would be considered a fair pledge from each of his prospects.

4. To provide an answer to the prospect when he wonders: "What is my fair share? How much should I give?" Too often we have failed to help the man who, sincerely asking this question, desires an honest reply.

The appraisal procedure used by the Resources Committee has been tested in over one thousand churches. *Opinion is agreed that here is the one step that accounts for the greatest increase in giving.* It is also the step, which, if omitted, will be most costly to the church. A survey of ninety churches in sector projects during the spring of 1952 revealed that seventy-seven followed the appraisal procedure and received an average increase of 78 per cent. The remaining thirteen churches obtained an average increase of 41 per cent.

John D. Rockefeller, Jr., speaking in 1933 before the Citizens Family Welfare Committee of New York City, stated that there are five factors to a successful solicitation: (1) The cause must be worthy, and you, the solicitor, must be informed. (2) You should know as much as possible about the man you are calling on. (3) You should give him an idea as to the contributions others in his group are making. (4) You should suggest what you might like him to give, leaving it to him to make the final decision. (5) You should be kindly and considerate: "Thus you will get closest to a man's heart and his pocketbook."

If your Proposal Committee has drawn up a worthy program (point 1), if each visitor prepares himself carefully (points 2 and 5), then the Resources Committee will provide the answers to points 3 and 4.

SELLING THE APPRAISAL IDEA

The appraisal procedure requires more selling than anything else in your canvass. Because the idea is new to so many, and because many misunderstand it at first (believing that someone is going to dictate to them what they must give to the church), it is generally the biggest hurdle in the enlistment. "Men usually scorn," declared Conan Doyle, "what they do not understand." If the General Committee will be prepared to face misunderstanding and scorn at first, always answering with a careful explanation of the procedure, the church will be won over. "We put the appraisal idea in our mental incubator," said a New Hampshire clergyman, "and let it hatch out in time." Two things need to be repeated again and again: *why* we appraise, and *how* we appraise. Church leaders should expect much rumbling and even anger when the idea is first proposed. Then one week later a second explanation is given. The rumbling becomes less violent. By the third week it has ceased (if the General Committee keeps selling), and by the time the visitor calls each prospect is thinking: I wonder what my suggested share will be?

The General Committee needs constantly to repeat what the appraisal is *not*, as well as what it *is*. It is *not* an attempt to tell anyone what he *must* give to the church. It is *not* an assessment. It is *not* a prying into anyone's personal affairs, since no information is given to any of the Resources Committee.

It *is* an intelligent, democratic way to arrive at a potential goal. If a small group of three or four sat down to discuss each name, there could be mistaken judgments and perhaps resentment from others. "In a multitude of minds, there is wisdom." Hence a large committee is used, some of whose appraisals will be too high and some too low, but the average will be amazingly fair.

The appraisal *is* a suggestion to each individual. It is as close to a scientific approach as has yet been devised. Each man must be shown that *if he could* reach his suggested figure, and if each other person *could* reach his, the total goal *would* be achieved. Each must make up his own mind whether he *will* give the appraisal amount.

The *real objective* of the appraisal is not that each individual reach his suggested figure but rather that the total group underwrite the total goal. The system works like this: Mr. A is appraised at $3, Mr. B at $4, and Mr. C at $5. Their total goal is $12. During the visitation, Mr. A decides to pledge $4, Mr. B $5, and Mr. C $3. No one of the three gives his exact appraisal, but the total is reached, and therefore the advance program is assured.

Some people may grossly distort the idea, like the little girl who rushed to her mother, exclaiming: "Next week some one from the church is coming to our house and is going to look at all our furniture and then tell us what we've got to give!" Some members may incorrectly prejudge the reaction of others. The Federated Church at Norfolk, Massachusetts, became disturbed when it was rumored that a very influential person threatened to leave the church if anyone "tried to tell her what to give." The pastor, Arthur Samuelson, called and was delighted to hear her state that she considered this method the most businesslike procedure in the church since she had been there. She later increased her giving fourfold. This gift led the way for a church increase of 170 per cent. A woman in New Hampshire became angry at the appraisal meeting. The chairman took pains to explain the method to her personally. She later doubled her pledge. Pastor Hartley Johnson, when at Damariscotta, Maine, stated that he had two reactions from his people. One was the usual misunderstanding. The other was stated by a man who said: "I have given 50 cents all my life. Nobody ever told me the church needed more." Churches which have used the appraisal method agree that criticisms disappear as people come to a fuller understanding of the process.

Many churches, of course, have no trouble with this evaluation. Charles Weller, general chairman at Trinity Union Methodist Church in Providence, declared that his church leaders were astonished at how well all took to the idea. No visitor, he stated, felt that he was appraised too high. Almost everyone on the advance pledge list subscribed his suggested figure. The steps this church took to sell the idea were well executed:

1. Weller first went to the church official board and explained the procedure at great length.

2. The appraisal was again explained at a church business meeting.

3. The bulletin mailed to every home had a statement each week on the evaluation method.

4. The minister, Rev. Harold Metzner, kept talking about it from the pulpit.

5. The entire official board served as the Resources Committee. Such careful selling paid off. The church increased its pledges from $15,000 to $28,000.

Harry Birch, of the United Baptist Church in Concord, New Hampshire, told of his early antagonism and gradual conversion to the evaluation technique. "It works like this," he declared. "Let me ask a group of people to estimate my age. One will say forty-eight, another fifty-three, and so on. If a dozen or so make guesses, the average is liable to be right. So it is with the appraisal. No one knows what anyone else's income is, and for this purpose no one is interested. But if a representative group makes estimates of what I might be able to give to the church, the average is going to be close to the truth."

It is often surprising how close the averages do work out. "We were amazed," said Dr. Alger Geary (Columbia Street Baptist Church in Bangor), "at the accuracy of the appraisals. Several members stated that the suggested figure was just what they planned to give." In the North Abington, Massachusetts, Church the advance pledgers were appraised at $262 a week and actually gave $254. In the First Baptist Church of Springfield, twenty-five of the advance pledgers gave more and twenty-four gave less than their suggested amount. The combined group pledged within fifteen cents of their total appraisal.

There are people in every church who will pledge more than the suggested amount. Three Baptist churches in Providence have supplied their figures in this regard: 52 members of the Roger Williams Church met the appraisal and 18 exceeded it; 64 in the Pond Street Church equaled and 24 exceeded the figure; 25 in Lonsdale reached and 2 exceeded the appraisal. In another city a man who last year had given $400 to local expense and $1,000 to a renovation fund was appraised at $2,000 for the year. Upon signing his pledge he handed the pastor a check for $1,000 and told him to come back in a month for the rest. This second time he handed out a check for $2,000. "You must have forgotten," said the pastor, "that you gave me $1,000 last month." "No," he replied, "I just supposed the church could use it."

The most common danger that the Resources Committee faces is that of being overcautious in their estimates. More people in the Mittineague Congregational Church of West Springfield complained of being appraised too low than about being too high. "That's not high enough," stated several in the Second Baptist Church of Holyoke. One young couple stationed at Westover Field in Massachusetts, newcomers in the church, were told by their visitor: "We thought you might like to think in terms of $1." A hurt look flashed across both faces. "But," blurted out the wife, "we are already giving $5!" In another church a man giving $1.25 a week was evaluated at $4. The minister thought he could give $10 and so suggested. Within five minutes the man agreed and went on to say that he might make an additional gift later in the year.

SIZE OF THE RESOURCES COMMITTEE

In a church of less than 150 members, this committee should consist of twenty members. Some small churches have asked the entire congregation to serve as the committee. In larger churches the number should be thirty. The size of the committee has a threefold importance:

1. A large committee will ensure more accurate results. Whereas a few will appraise too high and a few too low, the average will be fair when a number of estimates are made.

2. The appraisers begin to see the importance of the church work and to compare their probable giving with what they think others could do. This appraising of others tends to raise a man's own sights. In one church the General chairman appraised himself at five dollars. When he came to his pastor's name, he wrote down five dollars for him. Then he reasoned: If my pastor could give five dollars (as I believe he can), then I could give ten dollars. Whereupon he raised his own appraisal. It is important that a number of the larger givers be included on this committee.

3. You can count on there being some talk throughout the parish when this day's work is done. The more talk there is, the better. Of course no one yet knows what the average figure will be for any individual. He knows only what he himself suggested.

HOW THE RESOURCES COMMITTEE WORKS

A great deal of preparatory work must be done before the committee of thirty meets. The Resources chairman asks the Publicity chairman to mimeograph fifty copies of the appraisal list (see Form D, Fig. 4-1). The following points must be kept in mind in preparing these forms:

FORM D

To be prepared by the Publicity chairman on WEDNESDAY, Week 2, for use by the Resources Committee on Sunday, Week 4.

			Resource appraisal sheet					Page No. 1
No.	Name	Address	Member or nonmember	Phone	Would he or she make a good:		Estimated giving potential
					Leader	Worker	

(Courtesy of American Baptist Convention)

The first five columns are to be filled in when the form is prepared. The remaining columns will be completed by the Resources Committee at its meeting, SUNDAY, Week 4. Provide one copy of the entire list for each member of the Resources Committee plus an extra twenty copies for use in other ways. Cut each stencil as above. But do not put it on the mimeograph machine until the names, addresses, and telephone numbers are cut in.

FIG. 4-1

1. All names are to be listed alphabetically and numbered.

2. The listing of members is to be done by *income units*. Thus, if Mr. Jones is producing the only income in his family, they will be listed on one line: E. S. Jones and family. If, however, there is a daughter now working, the listing will be on two lines:

Mr. and Mrs. E. S. Jones

Elsie Jones

3. Each address must be included.

4. All telephone numbers are to be given.

5. Nonresident members are put in a separate listing.

6. Churches of five hundred or more should list separately all shut-ins, pensioners, and others with greatly limited incomes.

7. Names of all friends are put in another separate listing. This includes parents of Sunday School children, members of the congregation, and summer or winter visitors.

Since the committee will use only thirty sets of the appraisal sheets, there will remain twenty sets for the telephone squad and for other uses throughout the year.

The committee is asked to meet on a Sunday afternoon for two hours. They need not be told beforehand what the job is to be except that it will be "important." See Form O (Canvass Kit) for agenda for this meeting.

The group must work in the spirit of prayer. If the work is so done, the church will benefit for many months to come. "We are instruments of the Holy Spirit and we ought to be willing to be used," Bryan Archibald told the Resources Committee in the First Baptist Church of Springfield. Open the meeting with the reading of II Corinthians 8:8–15. Have the Proposal chairman speak on the dream of the church for next year. Mention several items being considered for the new budget and state how these new projects can become reality as the people have faith and are willing to work for them. Emphasize the spiritual import of the canvass —the purpose being not to raise more money but to strengthen the Kingdom and to bless the givers.

The Resources chairman may state to the group that success for the enlistment will be won as three principles are followed:

1. A personal call will be made upon every prospect.

2. Each will be encouraged to subscribe in proportion to his ability.

3. Every name will be treated in the same manner.

The chairman should then go over the following points with the committee, encouraging all to ask questions. It is better to delay the work one-half hour in selling the idea than to ram things through and end up with a set of appraisals that show no faith or imagination. You may wish to distribute mimeographed copies of the following to all present:

DISCOVERING OUR RESOURCES

1. Our work must be done in a spirit of prayer. The purpose is to glorify God by enlarging His work.

2. Members of the committee should not work as a team; each appraisal should be made independently of each other. Work in privacy by separating around the room.

3. Members of the committee should check their lists for accuracy and make any necessary corrections in the spelling of names and addresses. This is important since the master list and pledge cards should be absolutely correct in every detail. Committee members should also add the name and address of any prospect whom they find missing from the list.

4. The *first* task is to find leadership for the canvass. Check whether "he" or "she" would make a good "leader" or "worker."

5. The *second* task is to secure an average judgment of what the church as a whole can reasonably expect to raise. This amount is the sum total of what each member can give.

6. The *third* task is to make an intelligent estimate of what each person might like to give per week to our advance program.

7. All judgments will be confidential, since the lists are not to be signed by anyone.

8. It is important for everyone possible to increase his giving in proportion to his ability. Only in this way can the church realize its potential. No adult with a regular income should be appraised for less than one dollar a week.

9. The one appraisal will cover both local expenses and benevolences. It is to be on a weekly basis.

10. The question to be asked each time is: "What could this person give if he were vitally interested in this proposed program?" The question is not "what *will* he give" or "what *must* he give," but "what *could* he give."

11. Avoid uniformity. Consider each case on its own merits. Any appraisal placing every person in the one-dollar-a-week category is worthless.

12. Do not guess, but make it a matter of best judgment. One does not need to know a prospect's earning capacity; one can make the judgment on the basis of whether the prospect has more responsibilities or less than the appraiser, and whether his income would seem to be more or less than that of the appraiser. While some appraisals will be too high, others will be too low. However, the average of twenty to thirty independent appraisals will be amazingly fair.

13. If any person listed is not known, no appraisal should be made. No appraisal should be made for children or for those without a regular income.

14. Begin by evaluating yourself. This will not be a pledge since the lists will not be signed. The question still is: "What *could* I give next year if I became really interested in this new program?"

15. Next, evaluate the minister, then the General chairman. Now proceed alphabetically with all names.

16. You may leave when finished. Hand your list to the Resources chairman. Do not sign it.

AVERAGING THE APPRAISALS

That same evening the Resources chairman solicits the aid of several other persons to help him strike an average for each name. There should be an adding machine available. Large churches may desire a second adding machine or a calculator.

The chairman will have prepared his form beforehand (see the next page). Since he needs more work space beside each name, he cuts the name and the address section from the Resource Appraisal Sheets (Form D) and pastes each onto a sheet at least 14 inches wide. He divides each sheet into six columns as shown in the Summary Appraisal Sheet (Form E). Onto these sheets he will copy all the estimates made for each name.

One way to expedite the averaging of appraisals is to have the group of helpers sit at a large table with the chairman at one end. Each assistant holds five or six sheets of page 1 of the appraisal list. The man next to the chairman begins reading: "Mr. A—$5, $4, $3, $4." Then the next assistant reads: "Mr. A—$2, $6, $5." This continues around the table while the chairman writes down each figure for Mr. A in column 2 (Form E, Fig. 4-2). As soon as the chairman finishes all the names on page 1, another helper takes this page to the adding machine for tabulation, then fills in columns 3, 4, and 5 on the right side of the sheet, leaving column 6 for a final revised figure.

THE RESOURCES REVIEW COMMITTEE

A check with the church financial secretary quickly reveals that the "average" for a number of members (perhaps 10 per cent) is less than that person is already giving. A few appraisals may be too high, particularly where there are cases of need known only to the pastor. Thus there is necessity for a Review Committee.

The Review Committee is made up of the Resources chairman, the General chairman, the Advance Pledge chairman, the financial secretary, and the minister. The financial secretary will state whether any person is already giving as much as or more than the appraisal average. The minister can provide information such as no other person can give. The feeling that he should not know what his members give to the church is to me a bit of prudery. Many years of facing this question have led to this conclusion: There may be several minor reasons why members do not wish

FORM E

SUMMARY APPRAISAL SHEET

(For use of Resources chairman and Resources Review Committee)

Date   Sheet

(1) Name and address	(2) List of individual appraisals	(3) Total of appraisals	(4) Number of appraisals	(5) Average appraisal	(6) Revised appraisal
Here paste column of names and addresses clipped from an appraisal sheet	This sheet should be at least 14 inches wide, giving column 2 all the extra width.				
Total names				Total of revised appraisals	$

FIG. 4-2

their pastors to see the financial record book, but the one major reason is that the objectors desire to keep their giving from the pastor's eyes because they wish to protect their consciences or their purses.

Mr. Fifty-Cents-a-Week is an important man since he is found in every church. He has not a financial, but rather a spiritual, problem. Hence, it is imperative that the minister know of this need so that he can best answer the spiritual problem.

"It is not good," some churchmen say, "for our minister to know what our people give. He might show favoritism to those of greater wealth." Answer: If any clergyman does not know within one month of his arrival in any parish who apparently has ample funds—as judged by automobile, home, clothes, and business—he is not a very observant Man of God. Should, in rare cases, the minister play favorites, he would not need the church books to tell him which members to choose.

The Review Committee will consider each average appraisal. In only a few cases should the figure be reduced. The committee must avoid the temptation of reducing all averages on the assumption that a man who never has given a high amount never will. Such action is playing fair neither with the committee of thirty nor with the members themselves. The only question these reviewers ask is: "What *could* this man give?"

What should be done with the person who is already giving as much as, or more than, his average appraisal? Such will be the case with 5 to 10 per cent of your people. Experience has shown that in almost every such case the appraisal should be revised to at least one dollar a week *above* the present sum. The reason for this blanket rule is that persons who are underevaluated are generally those who love the church a great deal. They are interested in a program of advance. Receiving the same publicity as everyone, they begin to think of increasing their pledge. If the visitor then suggests the same amount as last year, the prospect suffers a spiritual letdown. It is far better to suggest a figure a little too high than one too low. We are dealing in this process with man's highest aspirations. We dare not aim low.

"My wife and I had been pledging seven dollars to our church," a layman confided to me. "When our Proposal Committee presented a forward program, we began thinking of how much to increase our gift. Then the visitor called on us, and when we came to the appraisal he suggested four dollars. (The church had not used the Review Committee.) The two of us had a distinct disappointment."

"What did you pledge?" I pursued.

"We reasoned this way: Since we were already giving more than the church wanted, we would keep our pledge at seven dollars."

As the Review Committee agrees on the final figure for each name, the appraisal is written in column 6 of the Summary Appraisal Sheet (Form E). Names of nonresidents, pensioners, and nonmembers are not to be appraised so high as active members. Whenever it is agreed that a person cannot pledge one dollar, he should not be given any appraisal figure. The amount of his pledge will be left completely up to him.

After all amounts have been reviewed, the figures in column 6 are added up to discover the total *ideal* potential of the church.

CUTTING BACK THE TOTAL APPRAISAL

No church will be successful in having every member pledge the suggested figure. In fact, one or two persons out of every ten will not pledge. A study of two hundred churches reveals that the average church should cut back its total *ideal* appraisal by 30 per cent. In other words, *each church should set as its goal a figure which is 70 per cent of the total appraisal.* Each church may then, by following the plan carefully, expect to reach and perhaps exceed its goal. It is better psychologically to exceed a moderate goal than to miss a high one.

Should this figure of 70 per cent of the total appraisal prove too low (because of timid appraising), the Review Committee is *not* to cut back the *total* less than 30 per cent. It must instead review the list again, raising *individual* appraisals until the 70 per cent total reaches the desired Proposal figure.

Cutting back the total appraisal by 30 per cent does not mean that the church cannot raise more money than this revised figure. The cutback is to assure each church (through prayer, perspiration, and the ten-step plan) of reaching its Proposal. Some churches will exceed this figure. Thus the Portland Street Baptist Church of Haverhill, Massachusetts, exceeded its Proposal of $12,700 by over $2,000. Two smaller churches, in the Attleboro Area Council of Churches, Hebron Methodist and Chartley Methodist, surpassed their Proposals by $1,000 each. Many churches have exceeded their goals by several thousand dollars.

It is important not to discuss publicly this cutback of 30 per cent. To do so would be to encourage your prospects to think of cutting their individual pledges.

PREPARING THE PLEDGE CARD

Once the individual appraisal figures have been reviewed, they should be rounded off and grouped into categories. Thus, an appraisal of $4.50 would be rounded off to $5.00, while one at $2.10 would be placed at

$2.00. All appraisals are then listed by groups in descending order:

1 at $12.00 per week
3 at $10.00 per week
2 at $ 8.00 per week
6 at $ 7.00 per week
14 at $ 5.00 per week

. . . . .

47 at $ 1.00 per week
Total proposal—$23,420

Only children or unemployed youth should be evaluated at less than one dollar. The total *Proposal figure* is to be given at the bottom of the listing. This figure is the one used on the Proposal. It is not the actual addition of all the appraisals, but rather 70 per cent of that total. Should anyone question the addition (no one ever does, even though committee members are afraid some one will), the reply is that, if the actual total were to be reached, it would necessitate a *perfect* campaign. There will be no perfect campaigns. The 70 per cent figure is a realistic one based on the experience of many churches.

This table of appraisal figures is then given to the Publicity chairman for printing on the pledge card, using Forms H-1 and H-2 in the Canvass Kit. See Fig. 4-3 for a sample pledge card.

Before this card is taken by the visitor, it is numbered (both the stub and the original) to correspond with John Doe's number on the master list. The name and address is put on the top of the card by the Publicity Committee. Finally, the Resources chairman checks the suggested pledge figure in the right-hand column (in John Doe's case at $7.00 per week). This box of appraisals makes fascinating reading for every church member. He is interested to see how much the top givers will be subscribing. He is eager to see how the committee of thirty estimated his ability. He wants to know how many others are in his giving bracket.

In the 1951 Boston sector project the eleven churches using this "pattern-of-giving" pledge card received an average increase of 82 per cent. The nineteen churches using standard cards received an average 46 per cent increase. Since then most churches in sector projects use the card illustrated.

Although the Resources chairman has now finished with the appraisal sheets, there remains one more job to be done. He is to turn over all these sheets to the Publicity chairman who will direct his committee in making up a list of all prospective workers.

COORDINATION WITH PROPOSAL COMMITTEE

While the Proposal Committee is dreaming its dream, the Resources Committee is discovering how much of that dream may become reality.

Name...

Address...

Card No...

MY PERSONAL COMMITMENT

In recognition of my time, talent and treasure as gifts from God, I am happy to join with others in the following commitment to:

FIRST BAPTIST CHURCH, Brookline

GIVING PLAN PER WEEK

Local Expenses $................

Missions and Benevolences $................

TOTAL $................

Signature:..

This pledge may be increased, decreased, or canceled by notifying the treasurer or financial secretary.

These Commitments Will Underwrite Our Church Proposal

5 at	$25.00	per week
2 at	20.00	per week
2 at	15.00	per week
7 at	10.00	per week
2 at	8.00	per week
10 at	7.00	per week
5 at	6.00	per week
10 at	5.00	per week
10 at	4.00	per week
35 at	3.00	per week
85 at	2.00	per week
83 at	1.00	per week

TOTAL PROPOSAL—$43,800

The Committee believed you would want to be in the group checked.

Card No...

This card taken by...

Team No...

(*Courtesy of American Baptist Convention*)

Fig. 4-3

Thus it is necessary that the Resources chairman meet with the Proposal Committee before it finishes its work. At this meeting he will state what the financial resources of the church are (70 per cent of the revised appraisal total). If the proposed budget is higher than this figure, the Proposal must be reduced. If it is lower, some new items may be added. Thus coordination of the two committees is essential. Each must be certain that it closely follows the calendar. Refer to Fig. 3-3 on page 43.

There are TEN steps to Victory. Step FOUR is discovering your resources.

"Our Father, we know that all we have is really Thine.
But so often we forget that fact and selfishly think of it
as our own. Help us to be honest with Thee and give back to
Thee a definite portion of that which Thou hast entrusted to
us. And so wilt Thou bless us as we give regularly and
honestly to Thy kingdom work. In Thy name and for Thy sake
we ask it. Amen."

> *W. S. Abernethy*
> PASTOR EMERITUS
> CALVARY BAPTIST CHURCH
> WASHINGTON, D.C.

IMPORTANT DATES FOR THE RESOURCES CHAIRMAN

THURSDAY *Week 1*   Resources chairman agrees to serve.

FRIDAY *Week 1*   With help of pastor and General chairman, compile list of those who will be asked to serve on committee. To be sure of thirty in attendance, ask sixty. Include key leaders, the General Committee, and several leading givers in the church.

MONDAY *Week 2*   Attend meeting of General Committee. Report on progress of securing committee of thirty and request entire General Committee to serve.

WEDNESDAY *Week 2*   Remind Publicity chairman of need for fifty mimeographed appraisal sheets (see Form D, Fig. 4-1). Publicity chairman has been asked to be responsible for preparing the appraisal list. If he has begun to make up a composite master list of all members and friends of the church, he and Resources chairman should now make necessary additions and corrections to the list. The names should then be placed in alphabetical order and numbered consecutively, using Form D. As soon as original appraisal list is completed, stencils may be cut and copies mimeographed for all members of the committee. Make about twenty extra copies. The telephone numbers on this list do not have any significance for the Resources Committee but will be used later by the Publicity Committee.

Because only twenty to twenty-five names can be included on a page, larger churches will need to cut several stencils—be sure to allow enough time. The lists must be completely mimeographed by THURSDAY, Week 3.

Every prospect with a separate income should be listed separately on the appraisal form.

TUESDAY *Week 3*   Remind pastor to send Letter A to sixty members, requesting attendance next Sunday afternoon.

THURSDAY *Week 3*   Obtain from Publicity chairman one set of appraisal sheets. Prepare Summary Appraisal Sheets (Form E) for averaging appraisals (see Fig. 4-2).

SUNDAY *Week 4*   Resources Committee meets and completes its work (see instructions, pages 56 to 58).

At end of meeting, gather all sets of appraisal sheets. In larger churches it is recommended that you begin that evening to tabulate all appraisals.

MONDAY *Week 4*   With the aid of several others, tabulate all appraisals and determine average for each name (see instructions, page 58).

TUESDAY *Week 4*   Review Committee goes over each appraisal (see instructions, pages 58 to 61).

WEDNESDAY *Week 4*   Round out all appraisals, grouping them into not more than twelve categories. List these, counting the number of names in each, and arrange them in descending amount (see instructions, pages 61, 62). Give listing to Publicity chairman for printing on pledge card, using Forms H-1 and H-2 in the Canvass Kit.

Give all appraisal lists to Publicity chairman for making prospective workers' cards.

SUNDAY *Week 5*   Meet with Proposal Committee to state total appraisal figure (using 70 per cent of appraisal total). Insist upon Proposal not exceeding this figure, except where there are invested funds or other unusual sources of income to make up the difference.

MONDAY *Week 5*   Appear with General Committee before the church council to state why the high goal is possible. Explain in detail (except for the 30 per cent cutback) the workings of the committee. Remember that the more the work of the Resources Committee is talked about (always with a proper explanation), the easier it will be to sell the appraisal figure later to each prospect.

WEDNESDAY *Week 5*   Attend Congregational Meeting and explain in detail the appraisal procedure. Tell why and how, emphasizing that everyone—even the pastor—is treated the same way.

SUNDAY *Week 6*   Assist at first meeting of Advance Pledge Committee.

SATURDAY *Week 6*   Check appraisal figure on each advance pledge card.

WEDNESDAY *Week 7*   Check appraisal figure on remainder of pledge cards.

SUNDAY *Week 8*   Attend First Workers' Training Conference to explain appraisal procedure and to train visitors in restating this story (see pages 143, 144).

FRIDAY *Week 8*   Second Workers' Training Conference. Explain appraisal and teach how to retell appraisal story.

SUNDAY *Week 9*   Dedication Day. Attend workers' luncheon and make sure all visitors know how to retell appraisal story.
First Report Meeting.

WEDNESDAY *Week 9*   Second Report Meeting.

FRIDAY *Week 9*   Third Report Meeting.

SUNDAY *Week 10*   Fourth Report Meeting.

WEDNESDAY *Week 10*   Victory Report Meeting. General Committee evaluates canvass and plans follow-up.

See Calendar for Resources chairman on next two pages.

TIME SCHEDULE

RESOURCES CHAIRMAN

For detailed information consult the "Important Dates for the Resources Chairman" in this chapter.

Insert the proper date in the upper right-hand corner of each calendar square.

	SUNDAY	MONDAY	TUESDAY	WEDNESDAY	THURSDAY	FRIDAY	SATURDAY
WEEK 1					RESOURCES CHAIRMAN AGREES TO SERVE	CHAIRMAN SELECTS 60 NAMES FOR INVITATIONS	
WEEK 2		FIRST MEETING OF GENERAL COMMITTEE		CHAIRMAN ASSISTS PUBLICITY CHAIRMAN IN PREPARING APPRAISAL LISTS			
WEEK 3		APPRAISAL LISTS MIMEOGRAPHED	MINISTER MAILS LETTER A		CHAIRMAN RECEIVES APPRAISAL LISTS		
WEEK 4	RESOURCES COMMITTEE MEETS	RESOURCES CHAIRMAN TABULATES AVERAGES	REVIEW COMMITTEE MEETS TO STUDY APPRAISALS	CHAIRMAN PREPARES APPRAISALS FOR PRINTING, FORM H			
WEEK 5	JOINT MEETING OF PROPOSAL COMMITTEE AND RESOURCES CHAIRMAN	RESOURCES CHAIRMAN MEETS WITH CHURCH COUNCIL		CONGREGATIONAL DINNER MEETING TO ADOPT PROPOSED BUDGET			

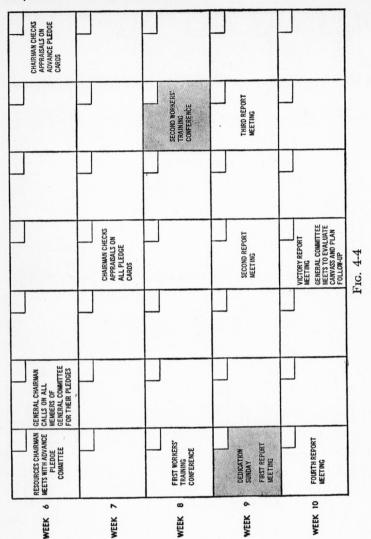

FIG. 4-4

STEP 5: *Telling the World*

*"As never before we begin to see the value of
publicity in the overall picture of church promotion.
. . . All of this means more money, more members,
more missionary interest, and more concern for people."*
REV. RICHARD L. KEACH
FIRST BAPTIST CHURCH
WATERVILLE, MAINE

People do not give according to their ability. They give according to their ability plus their interest, with the latter often the more important. Read again the story of Jesus at the temple treasury (Mark 12: 41–44). It is the work of the Publicity Committee to arouse interest—by showing the people how the church can in larger measure satisfy the needs of themselves and of others.

Many campaigns fail because of a lack of education. The General Committee, enthusiastic about the program, does not realize that the people are not so informed, nor enthusiastic, as the leaders. No matter how high your ideals, nor how necessary your expansion, if the congregation is not convinced of the value of your program, it will not support it. As the salesman attempts to show the purchaser how he needs his product, so must the General Committee convince the church members of the value, the needs, and the challenge of the church.

The church has much to offer—peace of heart and mind, comfort for broken hearts, knowledge for inquirers, salvation for the lost, challenge for the adventuresome, and opportunity for service. When men understand that these spiritual treasures are offered by the church through its various ministries, they will turn to the church in increasing numbers. They will give to its support.

DUTIES OF THE PUBLICITY CHAIRMAN

The work of the Publicity Committee falls into seven divisions:

1. Order all supplies
2. Prepare all forms, letters, and pledge cards
3. Mail all letters on proper dates
4. Remember the nonresident members
5. Prepare the Proposal
6. Prepare and display posters; show films
7. Encourage full attendance at all meetings

These duties are only mechanics to aid the performance of the larger task—namely, to get the facts before the people and to do so enthusiastically. The Publicity chairman, and the entire canvass organization, must work expectantly and optimistically. They must enter into their work wholeheartedly, presenting new ideas and constantly repeating the aims of the canvass.

This committee is responsible for far more than publicity. Perhaps a better title for the chairman would be Office Manager. He is above all else the detail man of the campaign. He is the "advance man" who has everything ready before each meeting opens. Such careful planning, together with the quality of his publicity, helps to create enthusiasm for the campaign.

The Publicity chairman must select a capable committee to aid in performing these duties. Among other members, this committee should include

Telephone lieutenant, to recruit and supervise a squad of women who will call every home on two specified dates.

Dinner lieutenant, to make all arrangements to serve all meals as agreed upon by the General Committee. She will clear dates, obtain reservations, arrange dining places, and solicit help.

Office lieutenant, to supervise all office procedure of the Publicity Committee and to order all supplies. She will enlist help for mimeographing, mailing, preparing lists, and designing posters.

1. *Order All Supplies*

The Publicity chairman is responsible for securing all Every Member Canvass supplies—or for delegating this responsibility to the General chairman. He must order materials and see that a sufficient quantity is on hand when needed. His duty is not to save expenses but to provide the tools that will make the entire job easier. The various items offered by denominational headquarters will pay for themselves many times over if used as suggested. This is noteworthily true of turnover charts. Some of the items to consider ordering are the following:

> Weekly envelopes for next year
> Stewardship Sunday bulletins
> Stewardship folders
> Posters
> Workers' information booklets
> Training film
> Turnover charts
> Pledge cards
> Proposal blanks

2. *Prepare All Forms, Letters, and Pledge Cards*

The successful carrying through of an intensive enlistment calls for many forms and letters, all to be prepared by the Publicity Committee. The Publicity chairman acts as office manager, not doing the actual mimeographing and mailing himself, but seeing that others do it. Some churches will wish to add to the General Committee a secretary, whose task it will be to supervise this clerical work. Churches of over 500 members may decide to engage part-time professional help. Volunteers can be used if they are instructed far enough ahead. Care must be taken, however, not to overload a few workers but to plan the work so that there will be no conflicts over use of office equipment.

The forms to be used by Proposal and Resources Committees are especially important. The Proposal Committee needs several forms early in the program. The appraisal sheets for the Resources Committee will require several days to make up. All letters can, and should, be prepared days or weeks ahead (see the Canvass Kit for sample forms and letters). Cecil Goddard organized a corps of women typists at the First Baptist Church in Waterville, Maine, so that every letter—over one thousand— was individually typed. "If a person," he believes, "is good enough to give us a pledge, he is good enough to receive a personal letter from us." Of course each letter is to be personally signed. It is wise to vary the use of letterheads in an enlistment. Use the General chairman's business letterhead if he has one.

The Publicity Committee will also

> Prepare the "prospective workers'" cards
> Type name and address on each pledge card (when delivered by printer)
> Prepare master list for the General chairman

3. *Mail All Letters on Proper Dates*

If letters are prepared and envelopes addressed and stamped well in advance, there is no problem in mailing. The Publicity chairman will be responsible, however, for seeing that the letters do not get left on the shelf for a day or two after the mailing date. Two mailings of the Proposal are called for—one to advance pledgers and one to regular givers. Envelopes for Proposals should be obtained early from the printer so that they may be addressed and stamped before the Proposals are printed.

4. *Remember the Nonresident Members*

Do not neglect your nonresident members. It was once felt they would return enough to cover the postage costs of writing to them. Churches following this intensive enlistment, however, report that if the two suggested letters are sent to each nonresident, enclosing a Proposal and pledge card, the average church might expect the gifts of these persons to cover the costs of the entire campaign. Now and then there is an agreeable surprise. The Rev. Benjamin Lockhart of the Baptist Church in Agawam, Massachusetts, sent a Proposal and personal note to a nonmember in California. The man's mother was an active member, and her picture was in the Proposal. Back came a check from the son for $500. Some churches state to their nonresidents that, if they do not wish to pledge, they might wish to transfer their membership to a nearby church. The church offers to grant them a letter of transfer.

5. *Prepare the Proposal*

Each church needs to mail one major publicity piece. Known as the Proposal, this will present the program of advance and its cost, as drawn up by the Proposal Committee and approved at the Congregational Dinner Meeting. It will be printed in color on heavy enamel stock and contain several pictures.

The printing of this Proposal may be the most expensive item in your campaign budget. It is well worth its cost, for an attractive prospectus prepares the way for the visitor, making it easier to obtain an increased pledge.

The Publicity chairman must prepare this mailing piece. He purchases the Proposal stock from some church headquarters, from the United Church Canvass office in New York, or designs one for his own printer to set up. The American Baptist Council on Missionary Cooperation, 152 Madison Avenue, New York, has for several years provided such Proposal stock. The chairman should select a good printer, one who knows how to handle fine-line halftones. The printer must agree beforehand to deliver all finished work on or before FRIDAY, Week 6.

The chairman arranges for the making of halftone engravings through the printer (following his advice on the screening). These halftones are made from professional photographs taken on a recent Sunday morning. Newspaper photographers often prove more satisfactory—and less expensive—than studio photographers.

Comment on this piece of publicity has been universally commendatory. Many receive this Proposal as a welcome "souvenir" and even request extra copies. Declaring that it was the best church publicity he had ever seen, a man in one congregation increased his pledge enough to pay the entire printing costs.

6. *Prepare and Display Posters and Show Films*

Attractive posters are colorful and constant reminders of the task facing the church. Individualized posters being preferable to stock posters, the Publicity chairman should search out talent to prepare such visual aids. All posters and other displays should be placed in prominent places three or four weeks before Dedication Sunday.

There are available many good stewardship and missionary motion pictures. These visual aids should be ordered from your film depository several weeks ahead, and their showing should be well advertised to ensure good attendances. The Rev. Otto Loverude was so impressed with the stewardship film, "And Now I See," after showing it to his midweek prayer service at the First-United Baptist Church in Lowell, that he decided to omit the sermon the next Sunday morning and show the film instead.[1]

A training film to use at the visitors' training session is essential. There are several available. If your denomination does not have one, you might purchase "Thy Mission High Fulfilling" from the American Baptist Convention or the National Council of Churches. Only three out of sixty frames are distinctly Baptist. Many churches will show the training film three or more times to the workers, sometimes showing it twice in the same meeting.

Some churches may wish to use lay speakers at Sunday services to publicize the program. These men add a new note of authority and approval. The danger is that laymen may speak too long. They should be coached beforehand so as not to exceed three minutes. A layman speaking to the congregation of the First Baptist Church in East Providence stated:

"I fought with the Lord. Jacob could not hold a candle to me in my wrestling. Finally I lost, and I have been paying 10 per cent of my income to

[1] A Cathedral Film produced for the United Lutheran Church.

the Lord ever since. I make $7,000 a year. The church can count on getting $700 of it."

His testimony helped the church win four new tithers.

7. *Encourage Full Attendance at All Meetings*

There are definite techniques that the Publicity Committee will use to encourage attendance at two crucial gatherings—the Congregational Dinner Meeting and Dedication Sunday. The first is a letter to everyone, with a return post card enclosed. The second is announcements in the parish paper and from the pulpit. But most important is the telephone squad.

There is nothing as effective as the human voice in getting a response. It is so easy to forget or misplace a letter. The United Baptist Church of Concord, New Hampshire, used the telephone squad to build up attendance at their congregational dinner. The letter brought responses from only sixty people. The use of the telephone increased attendance to 160.

The Publicity chairman has previously made sure that all telephone numbers were mimeographed on the appraisal sheets. Since fifty of these lists were run off, there are now extra copies available for the telephone squad. The chairman assigns a woman as telephone lieutenant, who in turn enlists a number of other women to do the actual calling. One church gave this task to shut-ins, who were delighted with their responsibility. Each worker is given a couple of appraisal sheets and is asked to call all the persons listed. She records all pertinent information on the sheet, such as, "will attend," "will not attend," "illness," or "call back." The telephoning is to be done on the Saturday preceding the Wednesday Congregational Dinner and on the Saturday preceding Dedication Sunday.

The telephone squad must be carefully organized to be most effective. They should meet for instructions a day before their first telephone assignment. Then on the day scheduled for the telephoning, the lieutenant should call each of her squad every hour to determine progress. Without this tactful reminder, several of the workers will put off the task. The final tabulation of all the calls is given to the Publicity chairman so that he may notify the dinner lieutenant and the General chairman how many will attend the dinner.

The Publicity Committee may prepare news releases for the local newspapers. Papers are glad to get church stories if they contain local names and items of interest. The stories must, however, be fresh. It is always better to write the story and give it to the editor *before* the event takes place. Do not *tell* the editor to run it, since it is his privilege to accept or reject it. Offer him the story and leave the rest to his discretion.

The Publicity Committee has more details to handle than any other committee. Its work ties into the work of every other committee, and in many cases its assignments must be completed before other committees can begin their work. It is imperative, therefore, that they keep up with the calendar. Coordination at every point is demanded.

There are TEN steps to Victory. Step FIVE is telling the world.

"Almighty God, from whose bountiful hand comes all the gifts that enrich our lives, we thank Thee that Thou hast entrusted to us the means by which we can enter creatively with Thee into the enlarging of the Fellowship of Life Eternal. Forgive us if we have ever thought of the giving of a just proportion of our material gains for the work of Christ's Kingdom as a burden to be borne. Give us, we pray Thee, from this day forward a deeper understanding of the truth that Thou art the owner, that we are the stewards, and that in the wise and unselfish use of all Thy gifts to us we find our strength and joy and peace. Amen."

William C. Martin
BISHOP OF THE DALLAS–FORT WORTH AREA
THE METHODIST CHURCH

IMPORTANT DATES FOR THE PUBLICITY CHAIRMAN

THURSDAY *Week 1*   Publicity chairman agrees to serve. Begin to build committee, including women to serve as telephone, dinner, and office lieutenants. Prepare 6 copies of Form N.

FRIDAY *Week 1*   Mimeograph Form B. Type several copies of Form C.

MONDAY *Week 2*   Attend meeting of General Committee. Report progress in securing committee.

TUESDAY *Week 2*   Check with General chairman on ordering canvass supplies and weekly collection envelopes. Prepare Forms J, K, and L (Canvass Kit).

WEDNESDAY *Week 2*   Begin making appraisal list, using Form D in the Canvass Kit as a guide. A first question in any financial canvass is: "Who are the prospects?" This can be determined only by making a composite master list of all the members and friends. Make the following:

List A—Active or resident members

List B—Nonresident members

List C—Friends, including nonmember parents of church-school children, parents of Boy Scouts, and other groups served by the church who do not have regular church ties

Review all current church records, lists, and files in making up this first draft. You may want to call in a small group of church leaders to review this listing with you.

List prospects alphabetically, placing last name first. Add the address and telephone number. Allow one line to a family, unless they have more than one income. *List each person with an independent income on a separate line.* Check carefully the correct spelling of each name. Watch for incorrect addresses.

The quickest way to make the appraisal form is first to draw the necessary lines on the stencils (see Form D). Then type in the names, addresses, and telephone numbers. This procedure is easier than mimeographing the forms first and then mimeographing the names. Do not forget to number both the names and the pages consecutively. Be sure to mimeograph twenty or more copies of this list in addition to the number needed for the Resources Committee, since they will be used in various ways during the canvass and the rest of the church year. The American Baptist Convention has available a special die-cut stencil for this task.

THURSDAY *Week 2*   Engage a printer to print Proposals which are to be sent to every prospect. Emphasize your deadlines. Tell him you will supply pictures for engravings on WEDNESDAY, Week 4, and final copy on THURSDAY, Week 5. He must have proposals and pledge cards ready for you to pick up on FRIDAY, Week 6. Order Proposal envelopes from printer today. Decide what Proposal stock you will use—will your printer design it or will you order stock from some denominational headquarters or from the United Church Canvass office? Order at least 10 per cent more than the number of families on your mailing list.

A word of warning: Do not select a printer on the basis of economy alone. When this is the major consideration, few will be satisfied with the results. A cheaply prepared Proposal leads prospects to feel that the canvass program itself is a "third-rate" venture.

FRIDAY *Week 2*   Secure a professional photographer for SUNDAY, Week 4. *Do not attempt to use a nonprofessional photographer* since fine-line cuts must be made from the photographs for the printed Proposal. The 8- by 10-inch glossy prints must be delivered the following day (MONDAY, Week 4).

For the printed Proposals you will need some or all of these pictures:
1. Church building exterior
2. Minister
3. Choir or church at worship
4. Church-school class or youth group
5. General chairman

Do not use old photographs or cuts. The size of the cuts or screen may not match, and this will result in an inferior piece of literature. Photographs of groups must be new. The only exception is that studio portraits of the minister and General chairman may be used. The printed Proposal is a sales piece and therefore must be as attractive as possible.

SUNDAY *Week 3*   Discuss with all persons concerned the pictures to be taken next Sunday. Plan each picture in detail. For example, plan with the choir director to take a picture thirty minutes before or immediately following the service. Take two pictures of each group in order to have some choice. Make sure they are taken from the proper angle, showing faces and not backs of heads. Guard against unattractive or confusing backgrounds. Take pictures of two classes to provide a choice. An individual picture of the minister may be taken in the church study prior to the service.

TUESDAY *Week 3*   Mail Letter A to special list of sixty persons. Obtain list from Resources chairman. Prepare 4 copies of Form O.

WEDNESDAY *Week 3*   Prepare and mail, with postcard enclosure, Letter B, inviting all to the Congregational Dinner Meeting.

THURSDAY *Week 3*   Deadline for completing appraisal lists. Remind photographer about Sunday pictures.

SUNDAY *Week 4*   Have photographs for the printed Proposal taken by a professional photographer.

MONDAY *Week 4*   Photographer delivers prints to Publicity chairman.

WEDNESDAY *Week 4*   Give pictures to the printer for making engravings. Make sure each photograph is identified by writing (in ink) on the back. (Use of pencil cracks the gloss.)

Prepare cards of prospective workers, using appraisal sheets received from Resources chairman. Every name checked on these sheets as a possible leader is typed, with the address, on a colored 3- by 5-inch card. Every name checked as a possible visitor is typed, with the address, on a white card. Duplications are of course ruled out, and names that are checked as both leader and visitor prospects are typed on the colored card. Give the two stacks of cards to the Organization chairman.

THURSDAY *Week 4* Use appraisal lists to prepare the master list (Canvass Kit, Form F). Be sure all corrections and additions suggested by the Resources Committee are made before this final copy is begun. Only one master copy is needed—for the use of the General chairman. The columns calling for number, name, address, and "member" can be completed immediately. Secure information about present pledges from the financial secretary. Get the suggested appraisal figures from the Resources chairman after he meets with the Review Committee. You cannot fill out the remaining columns until after the workers' training conference. Now give the master list to the General chairman who will be responsible for completing it. Be sure each name is numbered since these same numbers will appear on the prospect's pledge card.

Mail Letter F.

Resources chairman gives Forms H-1 and H-2 (Canvass Kit) to Publicity chairman.

FRIDAY *Week 4* Telephone squad meets for instructions (see page 75). Mail Letter C. Prepare Form P.

SATURDAY *Week 4* Committee directs telephone squad in calling all who have not replied to the invitations for Congregational Dinner.

SUNDAY *Week 5* Publicity chairman and Proposal chairman prepare copy for the printed Proposal, using Form G in the Canvass Kit as a guide. Make certain that all proposed budget figures are accurate and that the spelling of each name is correct.

WEDNESDAY *Week 5* Participate in Congregational Dinner Meeting.

THURSDAY *Week 5* Deliver Proposal stock, Form G (copy for the printed Proposal), and Forms H-1 and H-2 (pledge card) to the printer. Make certain that the completed Proposals will be ready for you to pick up on Friday of next week.

FRIDAY *Week 5* Publicity Committee begins addressing and stamping envelopes for printed Proposals. (Envelopes were ordered on THURSDAY, Week 2.) Each family should receive one.

Deadline for completing the master list. Prepare Forms Q and R.

SUNDAY *Week 6* Place posters in a conspicuous spot in the church, and ask the minister to call attention to them during the morning worship service.

FRIDAY *Week 6* Pick up Proposals and pledge cards from printer. Advance Pledge chairman meets with Publicity chairman to select and pull out cards of all who are advance pledge prospects. Write "A.P." to the left of each name on the master list for which a card is taken. Begin preparing pledge cards, making up advance pledge cards first. Each prospect on the master list should have a pledge card with name, address, and master list number appearing on it. All cards for the same family at the same address should be clipped together and treated as one call.

Mail Letter D and printed Proposals to all advance pledge prospects.

SATURDAY *Week 6*   Absolute deadline for mailing Proposals and Letter D to advance pledge prospects.

SUNDAY *Week 7*   Assist at second meeting of Advance Pledge Committee.

TUESDAY *Week 7*   Mail Letter E to all advance pledge prospects.

WEDNESDAY *Week 7*   Mail Letter G to all workers. Prepare Forms S, T, and U.

SATURDAY *Week 7*   Mail printed Proposals to all who did not receive Letter D. Mail Letter H to all resident members and Letter J to all non-residents.

SUNDAY *Week 8*   Take part in First Workers' Training Conference.

WEDNESDAY *Week 8*   Mail Letter K to all resident members and Letter L to nonresidents. Prepare Form W.

FRIDAY *Week 8*   Take part in Second Workers' Training Conference.

SATURDAY *Week 8*   Telephone squad builds up Dedication Sunday attendance by calling all families, inviting them to attend church on Sunday. It should be mentioned that no pledges will be taken at the service.

SUNDAY *Week 9*   *Dedication Sunday* and First Report Meeting.

WEDNESDAY *Week 9*   Second Report Meeting.

FRIDAY *Week 9*   Third Report Meeting.

SUNDAY *Week 10*   Fourth Report Meeting.

WEDNESDAY *Week 10*   Victory Report Meeting.

General Committee meets to evaluate canvass and to plan for follow-up.

FRIDAY *Week 10*   Mail "thank-you" Letter M to all subscribers.

See Calendar for Publicity chairman on next two pages.

TIME SCHEDULE

PUBLICITY CHAIRMAN

For detailed information consult the "Important Dates" for the Publicity Chairman" in this chapter.

Insert the proper date in the upper right-hand corner of each calendar square.

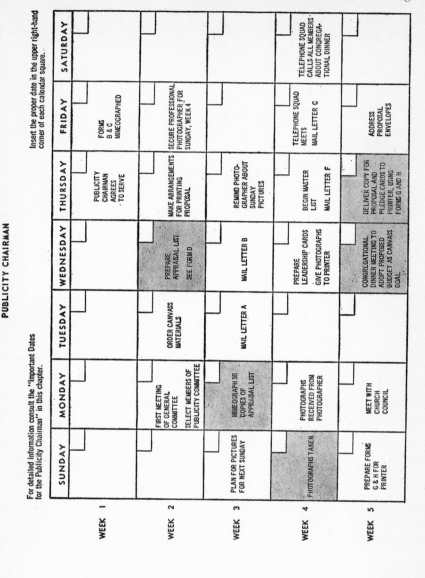

	SUNDAY	MONDAY	TUESDAY	WEDNESDAY	THURSDAY	FRIDAY	SATURDAY
WEEK 1		FIRST MEETING OF GENERAL COMMITTEE			PUBLICITY CHAIRMAN AGREES TO SERVE	FORMS B & C MIMEOGRAPHED	
WEEK 2		SELECT MEMBERS OF PUBLICITY COMMITTEE	ORDER CANVASS MATERIALS	PREPARE APPRAISAL LIST SEE FORM D	MAKE ARRANGEMENTS FOR PRINTING PROPOSAL	SECURE PROFESSIONAL PHOTOGRAPHER FOR SUNDAY, WEEK 4	
WEEK 3	PLAN FOR PICTURES FOR NEXT SUNDAY	MIMEOGRAPH 50 COPIES OF APPRAISAL LIST	MAIL LETTER A	MAIL LETTER B	REMIND PHOTO-GRAPHER ABOUT SUNDAY PICTURES		
WEEK 4	PHOTOGRAPHS TAKEN	PHOTOGRAPHS RECEIVED FROM PHOTOGRAPHER		PREPARE LEADERSHIP CARDS GIVE PHOTOGRAPHS TO PRINTER	BEGIN MASTER LIST MAIL LETTER F	TELEPHONE SQUAD MEETS MAIL LETTER C	TELEPHONE SQUAD CALLS ALL MEMBERS ABOUT CONGREGA-TIONAL DINNER
WEEK 5	PREPARE FORMS G & H FOR PRINTER	MEET WITH CHURCH COUNCIL		CONGREGATIONAL DINNER MEETING TO ADOPT PROPOSED BUDGET AS CANVASS GOAL	DELIVER COPY FOR PROPOSAL AND PLEDGE CARDS TO PRINTER USING FORMS G AND H	ADDRESS PROPOSAL ENVELOPES	

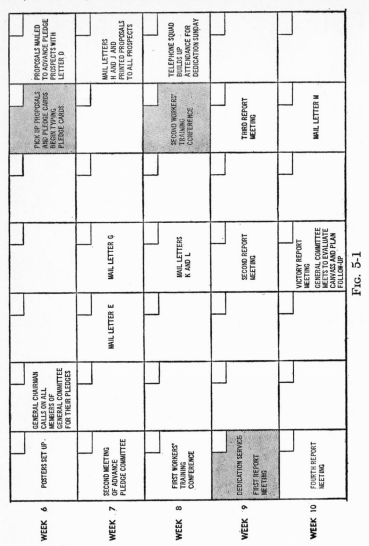

FIG. 5-1

STEP 6: *Leading the Way*

"*Our church, as result of Sector, has new
members—new in numbers, and new in spirit—
because their purses are consecrated.*"
                                A NEW ENGLAND PASTOR

"I love money for three reasons," William Allen White once said.
"First, I write a book and receive a good income. This I love. Secondly,
I love to invest my money and see it grow; to take care of it—to stroke it,
as it were. Thirdly, I love to give it away." George P. Nason, president of
the Charlestown Savings Bank—sixth largest savings bank in the Bay
State—invests as high as $2 million in a day. "The best investment I have
ever made," he has several times said to me, "is the money I have given
away." Tens of thousands of men in America who have prospered in
material ways feel as these two men. They want to make a contribution
to society, to help build institutions that will carry good will to all men,
now and after the death of the donor. Many such men and women are
waiting only for a sufficient challenge. This is true not only of families
that have had wealth for many years, but also of businessmen, professional men, and farmers who are today for the first time enjoying incomes
of $10,000 a year and up. It is to the everlasting shame of the church of
Jesus Christ that we have not challenged more of these people. We think
again of the Biblical admonition: "Ye have not because ye ask not."

The Old First Church of Springfield, Massachusetts, in 1952 had not
one contributor of $1,000 a year, stated John Wallace. Two years later
they had five men giving that amount or more. In the Brookline Baptist
Church, four men were evaluated at $57 a week, a considerable increase.
They actually pledged $90. The chairman of the Lanesboro (also Massa-
chusetts) Federated Church met with the Resources Committee and saw
that the figure to be suggested to him was increased to $4. "I think that
figure is wrong," he commented. "I have already decided to give $10 a

week." In the First Baptist Church of Springfield, it is the laymen who have been working on themselves. In 1945 the largest pledge to the church was $6 a week, with only four persons giving as much as $5. "I told them," Shepard Wright relates, "that this was Sunday School giving. We ought to be ashamed. Somewhat later two of the men half-jokingly filled out a pledge card for $20 and placed it before me, saying: 'Sign it, Shep, sign it.' I looked at it and then said: 'I'll sign it if I can make out cards for you two.' They didn't sign up for what I put down, but they did increase. Today we have one pledge for $30 a week, others at $20, $16, $15, and $12. There are now a dozen persons giving at least $10 a week."

When the minister states from his pulpit that the budget for next year will be raised if everyone increases his giving by 5 per cent (since the budget is up 5 per cent above the past year), he is injuring two members in his congregation. One is Widow Green who cleans by the day to support her two young children. She gives—no one knows how—$3.50 a week to the church, which she dearly loves. She also loves her pastor and desires to do what he suggests. But not seeing her way clear to increase her giving, she leaves the worship service with a heavy heart.

There is also at church that morning a man who is hurt by the minister's remark. He is our friend, Mr. Fifty-Cents-a-Week. For years he has been giving this same amount to his church. But now he has had a fine year, and something the minister says touches him. He does some fast figuring. "Five per cent of fifty cents. That is 2½ cents. I'll do better than that. I'll give 55 cents. No, it would be perhaps easier to give 60 cents. That's what I'll do. We are fortunate to have such a fine pastor." Mr. Fifty-Cents-a-Week steps forth from the church that morning with head high and heart light. He is proud that he has done four times as well as his minister suggested.

Perhaps of the two members, Mr. Fifty-Cents-a-Week is the more deeply injured. For he is not a stingy man. He is merely ignorant, and now his ignorance is deepened by a well-meaning clergyman. His problem is a common one, for he has relatives in every church.

Mr. Fifty-Cents-a-Week needs help, the kind of help that the ten steps of this program will give. The Resources Committee will give him some assistance. The Advance Pledge Committee will also.

WHAT ARE ADVANCE PLEDGES?

A number of homes in every church are called upon for their pledges prior to the general visitation. These persons will receive publicity ahead of the regular mailing, and a special committee of visitors will be trained for this advance calling.

Advance pledgers include the following:

Those able to give somewhat higher than the rest of the church
The leaders of the church and especially of the enlistment
Any "problem cases" requiring a special caller
All visitors in the enlistment

REASONS FOR ADVANCE PLEDGING

All churches, regardless of size or wealth, should have an advance
pledge program. There are several reasons:

1. No one should be allowed to seek another's pledge until he himself
has already pledged. Ethics dictates that visitors pledge in advance.

2. One who has signed a pledge becomes thereby a more enthusiastic
worker. He will turn in higher pledges than one who does not first commit
himself.

3. When church officials and visitors subscribe early, they build up
confidence throughout the congregation. Their endorsement of the program influences others.

4. Those able to give somewhat higher than others should be called on
early:

   a. They usually ask more questions, and so their call requires longer
      time.
   b. They like to discuss their giving with a layman of equal giving
      ability. When assignments are made early, it ensures the cards
      being distributed to the proper callers.
   c. This early approach helps "raise the sights" of the "special" giver
      when he is told how his gift will influence others.
   d. The top 15 per cent of your prospects may give 40 to 50 per cent
      of your goal. You cannot risk losing any of these pledges through
      the wrong visitor selecting these cards in the general visitation.

5. The announcement of the total of all advance pledges on Dedication
Sunday—provided it does not exceed half the goal—shows the congregation that victory is attainable if all pledge their share. "Success begets
success."

The minister of a prominent Boston church once asked me to go with
him to call on the leading member of his church to initiate their campaign.
After lunch, the conversation went like this:

MINISTER: "Mr. B, our new program will enable us to renovate those
rooms that so badly need attention. It will also allow us to finance our

church without dipping into invested funds and without further special appeals.

MR. B: "Your program sounds good. But will the people give?"

MINISTER: "We believe so. We are sending out good publicity, and interest is mounting. We are enlisting enough workers to go into every home for a pledge."

MR. B: "Well, I shall not increase my giving as long as the Sunday School is being run the way it is."

The minister discussed his objection for a moment, agreeing with the man's general observation. Then I said:

"Mr. B, we believe we can reach our goal. We have excellent leadership. The Resources Committee is making a suggestion for each member. If each gives approximately what we suggest, we will reach our goal. [Pause] We were wondering, Mr. B, whether you might like to give forty dollars a week."

His present giving was on the basis of thirty dollars a week.

MR. B: "I don't believe in pledges. I give once a year."

"That is entirely all right," I answered. "We were wondering whether you would like to make an extra gift now and then give your regular amount at the usual time."

We discussed the matter a little, not pushing it, since we wanted him to make up his own mind. Finally he said:

"I am not sure that your campaign will be a success. If it is, come back to me, and I will give you an extra $1,000."

He was now offering twice as much as we asked. Without hesitation, the minister answered:

"Thank you, Sir. That is generous of you. But we do not wish to accept it. We need your increased gift now at the beginning of our canvass. It will encourage everyone down the line to raise his pledge. Your $500 today means far more to us than $1,000 a month from now."

MR. B: "I see. Here is my check. You make it out and I'll sign it."

I turned the blank check over to the minister, asking him to do the honors. Suddenly, as he was writing, he gasped:

"I signed the check myself!"

Mr. B stated that it was the only blank check he had. It happened that I bank with the same institution and generally carry blank checks. Today I had none.

"Never mind," said Mr. B, "I will send the church another check this afternoon."

We thanked him and departed fearfully. The morning mail brought the check for $500.

The minister handled this interview in the proper way. Though the prospect offered him twice as much as requested, he was proffering it at the wrong time. The largest gift in the campaign was worth more at the opening of the canvass than an even larger check would have been at the end—if and when the enlistment were a success.

WHAT HAPPENED WHERE THE PLAN WAS USED

In churches that have used the advance pledge technique, two results are outstanding: the tremendous financial lift to the church program, and the genuine spiritual lift to those persons who increased their giving appreciably.

Of the thirty churches participating in the Boston sector project of 1951, twenty-four followed the advance pledge technique and received an average increase of 67 per cent to local expenses. The six churches that did not use this procedure obtained a 27 per cent increase. The first twenty-four churches received over 35 per cent of their total goals in advance pledges. The next year in New Hampshire the Baptist churches obtained the following per cent of their total goal in advance pledges:

Manchester, First	55%	Ashland	40%
Portsmouth, Middle St.	40	Exeter	50
Concord, United	40	Nashua	40
Whitefield	70	Milford	40

The following cases are typical of what has been happening in the advance pledge phase of the ten-step program:

Congregational Churches

"Last year only one person gave $25 a week. He has since died. Now we have one giver of $35 a week, one at $25, and one at $23. One nonresident has given us $600."

Rev. Charles Stanley Jones
Burlington, Vermont

"Only three advance pledgers did not meet their appraisal, while three others exceeded their appraisal."

Rev. Stanley Gould, South Church
Lawrence, Massachusetts

Baptist Churches

"Twenty-three advance pledges equal one-third of entire goal. Last year only two gifts at $20 a week; this year four such gifts."

Rev. Paul Sturges, Central
Providence, Rhode Island

"Fifty advance givers met their appraisal 100 per cent."
Rev. Horace Tatum
Wollaston, Massachusetts

"Of twenty-three advance pledgers, only one did not come up to appraisal. Five exceeded it."
Rev. Hubert Matthews
Reading, Massachusetts

"Our total budget last year was $3,200. Three advance pledgers have so far this year given $2,200."
Rev. J. Lee Ice, Horace Memorial
Chelsea, Massachusetts

"One-half of advance givers have pledged more than total amount pledged last year."
Rev. John Fitzpatrick
Thomaston, Maine

"Forty-seven persons are appraised at $10,000. Everyone of the one-half seen so far has reached or exceeded the appraisal. Our top gift of $10 a week was obtained when we asked the prospect to come into the church office to talk it over. He had been giving $5."
Rev. Richard Keach
Waterville, Maine

Something happens to the soul of a man who makes a large gift to his church. "When you get a man's money, you get his interest," declared Herbert Clark, president of the North Adams National Bank and leader in many philanthropic enterprises. Churches across the land are discovering anew this truth. Too often churchmen wait to get a man's financial investment in the Kingdom of God until they have won his hearty devotion. But devotion can be strengthened by first getting the gift. "Where a man's treasure is, there will his heart be also."

"The most attentive listener in my congregation," said one minister, "is a man who is giving thirty dollars a week. If preachers want people to listen better to their sermons, they should get them to give more. This same man is now teaching a class of young girls in the Sunday School and is heading up our corps of visitors who are making friendly calls in our homes."

In another church, a schoolteacher met her appraisal of five dollars a week. She then went to her dad and said that, if she could give five dollars, he could give ten dollars. For the next four Sundays this man, whose attendance had previously been spasmodic, was at worship. On the fourth Sunday, the minister twitted him for nodding during the sermon. "Yes," the man replied, "I am tired this morning. But you don't think I'd stay away, do you, when I'm giving ten dollars a week?"

HOW TO SET UP YOUR ADVANCE PLEDGE PROGRAM

1. Select the chairman. The General chairman, in consultation with the minister, names the Advance Pledge chairman. He should be a man who is able to make one of the highest pledges in the church. He must be thoroughly sold on the objectives of the canvass and able to influence other leading givers. He will need to give time and thought as to whom to approach and how to approach them. An important task will be that of assigning the right person to call on certain top givers.

2. Outline duties of the chairman:

   a. *Select the prospects.* Assistance will be given you by the minister, General chairman, and Resources chairman.

   There are three groups of prospects:
   (1) The top 10 per cent of your appraisal list
   (2) All leaders and workers in the canvass
   (3) Any "problem" cases

   b. *Select and secure committee members.* You must secure sufficient men to ensure all calls being made within two weeks. They should be men who are themselves able to give higher-than-average pledges. Work on this committee often appeals to men who may have time to give but have not been sufficiently challenged heretofore. Two retired men in the Court Street Baptist Church of Auburn, Maine, became inspired literally to "go the second mile." They made a trip out of town to see a nonresident member and returned with a check for $50. They then looked for another assignment and decided to call on a Roman Catholic widow whose husband had attended their church occasionally, though not a member. They suggested some memorial gift for her husband. She promised $500, giving them half of it immediately.

   c. *Serve on Resources Review Committee.* This group is sometimes tempted to lower all suggested figures, on the assumption that since the people never have given such high pledges they never will. You must remind them that the question they are to face is: "What *could* each man do *if* he became interested?"

   d. *Conduct two training sessions.* Even your most capable leaders will need the specialized help you will give at these sessions. Here you will explain the Proposal, guide in the making of turnover charts, and distribute prospect cards. Helps for conducting these meetings are given in the Important Dates at the end of this chapter and throughout Step 10.

    e. Hold at least two report meetings. See Step 10.

    f. Serve as supervisor.

        (1) Assign cards to visitors, making sure the best visitor calls on each prospect.

        (2) Give help with difficult cases, perhaps making the call yourself.

        (3) Keep up morale of your committee.

Since the advance pledge technique is based upon the influence of one man's gift upon other men, it is wise to secure your top gift as early as possible. Getting your top pledge committed before the pledge cards are taken to the printer will place your campaign in an advantageous position. Then should anyone exclaim upon seeing the card: "Somebody must be crazy. Nobody around here will give $20 a week," your answer is at hand: "We already have that pledge card signed and locked in our church safe!"

The minister, Advance Pledge chairman, and General chairman must give thought as to the best man to secure your number-one gift. Often it will be the minister, particularly if the prospect's ability is far above that of anyone else in the church.

"In forty-one years as a pastor," related the Rev. Lionel Whiston of Wrentham, Massachusetts, "I had never made a financial call. I decided, after attending the training sessions of the Attleboro Council of Churches, to do so. I did not believe that anyone gave eight or ten dollars a week to the church. Then I heard in these sessions of fifteen- and twenty-dollar pledges. Finally I went to our General chairman and said: 'Just for fun, is there anyone in our church who could give twenty dollars a week?'

" 'Yes' he replied. 'Mr. X could. He is now giving six dollars, but he could afford twenty dollars.'

" 'Good,' I said. "You call on him and ask him.'

" 'Not on your life. It's your idea. You call on him.'

"I finally screwed up my courage and went, plenty scared. As I walked down his driveway, I thought: 'I can't ask for twenty dollars. I'll ask for fifteen dollars.' Then I thought of our training: 'Let each man make up his own mind. Don't make it up for him.'

"I went in, told our story, and wondered whether he would like to consider giving twenty dollars.

"He said yes, and I almost tumbled off my chair. Then he added: 'You are now renovating your study at church. I shall be glad to give the rug, if it will help any.' "

Very often the advance pledge phase of the campaign is the easiest and most pleasant. For here we are dealing with outstanding men and women. Often they are the church leaders, resolved to do their part in lifting their church to higher levels. Many of them have been successful in business and farming operations. They tend to think high. They are quicker to see—and accept—the challenge of a forward program.

You will have fewer refusals to pledge—and fewer not reaching their appraisal—in the advance pledge campaign than in the remainder of your effort.

"Our first twenty persons were appraised at $56 a week. They pledged $66."

> Rev. Christian B. Jensen
> First Baptist
> Pittsfield, Massachusetts

"Our advance pledge appraisals came to $8,179. We received $8,068 from them."

> Rev. E. Joseph Woodbury
> Portland Street Baptist
> Haverhill, Massachusetts

"Not one of our seventy-six on the advance pledge list refused to subscribe."

> Rev. Alger W. Geary
> Columbia Street Baptist
> Bangor, Maine

There are TEN steps to Victory. Step SIX is leading the way.

"O Lord, help me to put nothing into my pocketbook that is not honestly made, and which has not been made in a vocation that honors both God and man. Help me not to keep in my pocketbook that which rightfully belongs to God, and that which will allow me to express my recognition of God's love for me, and of the world's need for Christ. Amen."

> *Porter Routh*
> EXECUTIVE SECRETARY
> OF THE EXECUTIVE COMMITTEE
> SOUTHERN BAPTIST CONVENTION

IMPORTANT DATES FOR THE ADVANCE PLEDGE CHAIRMAN

It is essential that the Advance Pledge chairman be well acquainted with Step 8.

THURSDAY *Week 1*　Advance Pledge chairman agrees to serve and, in consultation with minister and General chairman, begins thinking of persons to aid him.

MONDAY *Week 2*　Attend first meeting of General Committee and state progress in filling committee. Until the number of advance pledge prospects is known, ask only two or three to serve on committee.

SUNDAY *Week 4*　Serve as member of Resources Committee.

TUESDAY *Week 4*　Serve as member of Review Committee. Remind the reviewers that they are to be concerned only with the question: "What *could* each one do *if* he were sold on the program?"

THURSDAY *Week 4*　Select your advance pledge prospects. Meet with Resources chairman to mark off the top 10 per cent on the appraisal list. Minister and General chairman assist in adding other names. Secure the rest of your Advance Pledge Committee. There should be one committee member for every five prospect names. You may desire one or two extra visitors since you can generally expect one or two to drop out before the visits are completed. Should you need suggestions for additional visitors, refer to the Organization chairman's list of possible leaders. You may wish to make your own master list of your prospects. Secure forms from Publicity chairman.

MONDAY *Week 5*　Appear with the General Committee before the church council.

WEDNESDAY *Week 5*　Attend Congregational Dinner Meeting to give assistance.

FRIDAY *Week 5*　Deadline for completing Advance Pledge Committee.

SATURDAY *Week 5*　Call all committee members to remind them of first meeting tomorrow.

SUNDAY *Week 6*　First meeting of Advance Pledge Committee. This is the first of two training sessions for these workers. A complimentary dinner should be served in a home or a hotel private dining room. Although these committeemen should be among the most capable leaders in your church, do not neglect their training. Ask the minister and other members of the General Committee to be present and to aid you in presenting the program. Follow the agenda (Form Q) at the end of this chapter.

Review the enlarged program now being planned. Emphasize new features. State that success depends upon substantial support from those able to subscribe in larger amounts. Explain how enthusiasm engendered by "pace-setting" gifts influences the entire organization. Outline the objectives of the committee:

> To raise a large share of the total budget
> To set the pace for the canvass, thereby encouraging other large gifts
> To inspire confidence and enthusiasm throughout the entire church

Every visitor should be provided with a tool to aid him make as vivid a presentation as possible. The most effective aid is a turnover chart. Several denominations supply ready-printed charts. The newest development, however, is the personalized home-made chart (see discussion in Step 8). If your church decides to make its own turnover charts, it will be necessary that the advance callers make theirs at this first training meeting. Follow the instructions given in Step 8. Spend time discussing the Proposal as you make the charts. Aim to sell this program to your workers this evening. After you answer questions, read to the visitors a worker's information booklet and show a training film.

Committee members will each call on four or five prospects.

Each member should reserve the following dates:

SUNDAY, Week 7—Instruction Meeting

FRIDAY, Week 7—First Report Meeting

FRIDAY, Week 8—Final Report Meeting

Advance solicitation will begin MONDAY, Week 7, and end FRIDAY, Week 8, with all calls made in the homes. State that you will call on all your committee members this week for their pledges.

MONDAY *Week 6*   Called on by General chairman, you sign your pledge.

TUESDAY *Week 6*   You begin calling in homes of all committee members for their pledges. Demonstrate turnover chart to them as though they had never seen it. Sell the appraisal figure, knowing that, if your men meet their appraisal, they are more apt to get their prospects to pledge their appraisal figure the following week.

Deadline for completing calls on your committee is Saturday.

FRIDAY *Week 6*   Urge upon Publicity chairman the need for immediate mailing (first class) of Proposals with Letter D to all advance pledge prospects. Check with Publicity chairman to make sure all advance pledge cards are typed with name and address. Number on card must correspond with number on master list. Appraisals are checked in box on right of card. Pledge cards will be distributed at Sunday's meeting. Master list is marked "A.P." in left margin beside each advance pledge prospect. Perhaps you have made up your own master list of advance pledge names.

SATURDAY *Week 6*   Deadline for placing in mail Proposals to all advance pledge prospects. Call all committee members to remind them of tomorrow's Instruction Meeting.

SUNDAY *Week 7*   Advance Pledge Committee meets in afternoon for instruction and selection of cards. Begin with a complimentary dinner. It is important that pastor and General chairman be present to assist.

The purpose of this meeting is to train in the use of the turnover chart, and in the introducing of the appraisal figure, and to assign cards to each visitor. Follow the agenda (Form R) at end of this chapter.

Open the meeting with a discussion of how to use the turnover charts. Coach the committee in how to introduce the suggested appraisal figure. The appraisal is exceedingly important in this part of the campaign, since failure to secure the amount suggested from a couple of your top prospects can jeopardize the entire campaign. Advance prospects will be more interested in the appraisal procedure than will anyone else, and will wish a fuller explanation. Be sure to study Step 8 for further helps for this training session.

Distribute pledge cards. You will have already taken out any special cards that require calls by the pastor, General chairman, or yourself. The rest of the cards are selected by the members of your committee, not more than five calls per visitor. If the prospect list is not too large, all sit at table while you read off cards, handing each to a volunteer. If list is large, cards are best selected by spreading them out alphabetically on a couple of tables, allowing callers to walk around making their own selection. It is wise to have one or two reservists who are given no assignment at this time. Use them to fill in later as needed, to make sure all prospects are interviewed. If there are in any home two prospects, only one of whom is an advance giver, clip the cards together so that the caller may receive both pledges at the same time. No home should receive two calls to obtain two pledges.

As each visitor takes a card, he signs the stub, tears it off and places it in an envelope marked "stubs." Later you will add to the master list the name of each visitor.

Urge your advance workers to be present at each report meeting. These meetings not only inform the leaders as to the progress being made, they also stimulate discouraged workers, keep the callers on the job until finished, and allow for any reassignment of cards. The Advance Pledge Committee should complete its work so that an announcement of results can be made at the second workers' training session in Week 8. Without report meetings, these calls will lag for three or four weeks.

MONDAY *Week 7* Advance Pledge Committee begins solicitation of prospects.

TUESDAY *Week 7* Check with Publicity chairman to see that Letter E is mailed today.

THURSDAY *Week 7* Call all members to encourage them and remind them of report meeting tomorrow.

FRIDAY *Week 7* First Advance Pledge Report Meeting. Give each member a worker's report envelope (see page 153) before the meal begins. After supper, call upon each worker to state the number of calls completed, number of pledges obtained, and total amount pledged. Call for a couple of success stories. Answer each question fully.

State the number of calls yet to be made and urge their completion during the coming week. Announce the time and place of the final dinner as part of the general visitor's instruction meeting on FRIDAY, Week 8.

SUNDAY *Week 8* Report progress at First Workers' Training Conference.

THURSDAY *Week 8* Telephone committee members to remind them of the final report dinner tomorrow. Check to see that each one is working to have all calls completed by that time.

FRIDAY *Week 8*   Final Advance Pledge Report Meeting (held in conjunction with second workers' instruction conference). Report amount of advance pledging.

SUNDAY *Week 9*   Chairman attends Dedication Sunday services in morning and report meeting in evening.

WEDNESDAY *Week 9*   Second Report Meeting. Deadline for all advance pledges not previously reported.

FRIDAY *Week 9*   Third Report Meeting.

SUNDAY *Week 10*   Fourth Report Meeting.

WEDNESDAY *Week 10*   Chairman attends Victory Report Meeting.

Chairman meets with General Committee to evaluate canvass and to plan follow-up.

FORM Q   AGENDA

Advance Pledge Committee Meeting No. 1

SUNDAY, WEEK 6

(This may be a luncheon meeting if desired)

Presiding Officer: ADVANCE PLEDGE CHAIRMAN

1. Opening Prayer
2. Quick Review of Every Member Enlistment Organization   GENERAL CHAIRMAN
   a. Proposal for next year *(Proposal Committee)*
   b. Analysis of resources *(Resources Committee)*
   c. The time schedule
   d. Publicity and aids
   e. Advance Pledges *(Monday, Week 7—Friday, Week 8)*
   f. General Solicitation *(Sunday, Week 9 ff.)*
3. Why We Have a High Goal   PROPOSAL CHAIRMAN
   Needs
   Opportunities
4. How We Can Reach Our Goal   RESOURCES CHAIRMAN
   The appraisal figure
   Ten per cent of members will be called on early
   All workers will be called on early
   Need for all to increase giving
5. Why We Have Advance Pledging
        ADVANCE PLEDGE CHAIRMAN
   (see page 86)
6. How to Use the Turnover Chart *(or Making the Turnover Chart)*
7. Reading of Worker's Information Booklet
8. Showing of Training Film
9. Discussion of Film
10. Advance Pledge Calendar
    Sunday, Week 7—Cards selected
    Monday, Week 7—First calls made
    Friday, Week 7—First report meeting
    Friday, Week 8—Final Advance Pledge report meeting
11. Adjournment

NOTE: Pastor and General chairman should make their pledges *today*. General chairman should obtain pledges in home of Advance Pledge chairman on *Monday. Rest of week* Advance Pledge chairman obtains pledges of all Advance Pledge workers.

FORM R

AGENDA

Advance Pledge Committee Meeting No. 2

SUNDAY, WEEK 7

Presiding Officer: ADVANCE PLEDGE CHAIRMAN

1. Opening Prayer   MINISTER
2. Report of Progress to Date

ADVANCE PLEDGE CHAIRMAN

3. Second Reading of Worker's
   Information Booklet   PUBLICITY CHAIRMAN
4. How to Use the Turnover Chart   GENERAL CHAIRMAN
5. How to Introduce the Appraisal Figure

ADVANCE PLEDGE CHAIRMAN

   Tell story of committee of thirty
   Strive to get prospect to ask the question
   Show special pledge card

6. Second Showing of Training Film
7. Importance of Report Meetings

ADVANCE PLEDGE CHAIRMAN

   First report—Friday, Week 7
   Final report—Friday, Week 8 (*at Second Workers'
   Training Conference*)

8. Selection of Prospect Cards
9. Adjournment

See Calendar for Advance Pledge chairman on next two pages.

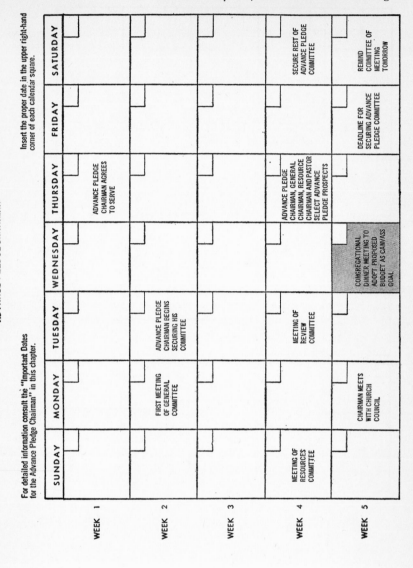

TIME SCHEDULE

ADVANCE PLEDGE CHAIRMAN

For detailed information consult the "Important Dates for the Advance Pledge Chairman" in this chapter.

Insert the proper date in the upper right-hand corner of each calendar square.

	SUNDAY	MONDAY	TUESDAY	WEDNESDAY	THURSDAY	FRIDAY	SATURDAY
WEEK 1					ADVANCE PLEDGE CHAIRMAN AGREES TO SERVE		
WEEK 2		FIRST MEETING OF GENERAL COMMITTEE	ADVANCE PLEDGE CHAIRMAN BEGINS SECURING HIS COMMITTEE				
WEEK 3							
WEEK 4	MEETING OF RESOURCES COMMITTEE	CHAIRMAN MEETS WITH CHURCH COUNCIL	MEETING OF REVIEW COMMITTEE		ADVANCE PLEDGE CHAIRMAN, GENERAL CHAIRMAN, RESOURCE CHAIRMAN AND PASTOR SELECT ADVANCE PLEDGE PROSPECTS		SECURE REST OF ADVANCE PLEDGE COMMITTEE
WEEK 5				CONGREGATIONAL DINNER MEETING TO ADOPT PROPOSED BUDGET AS CANVASS GOAL		DEADLINE FOR SECURING ADVANCE PLEDGE COMMITTEE	REMIND COMMITTEE OF MEETING TOMORROW

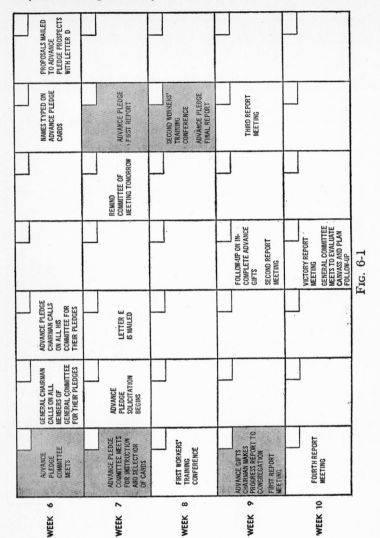

Fig. 6-1

STEP 7: *Enlisting Manpower*

*"Part of the value of our every member enlistment
was the great number of people it involved.
It was a good experience for all."*
                    REV. GORDON BIGELOW
                    FIRST BAPTIST CHURCH
                    BEVERLY, MASSACHUSETTS

The more people you enlist as workers in a campaign, the easier will be the reaching of the goal. Having many workers means not only lighter loads for everyone, but also a wider spreading of information. As these workers learn of the program by working from the inside, their enthusiasm mounts. Realizing the tremendous importance of the goals they are working for, they are willing to contribute larger amounts, their subscriptions often running to one-third of the goal. Their enthusiasm and benevolence then make them better salesmen as they talk with others.

HOW MANY VISITORS ARE NEEDED?

The number of homes in your church determines the number of workers you will need. If several prospects live at the same address, they are treated as one call. Likewise, if one home has an advance pledge prospect and other regular prospects, all are called upon in the advance pledge visitation.

Visitors may, if desired, go out two by two. A two-man team is good where one of the team is weak, for then the stronger one makes the presentation and helps to train his partner. Should both of the pair be strong, it is usually better to send them out singly. *One visitor with a good turnover chart is better than two without a chart* (see Step 9). Keep in mind that the more trained people you have at work on the enlistment, the higher will be the financial returns.

102

The following pages show the number of visitors needed for churches of different sizes. If your visitors go out in pairs, double the number of visitors here called for.

Church of 25 to 50 Members

Four visitors will be sufficient for this size church. The Organization chairman, with the help of the pastor and General Committee, selects the callers, who then report back to him. Your organization would look like Fig. 7-1.

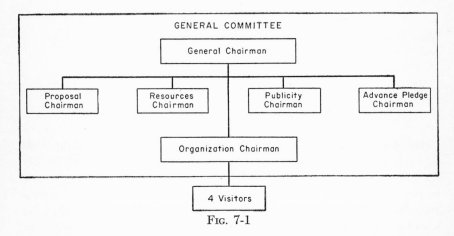

Fig. 7-1

If you prefer your visitors to go out in couples, double the above number of visitors.

This same setup is used in churches of 50 to 99 members. Merely add an extra visitor for every fifteen members above the first fifty.

Church of 100 Members

A church of 100 members needs an organization of about eight visitors, each working singly. The Organization chairman (conferring with minister and General Committee) selects two persons to act as team captains. Each captain then selects four visitors to work with him. The captain *chooses* these four, *helps* them work, and *receives* their reports. The two captains work as two-way channels between visitors and Organization chairman.

The organization for a church of 100 members would look like Fig. 7-2.

If you prefer your visitors to go out in couples, double the above number of visitors.

This same setup is used in churches of 100 to 499 members. Merely add

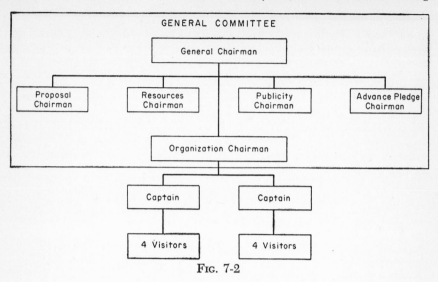

FIG. 7-2

an extra captain and four visitors for every seventy-five members above the first hundred. You may wish to add an additional captain and four visitors to serve as reservists. *Do not omit captains in a church exceeding 99 members.*

Church of 500 Members

A church of 500 members needs about thirty-two visitors, each working singly. If you send out two visitors to a team, you will need sixty-four. The Organization chairman (in consultation with the pastor and General Committee) first selects two division leaders. Each division leader chooses four captains. Each captain enlists four visitors. The division leaders *choose* their four captains, *help* them to organize, *assist* in training them, and *receive* their reports. In like manner, the captain works with his four visitors. Thus a division consists of twenty-one persons—division leader, four captains, and sixteen visitors. You may wish to add an additional captain and four visitors to serve as reservists. *Do not omit division leaders in a church exceeding 499 members.*

The chart for a church of 500 looks like Fig. 7-3.

If you prefer your visitors to go out in couples, double the above number of visitors.

For churches over 500 members, you add another division leader for every 250 additional members. Thus a church of 1,000 members will have four division leaders, sixteen captains, and sixty-four visitors, with an additional captain and his company serving as reserve visitors.

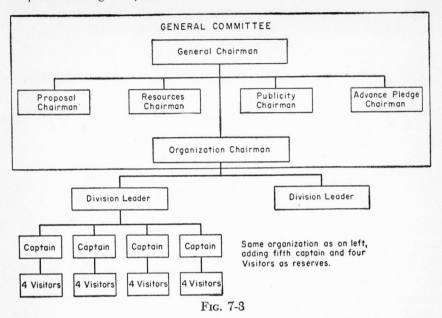

FIG. 7-3

Churches of More than 1,000 Members

If your membership is 1,250 you will need five division leaders; if 1,500 members, six division leaders. Then another tier of leadership will be added, since no one leader should be responsible for more than four division leaders. The Organization chairman will then select two colonels, each of whom will choose three or four division leaders. The division leaders enlist four captains, and the captains each enroll four visitors. The colonels *choose* their division leaders, *help* them to organize, *assist* in training them, and *receive* their reports. In like manner the division leaders work with their captains, and the captains work with their visitors.

The chart for a church with between 1,500 and 2,000 members would look like Fig. 7-4.

If you prefer your visitors to go out in couples, double the above number of visitors.

THE LIST OF PROSPECTIVE VISITORS

The character of your visitor is sometimes more important than the presentation he makes. If your members have faith in the caller, his word carries tremendous weight. The superintendent of public schools, Ernest R. Caverly, one of the visitors for the Brookline, Massachusetts, Baptist Church enlistment, was asked: "Do you really think this whole thing is a

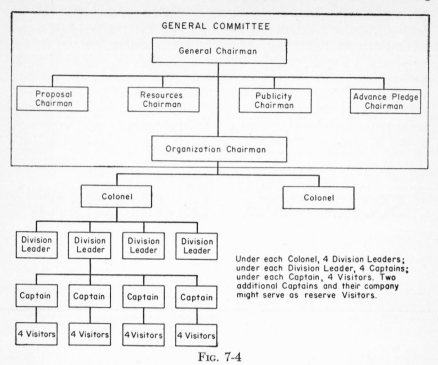

FIG. 7-4

good idea?" On being assured, the prospect gave a pledge for ten dollars a week. Select your canvassers with care. Do not call for volunteers.

Some churches enlist a few nonmembers as visitors. Often they make valuable workers. "I'm not a member," one man said to his visitor. "Why should I pledge?" "I'm not a member, either," replied the caller, "yet I'm going out to get pledges. I've signed one. Here is your card." He got the pledge—a good one. Many a man has been won to church membership through working at such a responsibility.

The Publicity chairman, using the appraisal sheets for suggestions, has prepared a card file of prospective workers for the Organization chairman. This card file is divided into possible leader and possible visitors. Use of these cards will greatly facilitate the securing of workers.

SECURING THE VISITORS

The task of enlisting visitors is lightened by the Organization chairman's sending out a letter to each prospective visitor, requesting him to agree to serve if he is asked by someone later on. Although this letter will aid the captains in securing their visitors, the selection of captains and division leaders cannot be delayed this late. In churches of over 500 members, division leaders are chosen during the second week of the canvass calendar. Captains are chosen in *all* churches (over 99 members) during the third week. Although three weeks are allowed for the enrollment of visitors, they should as far as possible be signed up within one week. This early selection gives you a better choice of visitors, before their date books are filled with other engagements.

The Organization chairman is responsible for securing only the top tier of workers. (In churches of over 500 members, this would be division leaders. In churches of 100 to 499 members, this would be captains.)

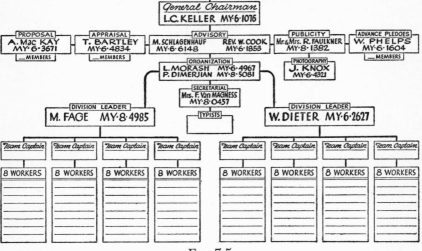

FIRST METHODIST CHURCH
SECTOR ORGANIZATION CHART
1954 GENERAL COMMITTEE

FIG. 7-5

Each division leader is responsible for securing four captains. Each captain is responsible for securing four visitors.

This enlisting must be done face to face rather than by relying upon the mails or telephone. The securing of visitors is such an important task that everything should be done to make it difficult for the prospects to decline serving.

Using a slight variation in organization, Thomas Brown of the Phillips Memorial Baptist Church of Cranston, Rhode Island, worked out a provisional organization chart, inserting the names of the men he desired as visitors. The chart was duplicated by photo-offset and a copy shown to each prospective worker with the statement: "Joe, we need you for a worker in our canvass this year. We have tentatively put you down here in this spot. Will that be O.K.?" These charts were also posted on the church bulletin boards. In those few cases where a prospect declined to serve, a new name was pasted over his spot. This procedure enabled the church not only to enlist an all-men group of visitors, but also to have sufficient visitors to limit their calls to four or five apiece.

Make a chart of your organization of workers, filling in the blanks from day to day. The Organization Chart of the First Methodist Church of Medford, Massachusetts, will show how this is done (see Fig. 7-5 and Form M in the Canvass Kit).

There are TEN steps to Victory. Step SEVEN is enlisting your man-power.

"Eternal God, whose power and presence enables us to perform our
daily work, to thee we dedicate the work of our hands and hearts.
Enable us, we beseech thee, to fulfill the partnership with which
thou hast endowed us. May the joy of sharing in the tasks of creation
ennoble every good work and become the symbol of our complete dedication
to thee, we pray in the name of Christ. Amen."

Gaines M. Cook
EXECUTIVE SECRETARY
INTERNATIONAL CONVENTION OF DISCIPLES
OF CHRIST

IMPORTANT DATES FOR ORGANIZATION CHAIRMAN

THURSDAY *Week 1*   Organization chairman agrees to serve.

MONDAY *Week 2*   Attend first meeting of General Committee. Report how many workers you will need. Ask for advice on selection of best men for top leadership in your organization.

The charts on the preceding pages outline the approximate number of workers you will need for your church. To be more exact, check for your size church with the following:

Find out the total number of calls (one per home) to be made. Subtract the number to be handled by the Advance Pledge Committee. Divide the remainder by seven. This is the number of visitors you will need. (Since each visitor will be called upon by his captain, there remain six calls to be made by each visitor.) Over every four visitors you have a captain; over every four captains, a division leader.

For churches of 250 members or more, it is wise to add another captain and four visitors to hold in reserve. This reserve team will be used only when other visitors drop out or when clean-up calls are necessary at the end.

TUESDAY *Week 2*   Begin enlisting division leaders, if your church has 500 members or more. If smaller, begin enlisting captains. Use Form J or K (in the Canvass Kit).

TUESDAY *Week 3*   Deadline for securing division leaders.

SUNDAY *Week 4*   Serve as member of Resources Committee.

MONDAY *Week 4*   Deadline for securing captains.

THURSDAY *Week 4*   Check with Publicity Committee on mailing of Letter F. Receive from Publicity chairman card file of prospective workers. Review names with minister and General chairman, eliminating any questionable ones. Total cards should exceed number of visitors needed by 50 per cent. If insufficient, other names are to be added from appraisal list.

FRIDAY *Week 4*   Check with Publicity Committee to see that Letter C is mailed to each prospective visitor.

MONDAY *Week 5*   Join General Committee in meeting with church council. At close of meeting, meet with division leaders and captains. Distribute prospective workers' cards to aid captains in enlisting visitors. Each captain selects six cards, from which he is to secure four visitors.

Instruct each captain to ask only the persons whose cards he holds. All visitors are to be secured by THURSDAY, Week 6. All cards are to be returned to you marked "accepted," "refused," or "not seen." Distribute Form L (Canvass Kit).

WEDNESDAY *Week 5*   Attend Congregational Dinner Meeting and report progress in enlisting workers.

WEDNESDAY *Week 6*   If your church has division leaders, you should (having already made your own pledge to General chairman) call in home of each division leader for his pledge. Use turnover chart in each home.

THURSDAY *Week 6*   Deadline for securing visitors.

Meet with division leaders and captains. Does each visitor know duties and dates? Has each received Form A (Canvass Kit)?

SUNDAY *Week 7*   Recheck your organization. Are all workers lined up? Should you have reserve captain and visitors to help only in an emergency? Have you made up a worker's chart? This organization chart of workers (see Form M in the Canvass Kit) should list the actual names of every captain under his division leader, and of every visitor under his captain. Make two charts, one to be carried by yourself and one to be posted on the bulletin board. Post chart before organization is complete, adding new names as they are secured.

MONDAY *Week 7*   If your church has no division leaders, you should call in the home of each captain for his pledge. Otherwise, division leaders make these calls. Use turnover chart in each home.

TUESDAY *Week 7*   Check with Publicity chairman. Will Letter G be mailed out tomorrow?

FRIDAY *Week 7*   Call your top leaders to request them to telephone their workers, reminding them of Sunday's important First Training Conference. Leaders are to call you back when their telephoning is complete. You then report to General chairman the number who will be present Sunday afternoon.

SUNDAY *Week 8*   Attend and assist at First Workers' Training Conference.

For additional dates for organization chairman, see end of next chapter.

See Calendar for Organization chairman on the next two pages.

TIME SCHEDULE

ORGANIZATION CHAIRMAN

For detailed information, consult the "Important Dates" for the Organization Chairman" in this and following chapters.

Insert the proper date in the upper right-hand corner of each calendar square.

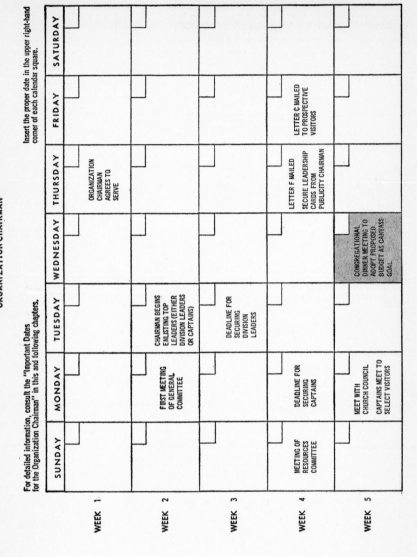

	SUNDAY	MONDAY	TUESDAY	WEDNESDAY	THURSDAY	FRIDAY	SATURDAY
WEEK 1					ORGANIZATION CHAIRMAN AGREES TO SERVE		
WEEK 2		FIRST MEETING OF GENERAL COMMITTEE	CHAIRMAN BEGINS ENLISTING TOP LEADERS (EITHER DIVISION LEADERS OR CAPTAINS)				
WEEK 3			DEADLINE FOR SECURING DIVISION LEADERS				
WEEK 4	MEETING OF RESOURCES COMMITTEE	DEADLINE FOR SECURING CAPTAINS			LETTER F MAILED SECURE LEADERSHIP CARDS FROM PUBLICITY CHAIRMAN		
WEEK 5		MEET WITH CHURCH COUNCIL CAPTAINS MEET TO SELECT VISITORS		CONGREGATIONAL DINNER MEETING TO ADOPT PROPOSED BUDGET AS CANVASS GOAL		LETTER C MAILED TO PROSPECTIVE VISITORS	

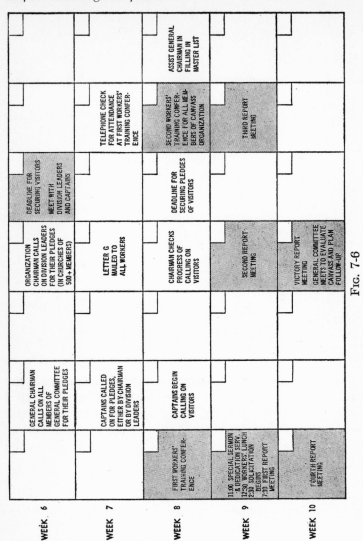

FIG. 7-6

STEP 8: *Training the Recruits*

*"The whole church is so encouraged and enthusiastic
about the church finances that it has brought a rebirth
of confidence in the church and in our world mission."*
REV. DAVID B. HOWE
UNITED BAPTIST CHURCH
SACO, MAINE

BASIC PRINCIPLES

1. *The Importance of Training*

"**The best thing** about the whole campaign was the cultivation of the
workers," declared Forest Parsons, minister of the Warwick Central
Baptist Church in Rhode Island. "One of our members went out several
years ago on a canvass and had a poor response, saying he did not know
what he was talking about. This year he knew what he was doing, the
response was fine, and he had a wonderful time."

When the visitor does not know what he is talking about, it is not
always his fault. If he has not been given the opportunity to attend at
least one thorough training session, and has no tools to make his presentation vivid, the fault lies with the General chairman.

The crucial point in any enlistment comes at the moment one man
talks to another about his share in the program. Though the General
chairman have the organizational ability of a du Pont, though his calendar
be as faultless as the Gregorian, though his publicity be written by a vice-
president of General Motors, and the sermons be preached by a Savona-
rola—all are largely in vain if the visitor blunder his interview with the
prospect. Ministers and chairmen agree that the training of the visitor
is the weakest point in most efforts. Since the effectiveness of the visitor
in the home is so crucial, churches should give prolonged thought as to
how to strengthen this part of the canvass.

114

2. Selling Is a Game

Every Member Enlistments go much easier, and are more productive, when you make a game of what you are doing. Working for the church is *fun*. Solicitation is fun, too, because you are not begging for money. You are giving an opportunity to your friends to take part in a glorious work for God. In the training sessions the visitors should be impressed that the interview can be an exhilarating experience. Often the call becomes a match of wits, with high stakes. Many a man who is first led to invest his money in the church then gets on fire for the Kingdom of Heaven's sake. The General chairman and the Organization chairman should encourage their visitors to become good salesmen for Jesus Christ.

In a Congregational church in Vermont, one church member had the preceding year given a total of twenty-five dollars to his church, believed to be his first gift in over fifty years. When he heard of the enlistment, he flatly said: "I will give fifty dollars—no more." He was appraised at two dollars a week. The General chairman, knowing that this man had successfully completed a sizable business deal, accepted the challenge and called upon him. He read his turnover chart and then quoted from a popular magazine that Americans should give heavily this year since taxes would be reduced the first of the new year. For several minutes the two men fenced until the prospect ended by saying: "I will give 10 per cent of the church proposal." His pledge amounted to $674.50. Engaging in a well-organized Every Member Enlistment can be fun for everyone. It is especial fun for the man who signs, according to his means, a large pledge!

TOOLS FOR VISITORS

The most effective visitor is one who, believing in his work and trained for his task, has been given the proper tools. Two tools are necessary—an instruction booklet and one or more visual aids. A third tool—mimeographed agendas of the training session—is helpful.

1. A *Visitor's Handbook*

Every visitor should be given his own copy of a set of instructions. This copy should be his to take home, mark, and study. Many denominational headquarters supply these for their churches. Especially helpful are the handbooks which contain a pocket to hold the pledge cards. Such a booklet has been prepared by the Council on Missionary Cooperation of the American Baptist Convention, entitled "Information for Those Who Make Calls in the Every Member Canvass." The following is from this handbook:

YOU

Can raise money for YOUR CHURCH . . . through a personal interview with friends

1. Tell the story of its services
2. Explain its present needs
3. Provide each prospect with an opportunity to act

YOU never know who will give until you ask!

Insurance companies are able to estimate *how many* will die this year, but they are not able to tell you *who* will die.

We can tell you *how many* will give to your church, if called upon in an intelligent way, but we cannot tell you *who* will give.

Irving Cobb said that he began life as an insurance salesman, but because he wasn't successful he quit. On calling upon his first prospect he said, "You don't want to buy any insurance, do you?" The prospect said, "No." He replied, "I didn't think you did." And he changed his job.

The only way to find out *who* will pledge is to tell your story positively and then ask optimistically and let each person make up his own mind.

Don't try to decide this in advance for him.

See each card properly and *7 out of 10* will give.

We cannot tell you which ones, *but* see every card and the law of averages will work in your favor.

See your cards, and *your church* will reach its goal.

YOU HAVE A WORTHY PRODUCT TO SELL

Your church's past record of achievement and present record of service merit support.

You are not selling an investment in mortar and bricks, steel and stones but a *program* and a *cause*. You are selling Christian homes, a Christian community, and a more stable and peaceful world. You are selling Christian training for children, moral guidance and encouragement for youth, and many other tangible and concrete values of life.

You are lifting the spiritual horizons of your church. *You* are projecting your own influence down across the years . . . and you are going to have an awfully good time in achieving a tangible goal for the Kingdom of God.

THIS IS A SALES JOB

But you don't have to be a salesman to do a good job. The best job is always done by those who know the needs and then explain them in a conversational way. The person who calls on each prospect conscientiously always turns in a good report.

You are going out to sell your church. Having done that you don't have to worry about the money. It will come and sometimes in much larger amounts than you could hope for. *You* do have to give each prospect an opportunity to *act*.

BEFORE SEEING YOUR PROSPECTS

1. *Be prepared for each call.* Elaborate preparations are not necessary. Think about your approach before you visit him. Consider what is likely to prompt him to give. Emphasize the phases of the program in which he is most likely to be interested. Individual attention pays big dividends to the church.

2. *Know the facts.* Some people give because of emotional factors. Others because a sense of duty compels them. Most prospects give only when they are convinced a cause is worthy and will accomplish something they believe in.

3. *You are not going out to see enemies,* you are going to meet with friends, most of whom love the church as you do.

4. *Be positive in your approach.* Do not be apologetic. You are not there to beg but to present an opportunity.

5. *Tell your story in an interesting way.* Catch his interest and you will gain his financial support. Take advantage of the turnover chart. Experience has proved that it will "sell" for you. Practice reading it aloud in a conversational manner . . . turning the pages quietly and quickly. When making calls in pairs, practice with your partner.

6. *Pray* for the success of your presentation.

ON SEEING YOUR PROSPECTS

1. *Before each call* . . . write the suggested appraisal of each prospect on the inside back cover of this book for easy reference. Insert the proper pledge cards for that call into the pocket of the last page of the chart. When calling in pairs decide in advance who will take the lead.

2. *On entering the home* . . . select a chair or small table and place the chart 3 or 4 feet from the nearest person. If calling at night check the light . . . you may need to move a floor lamp nearer the chart. Make sure all members of the family can see.

3. *How to begin.* The reader sits on the right of the chart turning the pages with his left hand. Adjust your voice to the size of the room so all may hear. Never let the family read the chart for themselves.

4. *Control the presentation.* Complete each page and answer all questions fully before letting the family see what is on the next page. If a question is asked which is covered by a later page say, "The answer to that question will be given on another page."

5. *Encourage your prospects to ask questions.* That is the only way to discover what they are thinking and how near they are to a decision. Be prepared to answer questions concerning the work of your denomination. If too many questions are asked, the continuity of your story may be lost. You can then say, "I'll answer that question after we have completed our story." Move rapidly. Do not let the presentation drag.

6. After you read the last page and present the family with their cards . . . *come to the point as rapidly and clearly as possible.*

7. *Suggest a definite figure.* The big question in the mind of the prospect is not, "Shall I give?" but "How much shall I give?"

He does not want to give more than his share, neither does he want to give less than his share. If he asks you what his share is, refer to the inside back cover of this booklet.

8. *The way you tell him is important.* Do not put it in an embarrassing or dictatorial way; nor should it be presented apologetically. Suggest it in a direct and friendly fashion.

Do not say, "We want you to give . . .

"We think you ought to give . . .

"You should give . . .

Say, "The committee thought you might like to give $_____ per week including local expenses and benevolences."

9. *The secret of success is BEWARE OF TOKEN GIFTS.* If offered a check or small amount of cash, explain that the Every Member Canvass is not that kind of program. Tell how the church hopes to eliminate guesswork and establish a sound program of finance by each member and friend giving regularly each week. Indicate that the church must plan its work months ahead in order to accomplish its real program.

10. *Talk in terms of a subscription.* Encourage a weekly pledge over a twelve-month period of time.

Every church member should be a "giver of record" to both local expenses and benevolences.

11. *Encourage each prospect to give in proportion to his ability.*

A prospect does not automatically give in proportion to his means. *He gives in proportion to his understanding of the needs.*

Emphasize the needs and indicate his responsibility for the program's success.

12. *Do not leave the pledge card.*

If the prospect cannot make up his mind and wants additional time to discuss it with his family or to think it over, suggest that you visit him again. Suggest a specific date and time for your return call.

13. Do not accept as final a refusal to pledge or an unsatisfactory amount on your first call.

But *leave the way open for another visit.*

14. Plan to *make at least one call each day,* and your cards will be completed in advance of the last report.

THE SUCCESSFUL COMPLETION OF YOUR CALLS WILL MEAN

1. *You help your prospect* . . . giving is a spiritual experience . . . money is time and energy . . . time and energy are life. Each time you secure a pledge, you help a person consecrate his life to a noble purpose.

2. *You help your church* . . . each pledge you receive helps it increase its services.

3. *You help yourself* . . . you are not only an ambassador of good will for your church, but your calls will deepen your friendship with those you visit. Your best friend is one you have just helped make a worthy gift to Christ's Kingdom.

2. *Visual Aids—A Second Essential Tool*

The best training is that which uses the eye as well as the ear. Put up around the room posters which outline the potential, the needs, and the challenge of the church. Make posters which tell your local story and your denominational program. Use of a missionary or denominational film is excellent if it does not exceed twenty minutes. A training film will greatly help everyone—if it is a genuine *training* film. It should be specifically designed to train the visitor in making his call. One dealing with any other subject is worthless at this point. Some churches show this film once, discuss it, then show it again. Others stop the film at strategic points and interpolate other helpful remarks. Several training films are available, such as "Thy Mission High Fulfilling," produced by the American Baptist Council on Missionary Cooperation.

Your visitors will be far more effective in their home calling if you give them a tool to handle—something to hold, show, and sell from. If you have no other piece, instruct the visitors to sell from the Proposal which was mailed into the homes a few days previously. The best selling tool to date is, however, a turnover chart. Stock charts telling the story of both the local church and the denomination are available from certain church headquarters:

> American Baptist Convention (152 Madison Avenue, New York City)
> Disciples of Christ (222 S. Downey Avenue, Indianapolis, Indiana)
> Presbyterian Church, U.S.A. (156 Fifth Avenue, New York City)
> American Lutheran Church (57 E. Main Street, Columbus, Ohio)
> Evangelical Lutheran Church (408 Fifth Avenue, S., Minneapolis, Minnesota)

Several denominations provide turnover charts on tithing.

In the interdenominational sector projects held in New England in 1952 and 1953, several churches of different denominations bought and adapted the Baptist charts. The Diocese of Western Massachusetts had several pages blueprinted, telling the story of Episcopalian missions. These were distributed to the parishes and pasted over the Baptist missionary pages. Other churches doing the same were the First Congregational of Burlington, Vermont, and Grace Episcopal of Lawrence, Massachusetts.

The turnover chart makes it easier for the visitor to tell his story, both under favorable and unfavorable conditions. One caller said he had always dreaded visiting in a home where there were children because of their distractions during his talk. But when he used the chart, the children sat on the floor before it and became his best listeners. One man found his prospect on the roof fixing his TV antenna. "If you want to see me," he called down, "you'll have to come up here." Thus challenged, the visitor climbed up, read his turnover chart, and descended with a signed pledge.

Although the chart (sometimes called a visualizer) has proved to be such a valuable tool, it has to be sold to the visitor. Some may think: "I am too intelligent to use such a silly thing." The answer: "Better salesmen, who have ever used a turnover, always want one when available." Others may think: "I don't need it." The answer here: The Rev. Frederick Gardner, pastor of the Roger Williams Baptist Church in Providence, said that he could tell who used the visualizers and who did not by the amounts on the returned pledge cards. When William Oldroyd of the Park Street Baptist Church in Framingham, Massachusetts, reported that they had received ninety new pledges, he gave credit for it to the turnover chart.

The most valuable visualizer, if well done, is one made by the local church. Ernest Cushing, publicity chairman of the enlistment in the First Congregational Church, Springfield, stated that they would never use a stock turnover after their experience with their own chart.

Cushing, who uses turnover charts in his work with the Blue Cross, used a specially made turnover to sell his pastor and his finance committee on entering the sector project. Later he made a large one for use in a Sunday morning service. For the call in every home he made a third one which he had each visitor copy. Since then he has used a turnover chart to sell the idea of turnovers! There are, he said, four reasons for using a visualizer:

1. It makes it easier to enlist workers. They appreciate having a tool.

2. It gives confidence to the visitors. They do not need to memorize their story, nor will they forget part of it. It permits turning back and repeating any page that awakened unusual interest.

3. It tells a good story. It builds up interest. The prospect waits to see what is on the next page. A visual story is five times as effective as an oral one.

4. It eases the explanation of the appraisal procedure and leads naturally to the presentation of the pledge card. The pledge card, inserted in the final page, has just enough showmanship to ensure a quick signature.

So enthusiastic was Old First Church over the results of their chart that not only did they make their own new turnover for the next year's campaign, but they then convinced eighteen other churches in the area to do likewise. Instructions on how to make a chart are given later in this chapter.

3. *Mimeographed Agendas—A Third Helpful Tool*

The giving of a mimeographed agenda to each attendant at the two training conferences is excellent procedure. This creates confidence in the worker by showing him that the General Committee has a well-organized campaign. It also helps the workers to follow and to remember what is said. The Second Congregational Church of Holyoke, Massachusetts, not only prepared agendas, they also included the salient points made by each speaker. Note how their four-page mimeographed agenda uses several different men in presenting the program, no one speaking over ten minutes at a time (except the minister who was limited to fifteen!). It is good technique also to put the time on the agenda. The workers will enjoy checking their watches with each presentation. At one of our sector project training sessions in Springfield, we asked William Appleton Lawrence, Bishop of the Episcopal Diocese of Western Massachusetts, to serve as chairman. Part of his charm in presiding was provided by his sense of fun. He brought along a referee's whistle, using it several times and threatening to blow down any speaker who took more than his allotted time.

The only suggestion I would add to this agenda is that *all* workers and visitors be urged to attend the report meetings. See the section on report meetings later in this chapter.

SECOND CONGREGATIONAL CHURCH
HOLYOKE, MASSACHUSETTS
SECOND TRAINING MEETING
TUESDAY, NOVEMBER *10*

General Chairman for Evening—Richard Read
What Division Leaders are responsible for—Richard Read
Seeing that all workers have turnover charts and workers' booklet and are educated in proper way to call (in case they had no training, give them copies of agenda).

Check up to see who has not been at these training sessions (the most important) and see that he or she is briefed on what went on.

Make sure all people in his division have made pledge before Loyalty Sunday.

Distribution of cards within division.

Make a list of who has each card in his division from stubs. Keep this list, but turn stubs in to Mrs. Doris Hathaway, who will post who has card in master list.

Get 100 per cent attendance on Loyalty Sunday.

See that any cards turned back are followed up and called on.

Be at all report meetings—send a captain to represent you if you cannot attend.

See that all pledge cards are turned in.

Duties of Captains

Follow instructions of division leader.

Do calling along with workers—necessary because we have not enough workers.

Turn in completed pledge cards of workers to division leader.

Supper—6:15–7:15

7:15—What are we going out to do?—Rev. Jerry W. Trexler

1. You are trying to persuade people to invest in the finest things in life—a Christian home, a better community, and a finer personal life.
2. People want to help when they thoroughly understand the opportunity and the need.
3. You never know who will give until you ask.
4. You have a worthy product to sell.
5. This is a sales job.
6. Things to do before going out and calling.
7. All these points (except 1 and 2) are covered in first four pages of workers' booklet.

7:30—Where do we stand now?—Donald McCorkindale

1. $54,000 and $10,000 and how we got there—appraisal—why. Proposal. Hand out proposal sheets.
2. Advance gifts report to date.
   Tell captains to complete calls on workers before Loyalty Sunday.
3. What to do about those 700 cards—900 total—200 done in advance (of 700, 250 nonpledging).
   a. Return extra two cards if you just can't do them.
   b. Division leader is person you talk to.
   c. Ten more workers will help a lot.
   d. One less packet than people in division—two less where division has sixteen or more in it.
   e. Captains to work.
   f. Cards broken down by deaconess districts.

7:50—Mechanics of call—James Laing and Richard Mathieson

1. Be prepared.
   a. Insert pledge card on the last page of chart before each call.
   b. Have a fountain pen that works.

     c. Know how to use the chart—use it—what are
     you going to say—use it.

     d. Mark appraisal figure on pledge card schedule.

     e. Notice whether member or not—whether ap-
     praised or not.

     f. Bring copy of proposal on call.

2. Make every call.

3. Never leave a pledge card—make a definite date to call back.

4. At door say, "Good afternoon, I am *(name)* from the Second Congregational Church. We're making our Every Member Canvass. May I step in and tell you about it?" (Step toward the door.)

5. In the home

     a. Try to get all the members of the family to-
     gether.

     b. Place the chart in a good light—3 or 4 feet from
     the people.

     c. Come to the point quickly.

     d. Be pleasant, interested, and sincere.

     e. Don't argue, don't apologize about your job of
     calling.

     f. Let the chart tell most of the story—only a few
     pages need extra explanation or enlargement.

     g. If there is something that the church should
     know about, note on canvasser information card
     and turn it in.

     h. "I'm not here to talk about that, but I'll tell the
     minister and he can work it out with you per-
     sonally."

6. Introduce chart.

7. How to handle last part of chart

     a. Those appraised—"Does that sound about right,
     or is the figure too low?"

     b. Those not appraised—

        (1) Where person called on is widow or there
        is a pension (no wage earner)—go through
        chart and then say, "We have not made an
        appraisal for you because we felt that in
        some cases we could not do so. However,
        you have been generous with the church in
        the past, and we know that you will do
        your best."

        (2) Where person called on is nonmember
        (most nonmembers are not appraised; a
        few are, however)—go through chart and
        then say, "Knowing you are a nonmember,

we did not feel we could make an appraisal. However, knowing your interest in the church, we wanted to extend to you the same opportunity we are extending to members to support God's work."
8. What to do if no one is at home.
9. If you cannot make all calls on Loyalty Sunday, let remaining persons not called on know you are not coming that day.
10. Turn completed pledge card back to captain with canvasser information card. Captain gives card to division leader—use report envelopes.
11. Turnover chart to be turned back to division leader when through using it. He turns it into church office. (Chart to be used by Sunday School later.)

8:15—Mechanics of records—Sidney Whiting
1. Explanation of three cards.
   a. Stub—sign and turn into division leader before leaving this meeting.
   b. Canvasser information card—*turn back with completed pledge card to captain.* Captain then gives to division leader. Explain figures on canvasser information card—last year's giving and appraisal figure.
   c. Pledge card—canvasser marks appraisal figure on schedule.
      (1) If person being pledged says he will give so much a year instead of weekly, indicate on card—cross out weekly and write in year.
      (2) Use of report envelopes, stub envelopes, captains, division.
      (3) Appraisal is a total figure—for instance, $1.00 a week per working family.
      (4) Exceptions where there is no appraisal.
      (5) Use chain of command—visitor reports to his captain; captain to division leader.
      (6) Benevolence giving—12 per cent figure.

8:25—Intermission

8:35—Steps ahead—James Laing
   Loyalty Sunday—November 15
   11:00 Dedication Service
      a. How canvassers participate.
      b. All canvassers be there with turnover chart and cards all prepared to go calling after luncheon.

        c. Division leaders responsible for attendance on Loyalty Sunday.

12:30 Luncheon (free) and advance gifts report—Ted Main.

2:00 Calling begins.

7:30 Report meeting in assembly hall. Report to division leader at his table first—all workers, all captains, all division leaders. Come to this report meeting whether you have anything to report or not and tell division leader your status.

REPORT MEETINGS FOR DIVISION LEADERS ONLY

If division leader cannot come, send captain to represent him or her.

    Second, Wednesday, November 18—7:30 P.M. at Church

    Third, Friday, November 20—7:30 P.M. at Church

    Fourth, Sunday, November 22—7:30 P.M. at Church

    Fifth, Wednesday, November 25—7:30 P.M. at Church

    Victory Sunday, November 29

8:45 *Division leaders' and captains' duties—Richard Read*

8:55 *Questions*

9:05 *Distribute cards* (Richard Read). Each division leader come and get his cards—explain again how divided up—tell about maps, making list of who has cards—

    Practice using turnover chart with person next to you.

9:20 *Training film*

THREE ESSENTIALS

There are three essentials in preparing the visitor for his work:

1. Two training sessions
2. Personal preparation and dedication of the visitor
3. Report meetings

1. *Two Training Sessions*

This book presents two training sessions. Those churches which work out a third session should produce even better results. The meetings are to be neither devotional exercises nor "pep rallies." Your workers come not to hear a sermon nor to be entertained. The meetings are to be what they are called—training sessions—with coats off and sleeves rolled up, with questions and answers, with demonstrations and practice periods. The sessions are to be so helpful that, like the Wesley Methodist Church in Springfield, Massachusetts, and the

Phillips Memorial Baptist in Cranston, Rhode Island, you will notice the difference in results between those visitors who attend the meetings and use the tools and those who stay away or scoff at helps.

Why two training sessions? Not merely to provide a second opportunity for those who missed the first session. Not merely to reiterate what was taught at the prior gathering. The emphases in the two sessions differ. The chief purpose of the first workers' training session is to raise the sights of the visitor so that he will make as large a pledge as possible when he himelf is called upon. Unless each visitor pledges, he should not be used to call upon others. Unless he himself makes a good pledge, reaching or exceeding his appraisal, he will not be successful in getting good pledges from his prospects. The subordinate purpose of this session is to train the worker.

In the second workers' training session, the stress is entirely upon how to make the best call. For by this date all visitors are assumed to have made their own pledges.

Both sessions will have as their motif the spiritual aspects of the proposed budget. The visitors should be reminded that the spiritual advance of the church—as represented by the Proposal—will be made possible as each member pledges the amount suggested to him.

The effectiveness of a training session begins with getting the workers to attend. This is the task of the workers' organization. Each captain is responsible for getting his four visitors to the meeting. Each division leader is responsible for his four captains. The Organization chairman is responsible for seeing that the division leaders are present. These meetings are so necessary for the success of the entire project that the General chairman will check closely with the Organization chairman to see that

1. There are enough workers lined up
2. They will be present at both sessions if possible; attendance at one session is imperative. Visitors who cannot attend at least one training session should not be used.

The organization will check one or two days before by telephone, each leader calling the four men under him. Each works for 100 per cent attendance at both sessions. Those who fail to attend

Do not understand the program
Cannot answer questions intelligently
Lack the enthusiasm of other workers
Usually return unvisited several of the cards selected for them

a. First Training Session. Following is a suggested agenda for the First Training Conference:

AGENDA

First Workers' Training Conference

(SUNDAY, WEEK 8)

Presiding: GENERAL CHAIRMAN

(1) 3:00 An Enlarged Program to Meet the Needs of Our Church and Christ's Kingdom
MINISTER

(2) 3:15 Showing of a denominational missionary film-strip if available

(3) 3:30 How We Shall Accomplish Our Program (our organization and timetable)
GENERAL CHAIRMAN

(4) 3:45 The Share of Each Worker in This Program: pledge and work MINISTER

(5) 3:55 Report of Progress: amount pledged to date
ADVANCE PLEDGE CHAIRMAN

(6) 4:00 The Importance of Making Our Pledges before Calling on Others
ORGANIZATION CHAIRMAN

(7) 4:10 Training film, such as the American Baptist sound filmstrip, "Thy Mission High Fulfilling"

(8) 4:25 Demonstration of Turnover Chart
—distribute to workers
GENERAL CHAIRMAN
or PUBLICITY CHAIRMAN

(9) 4:45 Brief Summary of Worker's Booklet
—distribute to workers
ORGANIZATION CHAIRMAN

(10) 4:50 What Happens at Our Meeting Friday
GENERAL CHAIRMAN

(11) 4:55 Questions

(12) 5:00 Prayer and Adjournment

NOTE: If this is a noon dinner meeting, move the time suggested here forward 1½ or 2 hours.

Be sure to use several leaders as suggested above.

Do not have one person speak longer than fifteen minutes at any one time.

Beware of using any lengthy motion picture. Your workers are not here to be entertained.

> Churches making their own turnover charts should
> allow forty-five minutes to having each visitor
> copy his chart from a master chart. When this
> is done, eliminate item 2, and shorten items 1, 3,
> 4, and 6 by five minutes each. Item 8 then be-
> comes "Making Our Turnover Charts."

The foregoing agenda naturally falls into two divisions. The first half (items 1 to 6) is designed to raise the sights of the visitors so that each will make the best possible pledge when called upon by his captain later this week. With the General chairman presiding, the minister opens the meeting with a challenge: the events of the next two weeks will determine how much greater program the church can undertake for Jesus Christ during the coming twelve months. An enlarged missionary work is presented either through the showing of a short filmstrip or motion picture or through a brief word by the minister. The General chairman explains the organization and calendar of the canvass, showing how both are geared to a successful outcome. Again the minister speaks, stating that each visitor has two obligations: to make his own pledge and to complete his chosen calls. Perhaps the highlight of the session will be the report of the Advance Pledge chairman. The purpose of this report is to spread optimism among the visitors. This chairman need not at this time report every dollar he has received; he should be sure that each of his succeeding reports is larger than the preceding. The Organization chairman or the General chairman then stresses that no one should ask anyone else for a pledge who has not already signed his own commitment.

The second half of the agenda (items 7 to 12) is designed to prepare the visitor for the calling he is to do a week from now. The major items here are the showing of a training film, the distribution and reading of a visitor's handbook, and instruction in the use of a turnover chart (or the actual making of the charts). As the handbooks are given out, the Organization chairman or General chairman should read the booklet aloud, asking each one to follow his reading. Although it is not advisable to read every word, the chairman should read aloud every salient sentence. The visitors are to take the booklets home for further study.

HOW TO MAKE A TURNOVER CHART

Should your church decide to make its own turnover charts, you will need to purchase artist's sketch pads or have your printer spiral-bind some sheets of paper together with a cardboard back. The churches in the 1953 Springfield interdenominational sector were able to purchase blank charts, similar to an artist's sketch pad. Each chart contained twenty-five pages, size 14 by 11 inches, with a cardboard easel so that it would stand upright. In each church the General Committee made a model chart which each visitor copied.

The church should supply large photographs of the building, to be pasted on the front cover of these home-made visualizers. One church used a moonlight photograph that had recently been displayed in a contest. Some churches make photo-offsets for this purpose. Old First Church ordered enough photo-offset copies of a fine drawing of the church so that one could be presented to each member when called upon. Many persons, stated the Rev. John Wallace, have since framed this sketch.

The text must be identical for all the charts. The General Committee prepares the text, revising it until the committee agrees it is as fine as possible. The text should not exceed twenty-five pages. Then the committee makes one model turnover chart. Each visitor copies this model at the first workers' training session.

At this conference each visitor finds on the table before him a blank chart, a church photograph, and a black marking pencil. (The best tool is a brush pen. It has a felt tip and uses an alcohol-base fluid which makes it instant drying. It costs about $3.50.) The General or Publicity chairman stands before the visitors, chart in hand. He tells why this tool is effective and introduces the technique of using it. (He will spend more time on the latter at the second session.) Each visitor, he explains, is to copy his own visualizer, making each according to the model now to be presented.

The chairman asks someone who is acquainted with the chart to assist him in dictating it. One man reads the first page, holding it aloft so that all might see. As soon as every visitor has copied that page, the second man reads the next page. And so on until the entire chart is read and copied.

It is best if each one is proofread before it goes out. Since these charts should be taken home that evening by each visitor so that he might practice the use of it during the week, this means that the turnovers will need to be collected as soon as finished and reviewed by one or two members of the General Committee. In cases of misspelling or inaccuracies, corrections should be made. In those few cases where the chart is too crude to be shown, a tactful suggestion should be made to the author that he might wish some assistance in making a new visualizer.

A little "home-made" look increases the value of the chart. The prospect is curious to know what the story is that this individually made chart is going to tell. He feels that this presentation is more personal. The visitor, too, takes a greater interest in his chart. Since he made it, he is eager and proud to demonstrate it.

The Centenary Methodist Church of Auburndale, Massachusetts, worked out a refinement of the foregoing technique. At the first training conference, the General chairman, Dr. R. E. Sylvester, stated that each visitor could immediately make his chart or could copy the text on a scratch pad and make the chart at home, decorating it anyway desired. Everyone of the sixty workers chose the latter and at the second conference turned up with the most attractive set of turnover charts I have ever seen. They had magnificent results.

Churches which successfully use a stock (ready-prepared) turnover chart the first year report that they need more of a surprise element the second year than a second stock visualizer seems to be able to provide. The home-made chart, built entirely around your church and telling of its individual ministry to the community and the world, gives the perfect answer for the second—or the third—year.

A poorly composed chart is, however, inferior to a stock chart. A good visualizer must be well written. It must be brief. It must often suggest, rather than tell a full story. It must be selective and yet broad enough to appeal to divergent interests. Certain rules of salesmanship should be incorporated. It would be wise if each church went to a professional publicity man—or at least to a sales manager who has used charts—for assistance in composing the text.

Three typical charts are shown on the following eight pages. A study of these three, actually used in Every Member Canvasses, should help you in preparing your own chart. The chart of the Bethany Congregational Church of Foxboro, Massachusetts, is on pages 131 to 133 (Fig. 8-1). The chart of the Old First Congregational Church of Springfield, Massachusetts, is on pages 133 to 135 (Fig. 8-2). The chart of the Wesley Methodist Church, also of Springfield, is on pages 136 to 138 (Fig. 8-3).

The Bethany Church affixed colorful plastic index tabs to the pages for ease in turning.

The chart used the second year by Old First Church of Springfield capitalized upon their success of the preceding year. Note how their chart thanked all for their part last year and then stated that this very success made another forward step imperative.

Their chart, kindly supplied me by John Wallace, is shown in Fig. 8-2.

Another successful visualizer was that prepared by the Wesley Methodist Church of Springfield. Pastor Leslie H. Johnson provided me with a copy. (See Fig. 8-3.)

The turnover chart used by the Bethany Congregational Church of Foxboro, Massachusetts, may serve as a sample in preparing your own text:

```
┌─────────────────────────┐   ┌─────────────────────────┐
│                         │   │   It                    │
│                         │   │       Needs             │
│                         │   │            your         │
│                         │   │                help     │
│                         │   │                         │
│   This is your Church   │   │                         │
│                    1.   │   │                    2.   │
└─────────────────────────┘   └─────────────────────────┘
```

```
┌─────────────────────────┐   ┌─────────────────────────┐
│     Our Church          │   │  Through Her Pastoral Ministry │
│       serves            │   │      Worship Services   │
│        You              │   │      Baptism            │
│   and the Community     │   │      Marriage           │
│     in Many Ways        │   │      Bereavement        │
│                         │   │      Illness            │
│                         │   │      Counseling         │
│                    3.   │   │                    4.   │
└─────────────────────────┘   └─────────────────────────┘
```

```
┌─────────────────────────┐   ┌─────────────────────────┐
│                         │   │     Each Sunday         │
│     We are              │   │   approximately         │
│      PROUD              │   │   250 Students          │
│                         │   │      and a              │
│     of our              │   │ Staff of 37 Dedicated   │
│   CHURCH SCHOOL         │   │     Teachers            │
│                         │   │ Seek to Learn about     │
│                         │   │       the               │
│                         │   │   Christian Life        │
│                    5.   │   │                    6.   │
└─────────────────────────┘   └─────────────────────────┘
```

```
┌─────────────────────────┐   ┌─────────────────────────┐
│   For the Teenagers     │   │                         │
│  there is an active     │   │  17 of the Members of   │
│  Pilgrim Fellowship     │   │   Pilgrim Fellowship    │
│ of some 30 members with │   │                         │
│  Excellent Leaders      │   │      attended           │
│      and a              │   │      Summer             │
│  Dynamic Program        │   │    Conferences          │
│                    7.   │   │                    8.   │
└─────────────────────────┘   └─────────────────────────┘
```

Fig. 8-1

Bethany Church
contributes to the
World Mission of the Church
by supporting
Miss Thompson

sponsoring
International Weekend
Missionary Speakers
Apportionment Giving

9.

Our Church Is the Home
for Such Activities as

Morning Worship
Woman's Union
Evening Division
Couples Club
Kindergarten
Choir
Study Groups

10.

The Church is

growing

The Activities are
Growing

The Challenge is
Growing

the need is
GROWING   11.

To Meet These

INCREASED NEEDS

We Must

RAISE

The sights of

OUR
GIVING   12.

With the
Increased Facilities
of
Bethany Church
Our Fixed Costs For
Heat Lights
Insurance
Parsonage
have

Increased   13.

Our Maintenance
Costs Have Increased

Paint Fund

Roof Fund

Landscaping

14.

WHAT DOES

A L L

THIS

C O S T ? ?

15.

This Is It:

Our Church Home	$ 7,700
Our Pastoral Ministry	$ 5,995
Worship Services	$ 2,215
World Service	$ 2,800
Christian Education	$ 1,000
Our Total Budget	$19,710

16.

FIG. 8-1 (*Continued*)

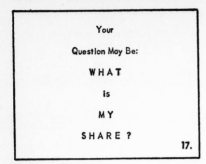

Your

Question May Be:

WHAT

is

MY

SHARE ?

17.

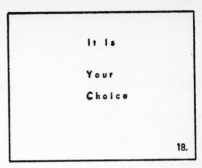

It Is

Your

Choice

18.

Our Resources Committee
has suggested an
Amount
which they believe
you
Might like to Consider

19.

*   *

Thank
You!

*   *

(pledge card inserted here,
and under the card "Thank You")

20.

Fig. 8-1 (*Continued*)

Our Church

ADVANCED

In

1953

1.

A NEW SPIRIT IS
AT WORK IN OUR
CHURCH !

BETTER CHURCH ATTENDANCE
_____
LARGER CHURCH SCHOOL
_____
INCREASED YOUTH ACTIVITY
_____
HEALTHIER FINANCIAL
CONDITION

2.

AND

WITH INCREASED
BENEVOLENCES

OUR CHRISTIAN WORLD
MISSION

REACHES

FARTHER THAN EVER

3.

Calkins Hall Decorated

New Roof

Tower and Steeple Rebuilt

Kitchen Remodeled

Outside Painting

These things done ──

The bills paid !

4.

Fig. 8-2

OUR

YOUTH PROGRAM

Advanced

with

New Leadership
More Camperships
Better Teacher Training
New Activities of
Interest to
Our Youth   5.

YES!

WE CAN BE PROUD
OF OUR

A D V A N C E

in

1953   6.

---

for

1954

THE CHALLENGE

IS EVEN

GREATER!

7.

A

CONTINUING ADVANCE
means —

Paint and Tile Rest Rooms
Decorate Halls and Stairways
Steam Clean Exterior Brickwork
Advance Music Program
and New Choir Robes

8.

IMPROVE CHURCH LIGHTING
FLOOD LIGHT EXTERIOR OF CHURCH

as well as

CONTINUE

BUILDING ORGAN FUND

INCREASED BENEVOLENCES
and
SUPPORT YOUTH PROGRAM   9.

But the real NEED

for 1954

concerns our Youth
Program

We have made a
Significant Start

We are Handicapped
by   10.

INADEQUATE

FACILITIES
———
WE NEED A
YOUTH ACTIVITY
ROOM
* * *
To Combine
WORSHIP, WORK, PLAY   11.

CHURCH MEMBERS
DISCUSSED THIS NEED
AT THE QUARTERLY MEETING
AND AUTHORIZED $8,000
IN OUR PROPOSED BUDGET
TOWARD THE COST OF
SUCH A ROOM !   12.

FIG. 8-2 (*Continued*)

EXTEND 'PECK' ROOM 50'

– parallel to church –

THEN

LATER A

CHAPEL

COULD BE BUILT

OVER THIS ROOM

13.

THIS ROOM COULD

SERVE OTHER SMALL

CHURCH GROUPS

AND

SOLVE OUR NEED

FOR A

YOUTH ACTIVITIES ROOM

14.

O U R

CONTINUING

A D V A N C E

WILL MAKE THIS

P O S S I B L E !

15.

HERE IS OUR PROPOSAL FOR

1954

CHURCH HOME	$19,075
MINISTRY	16,200
OUR CHRISTIAN WORLD MISSION	12,200
WORSHIP AND SERVICE	24,875
EDUCATION	9,750
	$82,100

16.

FIRST CHURCH
Has the

FAITH

PRAYER

VISION

TO MEET THIS

CHALLENGE !

17.

What is my Share

for 1954?

If This Is Your

18.

AGAIN THIS YEAR A

CHURCH-WIDE APPRAISAL

COMMITTEE SUGGESTS

AN AMOUNT WHICH THEY

BELIEVE YOU MIGHT

LIKE TO GIVE

19.

YOUR   CHURCH

THANKS
YOU
FOR

YOUR GIFT FOR 1954

20.

FIG. 8-2 (*Continued*)

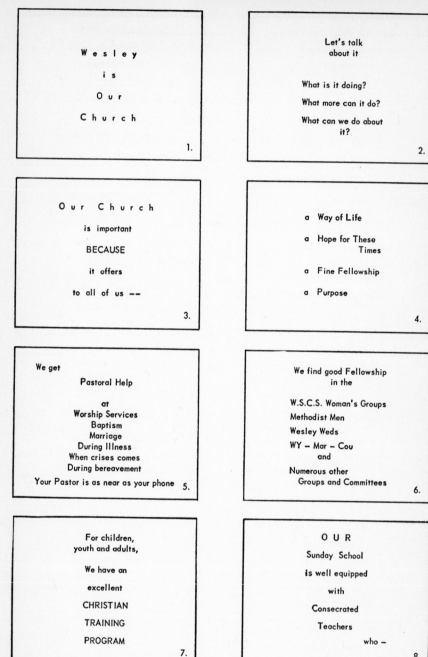

FIG. 8-3

benefit from
the BEST
available helps
and guidance
from our

Director of
Christian
Education

9.

Your Church

has

3 Sunday Evening
Youth Groups
Saturday Activities
A Bible School
Scout – Cub and
Brownie Groups

10.

Wesley is also
concerned with

OTHERS

its members are active
in
Greater Springfield
Council of Churches

United Church Men and
Women

Goodwill Industries

11.

We have a part in the

CONFERENCE

Advance Program

to relocate
and build

NEW CHURCHES
and a
Conference Center

12.

We participate in

OUR

WORLD MISSION

to take the

Gospel of Christ
to
Every Person

13.

But – OUR work
is never done.

NEW PEOPLE are
coming to town.

Wesley needs them!
They need the church!

We must help
win them to Christ!

14.

To do this –

YOUR CHURCH

needs

the additional
services of an

ASSOCIATE PASTOR

to seek out
these new persons

15.

Your Staff

in Wesley is doing

Wonderfully well –

But –

with this additional

help they can

do even better   *to* –   16.

FIG. 8-3 (*Continued*)

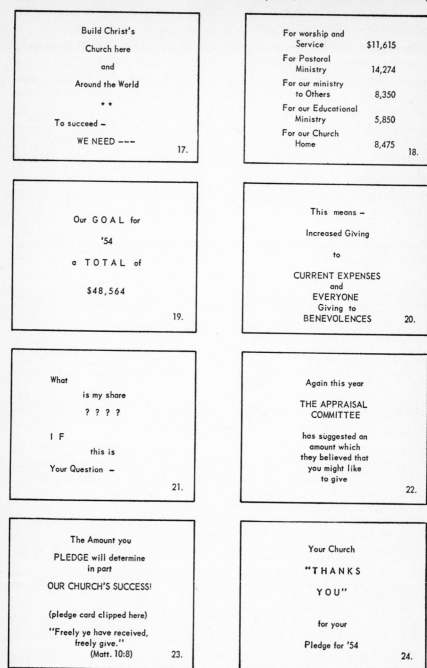

Build Christ's

Church here

and

Around the World

* *

To succeed —

WE NEED — — —

17.

For worship and
   Service $11,615

For Pastoral
   Ministry   14,274

For our ministry
   to Others   8,350

For our Educational
   Ministry   5,850

For our Church
   Home   8,475

18.

Our G O A L for

'54

a T O T A L of

$48,564

19.

This means —

Increased Giving

to

CURRENT EXPENSES
and
EVERYONE
Giving to
BENEVOLENCES

20.

What

   is my share

   ? ? ? ?

I F

   this is

Your Question —

21.

Again this year

THE APPRAISAL
COMMITTEE

has suggested an
amount which
they believed that
you might like
to give

22.

The Amount you

PLEDGE will determine
in part

OUR CHURCH'S SUCCESS!

(pledge card clipped here)

"Freely ye have received,
freely give."
(Matt. 10:8)   23.

Your Church

"T H A N K S

Y O U"

for your

Pledge for '54

24.

FIG. 8-3 (*Continued*)

HOW TO USE A TURNOVER CHART

The visitor must be trained in the use of the chart. It will be largely a waste of money to purchase printed charts and hand them out to the visitors without instruction in the use of them. Even the use of "home-made" charts—of which each creator is so proud—requires training. This instruction is to be given mainly or entirely at the second training session. At this first meeting, however, you might wish to hand out a mimeographed sheet of instructions. One chairman presented the following to his visitors. Father George Smith of St. Peter's Episcopal Church, Springfield, supplied me with a copy.

THE MASTER CONTROL CHART

Used extensively for over twenty years in sales training, the turnover chart is still one of the best devices in the field. Its use is comparatively new in our church. Here's what it does:

a. It tends to guarantee a uniform presentation in all territories.
b. The audience sees and hears at the same time, resulting in a more lasting impression.
c. It replaces the notes or manuscript of the speaker.
d. It furnishes a measure of audience participation, thereby retaining interest.
e. It is a substantial help to the less experienced speaker and a definite aid to somewhat colorless delivery.

Here's how to use it:

a. Keep it closed until you're ready to use it.
b. See that it is well illuminated so that everyone can read it.
c. Sit at the right of the chart and turn the pages with your left hand.
d. Roll the pages back over the top with a smooth continuous motion.
e. Don't reach for a page until you've finished reading it.
f. Know your chart thoroughly before presenting it.
g. Read slowly but with change of pace.
h. Write in ad-lib notes in lower right-hand corner.
i. Save the last word on the page whenever possible and use it as the start of the next. This gives continuity.
j. Be sure your ad-lib helps, not hinders, the presentation. Don't try to rephrase every page.
k. Face your audience as much as you can.

It's a good and faithful friend. Learn to use it expertly.

Each visitor shall have his visualizer available immediately after the First Workers' Training Conference so that he may practice using it all that week.

It should be stressed that every caller uses the turnover chart, making a game of his work. Each worker, having the chart read to him at the time he signs his own pledge, will attempt to read his chart more effectively when he himself goes calling. In the First Baptist Church of Holden, Massachusetts, the general chairman, Anker Nielsen, called on the pastor, Hartley Grandin, for the first pledge in the canvass, using the visualizer. Mr. Grandin then called on Nielsen, again using the turnover. Despite the fact that Nielsen had already decided on what he would pledge, the use of the chart (which he knew as well as the minister) caused him to raise his pledge an additional dollar a week.

The importance of each visitor making his own pledge before calling on others should be stressed by the Organization chairman. *It should be a rule that no one is to go calling who has not already signed a pledge.* Beginning the day after this first training session, each captain will call in the homes of his visitors. He will use the turnover chart as though the visitor had never heard of one. He will work toward getting each of his four visitors to reach his appraisal.

b. Second Training Session. Following is a suggested agenda for the second workers' training session:

FORM T

AGENDA
Second Workers' Training Conference
(FRIDAY, WEEK 8)

Presiding: GENERAL CHAIRMAN

6:30 Invocation and Dinner

7:30 Restatement of the Needs of Our Church
and Christ's Kingdom   MINISTER

7:35 The Canvass Goal   PROPOSAL CHAIRMAN

7:40 The Steps Already Taken   GENERAL CHAIRMAN

7:45 Report of Progress   ADVANCE PLEDGE CHAIRMAN
(After the Advance Pledge chairman reports the total received by his committee, have each division leader or captain stand and announce the total received from his workers. Add these totals to advance pledge totals)

7:55 The Steps Ahead   ORGANIZATION CHAIRMAN
Making the Calls
The Report Meetings

8:05 Another Look at the Training Film

8:25 Why Use the Turn-over Chart?
          PUBLICITY CHAIRMAN or GENERAL CHAIRMAN

8:40 The Workers' Booklet   ORGANIZATION CHAIRMAN

9:00 The Pledge Card   PUBLICITY CHAIRMAN

9:10 The Call in the Home   GENERAL CHAIRMAN
  1. Getting into the house
  2. Showing the turnover chart
  3. Introducing the suggested figure
  4. Presenting the pledge card
  5. Making the exit

9:40 The Minister's Final Word

9:50 Selecting the Pledge Cards

(SUGGESTION: If you are using a training film, it is good technique to train as the film is being shown. Stop the film and record to interpolate wherever you wish to emphasize some point. If you do, rearrange this agenda, allowing forty-five minutes for use of film.)

The second training session should be held as close to Dedication Sunday as possible, preferably Friday. The stress in this meeting is upon so training the worker that he can do his calling enthusiastically.

The Advance Pledge chairman at this meeting reports the total of pledges his committee has obtained. The Organization chairman then asks for a report on the totals pledged by the workers. Each captain arises and states the total received from his company of workers plus himself. The figures are written on a blackboard. As the workers see that they have already raised 35 to 50 per cent of the goal, enthusiasm mounts. They realize that victory now depends on the kind of job they do in their calling.

Greater time is given in this second training session to the use of the turnover chart and the retelling of the appraisal technique. A major portion of the evening is devoted to the interview in the home.

GETTING INTO THE HOME

The visitor is not to hold his interview on the porch or front vestibule. To show his chart and to lead in an easy, natural way to the pledge card, he must be seated with the prospects. Before he has gone up the front walk, he has clipped onto the last page of his chart the card or cards for this family. No other cards are to be in the chart.

As the door opens to him, he speaks, always using the name of the prospect:

"Good afternoon, Mrs. W. I am John Banks from the First Church. Our church is calling on every home this week. May I come in?"

The trainees are instructed that whenever they desire something, or are in a difficult position, or are facing a troublesome question, they are themselves to ask a question. Thus: "May I come in?"

A life-insurance agent told me that good procedure is to take *one step back* as the door opens and you give your name. Then *one step forward* as you ask the question.

If the woman hesitates, the caller brings his chart into play. Holding it in his hand, he lifts it so that she may see the cover—and only the cover—and says:

"This afternoon we are showing these charts in every home. May I come in to show it to your family?"

Her curiosity aroused, she invites him in. As he steps in, he glances over the living room to see where he can best show his chart. He should not sit with his back to a window. There should be nothing distracting behind him. If there is a table at the left of a suitable chair, so much the better for displaying the chart.

If only Mrs. W comes in and there are other church members at this address, Banks again asks a question:

"Is Mr. W, and are John and Mary home? Would you not like to invite them in. I believe they would enjoy seeing this chart. I made it myself."

Even children will sit quietly when there is something new to see.

Suppose the television set is on. Apparently the family has forgotten it. The caller, in a difficult spot, asks a question: "Would you mind turning off the television? This will take only a few minutes." If it is obvious that the family is absorbed in a particular program, it is better to wait until that show ends, then ask the question, or excuse oneself to come back at another time. The caller should not attempt to give his story if the TV stays on, or if there are guests present.

When all are seated, Banks opens the conversation with a few general remarks about the family. Are all well? If he discovers illness, or any trouble the minister should know about, the visitor is instructed to say:

"Mrs. W, our pastor will want to know about this. I'll jot it down now so as to be sure to tell him when I return."

SHOWING THE CHART

After one minute of general conversation, he says:

"I know you folks will be interested in this turnover chart. It tells something about our church."

Whereupon he immediately sets the chart up, preferably on a table at his left, so that all may see. He begins to read, not allowing the family to read for him. He reads with emphasis, stressing especially the word "you."

The opening pages are not apt to draw questions. As he gets to the church budget, he encourages questions, answering them as they arise. If, however, the question is answered later on in the chart, he replies:

"I believe that question is answered on the next few pages. If you don't mind, I'll hold it until then."

Banks has studied his prospects before he rang their doorbell. Now he observes them as he opens up the proposed program for next year. Discovering their particular interests, he will stress these items. Many a pledge has been obtained by selling only one item or one idea.

The caller proceeds to the benevolence pages, stating that it is the desire of the church that everyone support this phase of church life.

As he comes up to the closing pages, he works for full attention. The chart leads up to a natural "close." The prospects become aware that they are expected to have a share in the underwriting of the new program. The last page is turned up, and the pledge card appears. On it is typed the name of Mr. and Mrs. W.

INTRODUCING THE SUGGESTED FIGURE

The training for this step of the interview must be clearly and carefully done.

As the pledge card appears, the visitors are instructed *not* to pull it out. Banks is now to turn away from his chart and state:

"You folks may recall that three or four weeks ago a group of thirty members sat down one afternoon to determine what our church resources are. Each one had before him a list of the names and addresses of every member. There was nothing else on the sheet. Everyone worked alone, not discussing any name or looking at anyone else's sheet. Then each was asked: "What *could* you give next year if you became interested in our proposed advance?" Each first wrote down a suggested figure for himself. No one signed any sheet; so the work remained anonymous. Then each was asked to suggest a figure for the minister and for the General chairman. Then, in the light of what he had put down for himself, everyone put down a suggestion for each other name on the list that he knew. When all had finished, the chairman added the figures for every name and determined the average for each. All the averages were added. From this we know how much money our church *could* raise.

"Mr. W, there is a suggested figure for everyone. For the pastor. For the General chairman. For me. And for you."

On the word "you," the visitors are trained to stop. They must not say another word. Silence now becomes golden. Expectantly the visitor is to look at the prospect, anticipating the question.

Salesmen tell us that at this point we are not to get jittery. If we sit long enough, the question will come. Tell the workers to begin counting to themselves. Before they reach thirty, the question will be put:

"What are they suggesting for us?"

Banks: "Since you ask, Mr. W, the committee thought you might like to think in terms of six dollars per week."

Again there must be silence. If the first silence was golden, this one is uranium.

Fred Blenkhorn, General chairman of the First Baptist Church of Milton, Massachusetts, and a star sales manager, tells me that he instructs his salesmen at this point: "The first man to speak loses. If you can get him to speak first, you will almost always win the sale."

Some visitors here add: "But whatever you decide is up to you and your Lord." If, however, the leaders of the enlistment have done a good job selling the appraisal idea, such a sentence is unnecessary. If the visitor does not succeed in getting this question, or if he stumbles over the appraisal story, he may present the pledge card. If printed and checked as suggested, the card tells the story itself, indicating the prospect's appraisal.

PRESENTING THE PLEDGE CARD

The prospect's answer determines the next move. If he assents to the suggestion, Banks simply hands over the pledge card with a fountain pen, saying as he points:

"Mr. W, you sign here."

Every visitor should carry two pens with him.

Arthur Wilder, one of the aggressive leaders in the excellent Worcester United Church Canvass related to me how a friend of his sells. This man uses a hearing aid. When he comes to closing his sale, he always turns off his battery (unseen by the customer), and no matter what objection the customer raises, he says, pointing to the order blank: "You sign here." . . . "Mr. X, you sign here." Art says this man is one of the most successful salesmen he knows.

Should the prospect suggest a lower figure, the visitor gives a word of appreciation, then turns again to his chart. Having determined what Mr. W especially likes in the Proposal, he tells once again the story of this item. Suppose it is summer scholarships for youth attending camps and conventions.

"Mr. W," Banks continues, "this item for summer scholarships is a most worthy object. It is new in our Proposal. Whether or not it becomes a part of the new budget is determined by how our people pledge. If many do not reach their suggested figure, something will need to be dropped. Perhaps it will be these camp scholarships."

Again Banks becomes silent, expecting a favorable reply from W.

Should W reply in the first place that he does not wish to pledge, or that he does not like the way the Sunday School is run, or that the minister does not call often enough, he will have Banks on the negative if Banks takes issue with him. The statement given by the prospect is apt to be a camouflage for some other reason. Therefore Banks should not take time to answer the objection.

He should as soon as possible get from negative to positive ground. This is what I call the "yes, but" treatment.

Banks: "Yes, you may be right, Mr. W, but wouldn't it be a wonderful thing if we could have this new program next year. Etc."

Or Banks: "Mr. W, you may be right. I don't know. But this is a great idea here in this chart to send some promising youngsters to a leadership training camp, isn't it?"

The "yes, but" treatment. Tell your visitors to agree as far as honesty will allow. Then immediately turn back to their charts and begin reselling.

Mr. W may desire "to think this thing over," requesting Banks to leave the pledge card, since "I shall mail it to you." If this seems to be an excuse, Banks should resell. If it seems to be a valid reason, Banks should reply:

"Mr. W, we are asked never to leave a pledge card. It will be very easy for me to come back. Should I return tomorrow at 8 P.M. or would Tuesday be better?"

Here is the "fatal alternative," as one life-insurance salesman calls it. In his choosing between tomorrow or Tuesday, he forgets that he may not wish to have Banks return. Leave the prospect some choice. But make it a choice that will either way favor the caller.

If the caller cannot get the card signed at that time, he should make a definite appointment for returning. Then he must be sure to honor the appointment.

HOW TO MAKE AN EXIT

As the prospect hands back the pledge card, the visitor should be trained to look at the card and repeat the amounts of the pledge.

Banks: "Mr. W, I see that you have pledged four dollars a week to local expenses and four dollars a week to missions. Is that correct?"

This procedure will clear up any question if the card is not clear. Should the pledge be quite a bit below the suggested figure, it sometimes serves as a shock to hear the low figure repeated. Thus one man signed a pledge for ten dollars for the year. The visitor said: "Mr. D, I see your pledge is for ten dollars a year. That is only twenty cents a week. Is that what you mean to give?" The pledge was immediately increased.

Churches should never encourage the desire for secrecy of pledges. Thus no visitor should ever carry envelopes with him for the pledge card to be sealed in. Let us not be timorous about this matter of pledging. We have a goal we are trying to reach. It will cost so many dollars. These dollars will be obtained only as most people reach their appraisal. Let the visitor, therefore, look at the pledge card to see whether he has been a good salesman for his church. Let him read aloud the pledge to check on its accuracy. Such reading may lead to the raising of an inadequate pledge.

In a very few cases the prospect may state that he does not wish the caller to see the pledge. In this case the request can be honored by the visitor telling the prospect that if he will get an envelope (the prospect will be made to supply his own envelope) and seal it, it will be opened only by the financial secretary.

As soon as the prospect acknowledges that the pledge is correct, the caller thanks him and rises to his feet. He immediately moves to the door. Good salesmanship tells the caller to leave as soon as possible after the order is signed. Something may happen to unsell the prospect. It is not discourteous to leave at this point, since the call was primarily a business call. The business is finished. The family would like to get back to its regular routine. And the visitor has other calls to make.

When the pledge is signed, get out.

DISTRIBUTING THE PLEDGE CARDS

The selection of pledge cards is done at the *close* of the *second* training meeting. The cards, each typed with name and address and checked for appraisal figure, have previously been divided by the Organization chairman among his top tier of leadership. Thus in a church of five hundred members, each of the two division leaders would be given one-half the cards. The division leaders then divide their cards into four equal stacks for their captains. At the end of the training session, each captain gathers his four visitors around a table. The captain, with a pile of twenty-five or thirty cards, reads off the name on the first card, asking who desires it. As one visitor takes the card, he immediately writes his own name on the stub (and the name of the prospect if the stub and original are not already numbered), tears the stub off, and places it in an envelope marked Stubs. The captain continues reading until every card has been taken. When the visitor has signed and torn off all stubs, he puts a rubber band around his cards, with his name on the pile. The captain then collects all stub envelopes and all piles of pledge cards. Pledge cards are not to be taken away by the visitor until after the worship service on Dedication Day. Before he goes home, the captain gives all his envelopes and his cards to his division leader or to the Organization chairman.

It is better for the captain not to take any cards for his own calling. His duty is not so much to call as to see that all calls are made. He is then free to encourage and aid his visitors, and perhaps make a call or two with a timid worker. If a visitor finds it impossible to finish his calls, or if there are cards that none of his visitors will take, the captain will make these select calls.

Parker Calvert of the Auburndale Congregational Church in Newton, Massachusetts, devised a helpful system. He used a spare page at the back of his turnover chart to make a schedule of his calls, allowing one hour for each. This page was especially helpful when he made an appointment to call back again later in the week.

On Saturday the General chairman, with assistance, enters on the master list the name of each visitor opposite the prospect's name. Thus he can know at any instant who is holding every card. Only in this way can he make sure that each card is reported back to him.

2. *Personal Preparation and Dedication of the Visitor*

The alert General chairman will give "homework assignments" to his visitors. Each will take from the first training session a turnover chart and a worker's handbook. To become the most effective worker possible, each will spend time at home studying the chart and practicing with it. While visitors do not memorize the text, they almost do so. They should know their visualizer backward and forward. They should practice reading it aloud. Practice it on the wife. Practice it on the children, the dog, or the cat. Practice reading it before a mirror.

The visitor will also give individual consideration to each prospect upon whom he is to call. Having selected his cards at the second training session, he will the next day work out a talk for each individual call, tailoring it to fit the interests of the prospect. He will always end each talk with a brief outline of the appraisal procedure. Since he is engaged in the King's business, he will pray that God bless his effort and give him the words to say.

While each visitor will make his own personal dedication to God in this task, there will also be a public act of consecration. Sunday, Week 9, is known as Dedication Day. Because of the work of the telephone squad, there will be a large congregation present. All visitors will be instructed to arrive fifteen minutes early, bringing their turnover charts.

For this service at the Centenary Methodist Church in Attleboro, Massachusetts, the workers joined in the processional, following the choir down the aisle of the church, each carrying his own chart. The Old First Congregational Church of Springfield and the Central Methodist of Lawrence have also used this procedure. It is wise to have all workers sit together in the front pews. At the moment of dedication, all workers rise together. Some churches ask the visitors to line up around the walls of the sanctuary. Others have them come forward for the dedicatory prayer. A suggested order of worship is Form W (in the Canvass Kit).

The minister should announce at this service the total of all pledges received to date. He reminds the congregation that victory will be reached if each one pledge the amount to be suggested that afternoon.

Following the morning service a complimentary dinner should be served in the church to all workers. Sometimes the church pays for the meal, sometimes one or two members. After dessert, the General chairman speaks for a few minutes on the objectives of the campaign. The Organization chairman stresses the need for seeing every prospect, even though several repeat calls may be necessary. No pledge cards are to be left at any home. Everyone is expected back that evening at the first report meeting. Report meetings will also be held on Wednesday, Friday, and Sunday nights, with a Victory Report Meeting a week from Wednesday. Each visitor is urged to attend every report meeting. The minister closes the meeting with a word of encouragement, reminding all that they are going forth to glorify Jesus Christ. The pledge cards are handed to each caller as he leaves the room, each one being given a couple of extra blank cards.

3. *Report Meetings*

The idea of report meetings is difficult to sell. Experience has proved, however, that those churches which hold several of them make out better than those who omit them or hold only one. Report meetings will aid the church by

> Informing the leaders immediately as to the progress of the canvass
> Acting as a spur to the workers, keeping them on the job
> Encouraging those whose calls may not have been so successful
> Keeping up the enthusiasm of all
> Allowing for reassignment of cards
> Bringing the campaign to a quick end

The General chairman and the pastor should know from day to day how the canvass is progressing. If there are many incompleted calls, or if the goal continues to stay out of reach, the chairman can help the situation if he acts quickly. The spiritual height which the congregation reached on Sunday, following the dedication service and the receipt of the Proposal in the mail, will not continue for long. When the chairman sees that things are dragging, he can stir up the workers to renewed vigor. It is imperative that the chairman know at the end of the first day of visitation how much has been raised.

Regardless of how well-meaning your workers may be, there will be tendencies to put off the visiting, especially after the first day. The first pledges are always the best pledges. The longer your visitors wait before seeing their prospects, the less the enthusiasm of both visitor and prospect, and the smaller the pledges. The second report meeting acts to stir up the visitor again. It works like this:

On Wednesday morning the captain calls one of his workers to remind him of the report meeting that night. Captain: "How is it going, Charley?" Charley: "Uh—okay. Thanks." Captain: "Good. I knew you'd do a swell job. By the way, you'll be at the report meeting tonight, won't you?" Charley: "Yehhh. Thanks for calling."

Things had not, of course, been going so well for Charley. He had made two calls Sunday afternoon. Both were out. So he quit and went home. Sunday night was TV night, and Monday was lodge night. Tuesday it had rained. Charley meant to do a good job, but one does get busy. Now, when his captain hung up, Charley did some quick thinking. He was certainly not going to show up tonight (he had forgotten it until the captain called) without any pledge to report. He picked up the telephone and made a quick luncheon date with one of his prospects. Then at four o'clock he left the office early and made a call on the way to church. Results: Charley had two pledges to report that night.

Now and then one of your workers has a discouraging couple of days. Herb tried to make five calls—two of them were out, one address he could not find, and the other two he could not get to sign. By this time he is almost whipped. He begins thinking that no one is pledging this year. But at the report meeting he hears vastly different stories. Everyone else seems to be meeting with wonderful success. The goal has been 90 per cent raised. The enthusiasm of the other workers stirs him up again. This time Herb goes forth in confidence and gets his next three pledges.

Toward the end of the first week most of the visitors begin to slow down. They are still calling, but they are not selling with the same zest. The last few pledges reveal it—they should have been higher. Then at the next report meeting, Edith tells a story: She had called on the parents of three children in the Sunday School. They were not members, and it had been many months since they had been at church. But she wondered whether they might not like to pledge one dollar a week. They agreed, and then began asking questions about the church. Finally Edith quietly said: "You have given your money to the church, why don't you now give your hearts to Christ?" There was further talk, and then these parents said they wanted to become Christians. After prayer with them, Edith went directly to the pastor's home to tell him. He called, and next Sunday, she continues, all five in the family are joining the church. Because of this one story, visitors go out renewed spiritually.

Perhaps all the cards were not taken on Sunday afternoon. These need to be picked up by someone. Perhaps a couple of visitors brought back half of their cards not called upon, for one reason or another. These need to be reassigned. Perhaps Joe returned with no success from a call that should have meant a substantial pledge. He believes that someone else may be able to sell the prospect. All these problems can be handled at a report meeting. Some visitors who have completed their calling will be willing to take two more calls. Others swap cards (with the knowledge of their captains who report the exchange to the General chairman). Other changes are made. The campaign picks up speed again.

Report meetings are best when they are supper meetings. The supper should be quickly served and the meeting under way within forty minutes. While the visitors are eating, each should fill in a worker's report envelope, enclose the signed pledge cards, and hand the envelope to his captain. Each captain also fills in a captain's larger report envelope, enclosing all worker's envelopes. In larger churches, division leaders also fill in their envelopes, enclosing all captain's envelopes. In directing the reporting of pledges, the Organization chairman should write each report on a blackboard. He will first write the amount previously reported. Then he calls on the Advance Pledge chairman for any new pledges, writing them on the board. Next he calls upon each captain (or each division leader if in a larger church) to make his report. Each captain states the number of pledges his visitors obtained, the number yet to be called upon, and the total amount received. Applause for each announced figure will add enthusiasm to the meeting. Allow twenty to thirty minutes for reports, announcements, and reassignments. Dismiss without delay so that visitors will have time to make one call before going home. These calls, made upon the enthusiasm of a good report meeting, are some of the most profitable ones made.

Without report meetings most campaigns will drag on for several weeks, ending with a number of homes never called upon. Report meetings will speed completion of any effort. This is particularly true where the fifth meeting (ten days after Dedication Day) is called Victory Report Meeting. Such a name gives a deadline to all workers and helps them to complete their calling before then. Many churches make this affair a gala occasion, having all workers in for a complimentary banquet and thanking all for the fine work they have done.

Use of report envelopes similar to the three pictured will be of value both in speeding up the reports and in keeping records straight. Note that the worker's report envelope (Fig. 8-6) fits inside the captain's report envelope (Fig. 8-5), which in turn fits inside the division leader's report envelope (Fig. 8-4).

DIVISION LEADER'S REPORT

NAME_____

DIVISION NUMBER_____ DATE_____

HOW TO REPORT

1. Collect each Captain's Report envelope for your Division.

2. Write the total results of your Division below.

The total number of cards completed
and reported by my Division .... _____

The total amount of the pledges
reported by my Division .... $_____

(*Courtesy of American Baptist Convention*)
FIG. 8-4

Larger churches will find it valuable to prepare bulletins of each report meeting. These are mimeographed the evening of the meeting and are immediately taken to the post office for delivery to all workers the next day. These bulletins give credit to whom credit is due, reveal areas of weakness, inform absentees of progress made, and renew interest. The

CAPTAIN'S REPORT

NAME_____

TEAM NUMBER_____ DATE_____

HOW TO REPORT

1. Collect each worker's report envelope for your team.
2. Write the total results of the workers on your team below and hand this envelope to your Division Leader if your church has over 500 members, if not, hand it to the General Chairman.

The total number of cards completed and
reported on by my team.................................. _____

The total amount of the pledges reported
by my team.. $_____

(Courtesy of American Baptist Convention)
Fig. 8-5

accompanying report was used by the First Baptist Church of Westfield, New Jersey, Pastor Elbert E. Gates, Jr., during their building-fund campaign. It was kindly supplied me by Harold Dudley, church campaign director for Marts and Lundy, Inc. (See Fig. 8-7.)

St. Mark's Episcopal Church of Leominster, Massachusetts, held at the end of their visitation an Appreciation and Evaluation Night, to which all workers and their families were invited. The rector, George St. John Rathbun, pleased with the increase of $3,600, wished to show appreciation to the workers by analyzing results and planning for next year. Three large charts were shown by George Winterer, the indefatigable General chairman. They read:

WORKER'S REPORT

NAME..

TEAM NUMBER............... DATE...................

1. Be sure you have a separate card filled out for each pledge you are reporting. The card must be signed by the donor personally.

2. List each card you are returning, entering the number of the card in the first column.

   — If it is a *PLEDGE* enter the total amount of the pledge for the year, including local expenses and benevolences, in the second column.

   — If it a *REFUSAL* write the letter *"R"* in the second column.

   — If the person has recently *MOVED* out of the city write the letter *"M"* in the second column.

NUMBER OF THE CARD	RESULTS
1	
2	
3	
4	
5	
6	
TOTALS	

(*Courtesy of American Baptist Convention*)
FIG. 8-6

1. Our goal for 1954 was $11,292
   This was our Proposal
2. Our results
   Total pledged—$12,459
   110.4 per cent of our goal
3. Comparison
   40.1 per cent over total pledged last year
   30 new pledges
   94.7 per cent of appraisal pledged
   185 calls completed

There are TEN steps to Victory. Step EIGHT is training your recruits.

"O God, the Maker and Giver of life, all that we have is Thine.
Help us to use it to Thy glory and for the good of all mankind;
through Jesus Christ our Lord. Amen."

Theodore P. Ferris
TRINITY CHURCH
BOSTON

BUILDING FUND PROGRAM
The First Baptist Church—Westfield, New Jersey

SECOND REPORT BULLETIN
"Keep right steadily on."   "We can if we will!"
Your goal is in sight—a few more days of work and your

VICTORY IS ASSURED
Grand total to date: $60,820.50

The Score by Teams

Division 1: Fred Banes	Today	Total		Division 2: Frank Horn	Today	Total
1. Mrs. Allen	$370	$1,390		5. T. Balling	$450	$1,875
2. R. S. Hill	0	100		6. W. G. Clark	915	2,715
3. H. S. Jessee	330	2,090		7. G. L. Rust	450	2,250
4. F. B. Cleaves	415	1,245½		8. D. Weisbecker	710	1,640
Total Div. 1	$1,115	$4,825½		Total Div. 2	$2,525	$8,480

Division 3: Henry Mereness

	Today	Total
9. Wm. Sortor	$ 120	$ 570
10. D. Oakley	1,000	1,640
11. J. D. Ward	1,125	1,325
12. D. E. Webber	210	1,410
	$2,455	$ 4,945
Special Gifts	$9,105	$42,570
Total all divisions	6,095	18,250½
Total for Dec. 10	$15,200	$60,820½

High division tonight: Division No. 2 $2,525
High team tonight: Capt. Ward No. 11 $1,125

Let us reach the $65,000 on Wednesday and strive for our
Challenge Goal $75,000 on Friday
Congratulations to you all,
William A. McBride, Chairman

Fig. 8-7

IMPORTANT DATES FOR ORGANIZATION CHAIRMAN

(For earlier dates, see end of preceding chapter.)

FRIDAY *Week 7* Chairman calls division leaders or captains to remind them of important first training session Sunday. Each captain calls his four visitors to remind them. All work for 100 per cent attendance. Captains should report results of their telephoning to division leaders who report to Organization chairman. He in turn reports to General chairman who notifies caterer of final count.

SUNDAY *Week 8* *First Workers' Training Conference.* This may be a dinner meeting served in the church. If three dinners cannot be served, the next two dinners are more important—on Friday and on next Sunday. See agenda, Form S, earlier in this chapter for this First Training Conference. Call roll by asking each division leader or captain to report on number of visitors present.

MONDAY *Week 8* Captains begin calling on their visitors for their pledges. They use a turnover chart in every home.

WEDNESDAY *Week 8* Check on progress of calling on visitors for their pledges, using your organization to do so.

THURSDAY *Week 8* Deadline for securing pledges from every visitor. Call division leaders; division leaders call captains; captains call each worker to remind of Second Training Conference tomorrow. Attendance at this session is considered even more important than at last Sunday's meeting. Notify General chairman how many will be present for dinner.

FRIDAY *Week 8* *Second Training Conference.* Assist General chairman in training of visitors. See agenda, Form T, earlier in this chapter. Assist General chairman in entering name of visitor opposite every prospect name on master list.

SUNDAY *Week 9* Morning—Dedication Day.

Noon—Workers' dinner and final instructions. Note which visitors are not present and whether reserve visitors are needed.

Afternoon—Visitation.

Evening—First Report Meeting. Assist General chairman in tabulating pledges.

WEDNESDAY *Week 9* Second Report Meeting. If visitors are failing to report, check with division leaders or captains. Decide whether reserve visitors are needed.

FRIDAY *Week 9* Third Report Meeting.

SUNDAY *Week 10* Evening—Fourth Report Meeting.

WEDNESDAY *Week 10* Victory Report Meeting.

Evaluation of canvass and plans for follow-up.

STEP 9: *Calling in Every Home*

"There was terrific enthusiasm in the church. We called
in every home. From 129 calls we received 125 pledges."
CENTRAL METHODIST CHURCH
LAWRENCE, MASSACHUSETTS

WEAKNESSES IN MAIL CAMPAIGNS AND GROUP PLEDGING

Pledging in church has a tendency to keep most people at last year's level of giving. It is a human trait to assume, no matter how effective the sermon, that the minister's words are directed at someone else. To be sure, church pledging cuts down on the work involved. It also cuts down the receipts.

Even as the receiving of pledges in a church service or any gathering should be avoided, so ought we to keep from accepting pledges from any organization. Many church societies have sizable bank accounts. Others are avid to raise funds for the church. These suggestions must be gently but firmly turned down. The danger is that each member of the organization will consider the group pledge to cover all his personal responsibility. I know of a building-renovation campaign that was almost thwarted by twelve women of the Ladies' Aid who had made a nominal group pledge. Each of the twelve then refused to sign an individual pledge. Not only was there a large loss in dollars, but the indignation aroused in the other church members almost caused the entire effort to collapse. If organizations do insist on pledging, it should be done only after each individual has made his personal pledge.

An all-mail campaign generally brings the poorest response. Reliance on this technique must be avoided in any progressive effort. The mails are exceedingly useful, however, if employed to lay the groundwork.

VALUES OF HOME CALLS

The heart of the Every Member Enlistment is the call in the home. It is here where the prospect talks most freely. As the visitor states his

156

case, talking man to man, the prospect cannot think that these words are intended for someone else. There is a directness that is impossible in church. A church member who had once gone through bankruptcy declared that he would never again make a pledge. His children attended Sunday School, and he himself would continue giving $100 every Easter. The visitor stated that the pastor was giving three times that amount. After some discussion, the caller asked: "Would you be willing to give a definite proportion of the money you make next year?" To this he agreed and after further thought stated he would give a tithe. By the end of the year he had contributed over $1,100 to the church. The entire family is now one of the most active in the church. It took an intelligent personal conversation to win the man.

Calling upon every home in the parish will increase good will. The indifferent and the careless will often be changed. Many persons whose interest has lagged are stirred to renewed effort. Virtually every church in an intensive Every Member Enlistment reports that attendance increases, beginning even before the call in the home. Charles R. Sims, pastor of the First Baptist Church in Bath, Maine, tells of a visitor calling upon a young family who had been lax in attendance for a year. The visitor said to the wife: "We know you are a member of the church." Later the husband said: "He didn't say anything about me. I made up my mind I had better get back to church. I was being forgotten."

"Our Committee at first shied away from calling on some people," related Albert Baller of the Robbins Memorial Congregational Church in Greenfield, Massachusetts. "They said it would be wrong or useless to see M. X and Mr. Y. But we decided to omit no one. Almost all these marginal names have pledged, and that accounts for no small part of our increase." In another church someone said not to waste time calling on the Z couple. But this couple pledged $1.50 and are now coming to church, singing in the choir.

Besides being the organizing dynamo of the enlistment within the First Congregational Church of Springfield, Ernest Cushing made thirty calls to see how people responded. From one nonmember he received a two-dollar-a-week pledge. "Now," said Cushing, "if you are going to pay dues, you ought to belong." The man is now a member. Many churches seize the evangelistic opportunities opened by visits in the homes.

A home visitation will uncover cases of need and special problems. The pastor in the average-to-large-size church cannot visit most homes more than once a year. Yet family problems do arise at other times, often the minister never learning of them. Visitors in the financial enlistment will in many cases discover these needs and report them to the minister. Thus the church is placed in a better position to serve those who are in need.

If your church is attempting a long step forward in this campaign, you will need to follow the appraisal procedure. But most of the work of the Resources Committee is in vain if the suggested figure is not made available to each member. Some churches have followed the method of mailing this suggestion to every prospect. Such a system is only second best. A well-trained visitor will handle the entire matter far better than the most carefully prepared letter. He will be ready to clear up any misunderstanding and to dwell on the glorious results if all should meet the appraisal. The method of pledging in church makes it virtually impossible to present the suggested figure to each worshipper. The only way to get the greatest good from the appraisal procedure is to have one person present it to another in private conversation.

The sending of a caller into every home is the simplest and most effective way to have everyone reconsider his present giving. As the visitor succeeds in stirring up questions, he finds out what the particular interests of the prospect are. He then dwells upon these interests. Mr. Fifty-Cents-a-Week needs to see that his contribution is niggardly—in terms of the world's need and his own ability. Widow Green needs to be assured that the church is well pleased with her sacrificial giving. Only a personal conversation will afford the greatest help to these two people—and to all in between them. In Winthrop, Massachusetts, two men over eighty years of age who had never before pledged each subscribed one dollar a week as a result of calls in the home. In the Braintree Baptist Church, a woman who had been inactive became a visitor. She made a call in a wrong home, visiting the son of the man she should have called on. The son gave her a pledge, then insisted that he would supply maintenance for the Sunday School bus for the whole year.

Tremont Temple in Boston, First Baptist in Springfield, and many other churches have been so pleased with the good will arising from their every-home financial visitation that they have used their workers' organization to continue friendly visitation the rest of the year. Wilbert Delano became so enthusiastic after serving as Publicity chairman for the canvass in the Springfield Church that the following spring he organized a group of visitors to call in each home, asking the members to attend church every Sunday in Lent. Delano worked out an attendance card and organized the young people to keep a record of attendance, listing every member's name on a chart in the foyer. This project increased church attendance by fifty persons a Sunday.

"No use to call on the X family," someone in the small Baptist church in Grafton, Massachusetts, declared. The father, mother, and four children—all nonmembers—attended services very sporadically. But someone did call, receiving a pledge of $1.50. Ten months later (when this story was being told) mother and father had been present at worship every single Sunday. The parents and one daughter had joined the church, as had two grandparents. The father, now an officer in the men's group, became concerned over his neighbors and had induced one family of six to attend church.

Call in every home. Omit no one, even the seemingly most unlikely prospect.

Every home.

E-V-E-R-Y.

There are TEN steps to Victory. Step NINE is calling in every home.

"O Lord of All—including ourselves—help us to understand what it is that we say when we acknowledge that we belong to Thee. May we know that all our concerns are in Thy mighty hand and in Thy loving heart. May we be very sure that all possessions are given us to bring us closer to Thee, and only as we share them in the spirit of sacrifice can we come to know Thy love and receive Thy life. Amen."

Margaret Henrichsen
PASTOR, SEVEN STEEPLES
NORTH SULLIVAN, MAINE

STEP 10: *Collecting the Pledges*

*"We shall follow up on the collection of our pledges.
It is the church's duty to help our members."*
                    REV. ERNEST M. JONES
                    FIRST BAPTIST CHURCH
                    MILFORD, NEW HAMPSHIRE

Being human, church members tend to forget. They forget names and telephone numbers, where they placed that important letter, when they were due next at the dentist's. Sometimes they forget about very sacred things such as their commitments to their church. A gentle reminder in time will help save embarrassment.

The purpose of a church collection program is to help your people do what they want to do. When members and friends sign pledges, they mean to pay them. But they sometimes need help. "Pastor," said the General chairman in one church, "I have doubled my pledge. It will be hard to pay. Not because I can't afford it. But because I'm not used to it." There is a way to help this man, and every other pledger, to do the thing he wants to do. It is an intelligent collection program.

There will of course be shrinkage in almost every campaign. Some persons die, or move away, or become unemployed. A rare few may oversubscribe. Others get so far behind before it comes to their attention that they find it almost impossible to catch up completely. It is felt that a loss of 5 to 10 per cent in the payment of pledges is normal. If the loss is less than 5 per cent, the canvass may not have been thorough enough, or the people may be loafing along in their pledging. If the loss exceeds 10 per cent, the church is not giving enough help to its pledgers in reminding them of their commitments.

An alert church can by the end of the year raise more money than was subscribed. Although some pledges will remain unpaid in full, extra money may come from several sources. Such additional sources of revenue, however, will amount to but little unless there is a system for encouraging these gifts. The responsibility for such new contributors should be delegated to some permanent committee—perhaps the Finance Committee or a newly created Prudential Committee.

There are several groups that this committee would work with:

1. New members received into the church. These should be approached prior to—or within two weeks after—being received into membership. Some ministers give a certificate of membership and a box of offering envelopes to each new member at the time of his joining the church. The Rev. Livingston Lomas, pastor of the Lakewood Baptist Church in Cleveland, makes a practice of calling on each new member himself and showing each the turnover chart in order to obtain the first pledge.

2. Young people graduating from school and stepping out into their first full-time jobs. Their giving habits should be established early. The General chairman in one church reviewed the appraisal of his son, unmarried and with a good income. The father raised his boy's appraisal from one dollar to five dollars a week. "I have seen that youth's soul grow," declared his pastor a little later.

3. Persons now employed who were unemployed at the time of the enlistment.

4. Members who did not pledge but said that they would give later.

5. Members who enjoy sudden large increases in income. These would include bequests, dividends and prizes, and salary increases.

The General Committee of the Baptist church in Holden, Massachusetts, does not disband when their enlistment ends in December. They continue as a committee, holding monthly meetings, to check on collections and uncover new sources of income. On September first, one of this group becomes General chairman for the next campaign and then names his new committee.

The church that encourages each member to share a proportionate part of his material goods for the Lord's work (both locally and for missions) is not begging or soliciting. It is helping that man become a better steward for Jesus Christ. The blessing is then a double one—a blessing to the Kingdom and a blessing to the giver.

SEVEN PHASES OF A COLLECTION PROGRAM

1. Acknowledge each pledge
2. Provide church envelopes
3. Send statements
4. Publish weekly reports in the calendar

5. Tell the story in all publications
6. Set up a revisitation program
7. Keep accurate records

1. *Acknowledge Each Pledge*

A personal letter of appreciation should be sent to each subscriber. It should be simple and sincere, signed preferably by the General chairman. In some instances the minister also signs. State the total results of the campaign and what new projects or services the additional money will provide. Include in the letter: "We appreciate your pledge of five dollars a week for local expenses and five dollars for missions." Such a statement will serve as a reminder (many folks forget what they pledged, particularly where they do not pay weekly). It will also check the accuracy of the church books. Send this letter within the week that the canvass ends. Delay will weaken the value of the thank-you note (see Letter M in the Canvass Kit).

It is suggested that each letter include the words: "You may wish to begin paying this new pledge next Sunday. This will help you to establish a habit for your new giving." Pastors in the thirty Boston sector project churches who urged their people to begin their new pledge payments immediately reported less yearly shrinkage in payment of the amount pledged than those churches which waited six weeks until the new fiscal year began.

2. *Provide Church Envelopes*

Weekly offering envelopes remind the subscriber of his pledge, making it convenient for him to put in coins, bills, or a check. They keep track of his payments, reminding him how many weeks he may be behind. They greatly simplify the bookkeeping of the financial secretary. Make sure that large-size envelopes are ordered. Small envelopes not only irritate the giver who has trouble inserting bills; they also encourage smaller contributions.

Give a pack of envelopes to each subscriber, to each member who does not pledge, and to friends who may desire them. They should be given out within a week after the new pledge is signed. The visitors for the White Street Baptist Church in East Boston carried the packets with them, leaving one in each home as they received a subscription. In any event envelopes must be in the homes of all the members before the first Sunday of the new fiscal year. Some churches place the packets on long tables in the foyer, requesting the worshippers to pick them up at the close of the service. After the second Sunday they organize the Boy Scouts or youth group to deliver the remaining packets to each door. If this is done, a careful check must be made to prevent any boxes of envelopes not being delivered. Of course the simplest method is to place all boxes in the mail.

3. Send Statements

People appreciate receiving a report of progress on the program which they are helping to make possible. Their pledge represents a dedication of time, talent, and treasure to something they love. Telling them about this program is not a "dunning" process.

Do not send a statement only to those in arrears, for this may cause resentment. Send it to everyone, whether their payments are on time, ahead of time, or in arrears. Then you can truthfully say to any who might object the first time a statement is received: "Mrs. B, we are not singling out you or anybody else. It is the policy of our church to send statements to everyone, even to the minister." If anyone, however, insists on not receiving a statement, you should honor his request and so mark the collector's book.

The statement which asks that errors be reported to the collector will help to keep the church books correct. Sometimes there is disagreement over receipt of some money. The wise financial secretary, even though he is sure the complainer is in error, will accept the word of the member and will not persist in trying to collect any disputed "past-due" amounts. Most subscribers will appreciate a record showing where they stand, especially when they make out their income-tax forms.

Many churches which send out statements prefer the quarterly mailing. Where this is done, they should not be sent out regularly every three months. Rather the following schedule is suggested:

First statement *thirty days* after beginning of fiscal year. This helps to establish a pattern. If a new pledge goes unpaid for three months, it is very difficult to collect it 100 per cent.

Second statement after three months.

Third statement after six months.

Fourth statement after nine months.

Fifth statement after *eleven* months. The purpose is to remind all subscribers to be paid up before the end of the fiscal year.

A final statement after the books close may be sent out if desired.

If your statement reads as follows:

Total pledge per week $_____
Amount due to date   _____
Paid to date   _____
Balance   _____

I believe it is psychologically sound not to fill in the bottom line. Everyone can subtract for himself. If the recipient should be a little sensitive, the fact that you are not literally telling him how much he is in arrears removes any sting.

Churches are increasingly favoring the monthly statement. People are used to receiving monthly reminders from department stores, electric and telephone companies. Are not the claims of the church equally important? "If my pledge," someone said to me, referring to monthly statements, "isn't worth as much attention as my grocery and gasoline accounts, I don't think the church needs it very badly." One church which sends out these monthly mailings has printed across the top of the statement: "To err is human. It is possible that we have made a mistake in your account. Would you kindly check our figures to see if we are correct?"

Although most churches print a regular form for their statements, or send out a carbon copy of the collector's records, it is better to make up a different letter each time. The letter should be newsy, telling of actual progress made during the past month and giving announcements of the future. Such a letter should especially note new services and projects that have been made possible because of increased giving. A postscript would state:

We thank you for your faithful giving. Kindly report any error in the following record:

	Local	Benevolence
Pledge per week	$____	$____
Amount due to date	____	____
Paid to date	____	____
Balance	____	____

See Letters N, O, P in the Canvass Kit.

St. Andrew's Episcopal Church in Longmeadow, Massachusetts (Rev. Charles Havens), prints their statement on an envelope. After allowing a place for the name and for the amounts paid and due, the following line is printed: "Please enclose check and place on the offering plate." This church also distributes each June an envelope for prevacation payment of pledges.

4. Publish Weekly Reports in the Calendar

Everyone is interested in how his church is prospering. One indication of progress is the state of the treasury. Each weekly calendar should carry a report of church collections.

Place this information in a box, using the same location every week under the heading: "The King's Business." The pastor may occasionally call attention to it from the pulpit, particularly at the beginning of the fiscal year, the beginning and end of summer, and the end of the fiscal year. Such use will avoid repeated requests to give.

Herschel Rogers, pastor of the First Baptist Church in Rockland, Massachusetts, prints a financial statement each Sunday. On May 20, 1954, it read:

Our budget requirement for the week	$372
Our budget receipts for last week	$384
Total requirements to last Sunday	$4,092
Total receipts through last Sunday	$4,141

The wording should be changed every few Sundays and occasionally a new thought presented such as:

Toward Baptist missions for 1946–1947 we gave	$1,015
In 1953–1954 we increased our giving to	$3,426

In the Massachusetts Baptist Convention we are listed as 102d in size and 38th in our missionary giving.

Each week that this church had taken in a total for the year to date that was less than the budget requirements, the entire calendar was mimeographed in red ink. This system was inaugurated early one September, and for three or four weeks the calendar appeared in red ink. After that the calendar "stayed in the black" for the remainder of the fiscal year. One of Rogers's ushers has reported that early worshippers always turn first to the financial box to see how the church is progressing. Ten months after "following the book" in an intensive Every Member Enlistment, this church reported an increase in attendance of 40 per cent and an increase in giving of 66 per cent.

5. Tell the Story in All Publications

Weekly or monthly newsletters, bulletins, magazines—all regular church publications—should be used to tell the church's financial condition. Emphasis should be placed upon progress made because of increased giving and future programs to be adopted as funds are available. Stress should be given to *program* rather than to finances.

The First Baptist Church of Pittsfield, Massachusetts, and the Temple Baptist Church of Baltimore have used the honor roll so successfully employed by many other churches. This is a listing of all members who are paid to date on their pledges. A deadline is determined (perhaps twice a year) and announced several weeks ahead. All pledgers up to date in their payments will be included in the honor roll to be printed on a particular Sunday or Sundays. Amounts are not published. Such a method, while valuable, should not become a substitute for the personal statement.

6. *Set Up a Revisitation Program*

Nothing in the field of human relations can equal the power of a personal conversation. When a study of the financial secretary's book reveals that a number of persons continue to fall behind in their pledge payments after receiving statements and bulletin reports, the church owes it to these members to give further help. A visitation program should be set up. The callers for this revisitation should be chosen with unusual care. They must be spiritually minded men, tactful and courteous. In some churches this responsibility is given to the board of deacons. In many cases all that will be needed from the visitor will be a tactful question: "We note that your pledge payments are behind. Is there anything we can do to help you catch up?" The member will appreciate the interest shown in him by his church.

Sometimes there is a valid reason why the member's record shows a lagging. Perhaps the bookkeeping is in error or the pledge card was misinterpreted. Perhaps there is distress in the home—unemployment, prolonged medical expenses, or temporary financial embarrassment. Without a visit, these errors or cases of need might never be uncovered.

A personal conversation will sometimes reveal a great deal. Dr. Charles Stanley Jones of the First Congregational Church, Burlington, Vermont, tells of his conversation with one of his parishioners who suddenly and drastically increased his church giving. "How," Dr. Jones asked, "can you possibly give eighteen to twenty dollars a week out of your salary of forty dollars?" "It is because of your emphasis on St. Paul's teachings on stewardship," the man replied. "I have no dependents, and I believe that if I shall ever come on hard times, the church will take care of me." Several years later he lost his job, and the church made him sexton. After a few years of this service, he became too old to carry on. The church budget now provides him an annuity.

7. *Keep Accurate Records*

Churches often are guilty of keeping poor records—or none at all. Accurate records expedite the work of the officers, reveal the financial health of the church, and make possible easy comparisons with former years and with other churches. Poor bookkeeping not only prevents a church from having accurate knowledge of itself, it also irritates the individual member, particularly when his name or address or financial standing is incorrect. Your denominational headquarters or bookstore will help you select a standard record book from the many samples available.

COLLECTION EXPERIENCES OF CHURCHES IN SECTOR PROJECTS

"What is the collection experience of churches which have put on this intensive Every Member Canvass?" is the question of many. "Is there not a lot of high pressure in getting your pledges up so high in one year? Does not a large shrinkage occur?"

High pressure has been defined as doing a good work in too short a time. If, therefore, sufficient time is allowed, the prospect is not placed under pressure. He is given ample opportunity to study the Proposal and to make up his own mind about his giving. A large increase in this case does not mean high pressure. A sound Every Member Canvass involves no duress.

In the Boston pilot project, before we had worked out a collection program, I found that collection experiences varied from church to church. Invariably, however, they fell into two categories. Whenever a pastor stated that he did not send out periodic statements, did not mention finances in letters or from the pulpit, never reminded the people of what had been accomplished, his collections were slow. Whenever a pastor reported his use of most of these reminders, his collections were excellent. In every case the percentage of pledges paid depended upon the efficiency of the collection program.

Despite wide variance in the collection helps used by these thirty Boston area churches, shrinkage at the end of twelve months averaged only 11 per cent, while seven of the churches reported collections exceeding 95 per cent. Other sector churches which have since been aided in collecting pledges are reporting even better results.

Typical are the following cases:

Collections for thirty-five weeks:
Amount needed $12,460
Amount collected   12,557

> Rev. Victor Scalise
> Calvary Baptist Church
> Lowell, Massachusetts

Pledging increased from $8,800 to $15,000
Collections for five months of preceding year 90%
Collections for five months of new year   94%

> Rev. Ralph Lightbody
> First Baptist Church
> Wakefield, Rhode Island

Pledged for 1953　　　$26,974
Collected in 1953　　　26,100

Rev. A. P. Colbourn
Pawtucket Congregational Church
Pawtucket, Rhode Island

"Collections from our first sector project were 92 per cent the first year. They may reach 95 per cent this second year."

Rev. William Herman
Pawtuxet Baptist Church
Providence, Rhode Island

There are TEN steps to Victory. Step TEN is collecting the pledges.

"Gracious Father, all that we are and all that we
have come from Thy heart of love. We dedicate to Thee that which
is Thine own. Use us, we pray, our abilities and our substance,
in ministering to the needs of Thy children. Through Christ, Amen."

M. Forest Ashbrook

THE MINISTERS AND MISSIONARIES BENEFIT BOARD
AMERICAN BAPTIST CONVENTION

CHAPTER 11: *Strengthening the Whole Church*

"*The total benefits of the program extend beyond the significant financial gains, assuring any participating church a revival of interest and unity of purpose regarding the primary task of the Christian Church.*"

REV. WARNER R. COLE
COVENANT BAPTIST CHURCH
DETROIT, MICHIGAN

SOME SPIRITUAL FRUITS

"Our Every Member Canvass was like a spiritual revival," declared one minister. When the ten steps of this plan are faithfully followed, the result is far more than increased income. The almost universal testimony of pastors in this program is that spiritual results have been at least as valuable as the monetary returns. When so many laymen are engaged in so energetic a program, when the new goals of the church are kept before the people so long, when the Kingdom of Jesus Christ is given such renewed emphasis, something vital happens to the spirit of the churches. The life of the whole church is strengthened. Some of these intangible benefits are the following:

Spiritual Life Strengthened

If this plan raises only dollars, it is but half successful. A new sense of loyalty to God and the church is the most evident outcome. "The greatest benefit of the canvass," wrote the First Baptist Church of Exeter, New Hampshire, "is not the amount of money raised but rather the intensity of the spirit that was generated. As a direct result of the calling, many new families have been attending church and offering their services to our program." Such experience is typical of scores. The increased spiritual awareness of the First Baptist Church of Bath, Maine, was so marked that Pastor Charles Sims wished his church had had the project ten years

169

earlier. The little Union Church in Mystic, Connecticut, stated that, coming at a time of discouragement, the enlistment had restored faith in themselves.

Attendance Increased

Attendance increases in most cases. This is a natural result of the greater interest being aroused by publicity and by many volunteers at work. Churches reported record attendances at Sunday School, communion, and worship services. The First United Presbyterian Church of Central Falls, Rhode Island, noted a marked increase in both attendance and giving even before the visitation week began. A few weeks later, fourteen new members were received.

New Members Won

"Anytime you make visits on all the people who are connected with a church," stated Joseph Burnett, "you will find new prospects. We have done so in the Second Baptist Church (Holyoke, Massachusetts)." The following are typical of the results coming out of the financial enlistment:

"Between ten and thirteen new members discovered."

> Embury Methodist, Central Falls, Rhode Island

"Twelve new members." (Membership—57 before canvass.)

> First Baptist, Grafton, Massachusetts

"Sixteen new members as result of canvass."

> Emory Methodist, Pawtucket, Rhode Island

"Baptized ten, with ten more waiting to come into membership."

> First Baptist, Pittsfield, Maine

"One of our visitors was a nonmember, his children coming to our Sunday School. I had called on his father several times in the hospital. The elder man pledged a dollar a week—as a token of appreciation, he said. After the visitation I received the younger man and wife into membership. He then called on the people on his street and won four new members in addition to his own family."

> Leon F. Kenney, People's Baptist
> Cranston, Rhode Island

New Leadership Discovered

Many churches report with joy that the project enabled them to discover new leadership. John Tilton, prominent member of the United Baptist Church in Concord, New Hampshire, stated that he had been concerned about the future of the church when the present older leadership would have passed away. The enlistment, however, brought forth strong new laymen, leaving no question about future leadership. Three out of four chairmen in one church were new workers, causing one old-timer to remark that, even if the church had not gained a cent, it was worth the effort to see new faces in positions of leadership.

Lay Interest Awakened

A number of churches report a desire of the visitors to continue making friendly calls upon the people. Such work has not only built up attendance, it has also strengthened the leadership talents of all who have so worked. John Koehler, pastor of Calvary Baptist in Providence, said that the enlistment drew him closer to his committee of five laymen than he had ever been to any previous group of laymen during twenty years in the pastorate. When appraisers in this church discovered that they knew only about one-fifth of the membership, they immediately acted on the minister's suggestion that they make a point of introducing themselves each Sunday to persons they did not previously know.

The Men's Club of the First Methodist Church in Pawtucket, Rhode Island, asked to sponsor the enlistment. In this way the church not only had more visitors than ever before, but men became active who would not otherwise have been asked to serve. An eighty-year-old woman in this congregation caught the spirit of cooperation and volunteered her services, writing letters to nonresidents, one of whom sent fifty dollars by return mail. In the Second Baptist Church of Palmer, Massachusetts, the visitors formed a Men's Club following the canvass. Volunteers painted the parsonage and agreed to paint the church later.

Churches Become Self-supporting

Many mission churches were enabled to become self-supporting parishes through their enlistments. Although this forward step was made possible by increased funds, it meant even more—a sense of independence and a spiritual strength unknown before. St. Stephen's Episcopal Church in Westboro, Massachusetts, with a pledged increase of 64 per cent, was thus able to become self-supporting. Albert Ormondroyd, Jr., the General chairman, declared that their Every Member Enlistment made the church more democratic, interesting more laymen in the work of the church. Such enthusiasm was aroused that out of 134 communicants 110 attended their parish loyalty dinner. The Rev. Harold B. Keir worked himself out of a job, he stated. The Wachogue Congregational Church of Springfield had such a successful canvass that the members were able to take on a full-time minister instead of the part-time service that Mr. Keir had been giving them. Other Massachusetts churches becoming financially independent, or hoping to do so within a year, were St. Andrew's Episcopal of North Grafton, All Saints Chapel of Whalom, First Methodist of West

Springfield, Chartley Methodist, First Baptist in Grafton, First Baptist of South Hanson, and the Federated Church in Becket.

Church Property Renovated

Many have been willing to engage in a major renovation or new building project after getting inspiration from the every member effort. As Old First Church, Springfield, entered upon its second year in the enlistment project, it reported to its people the following projects completed and bills paid as a result of the first year's financial campaign: New roof, tower and steeple rebuilt, kitchen remodeled, fellowship hall decorated, outside of building painted. St. Paul's Methodist Church of Lawrence, Chartley Methodist, Hanson Baptist, and the First Baptist Church of Milton, Massachusetts, are among the many churches in the country whose Every Member Enlistment propelled them into building projects either new or already begun.

CAMPAIGN TECHNIQUES USEFUL FOR OTHER PROGRAMS

The experiences of churches putting on the ten-step enlistment have emphasized certain truths concerning spiritual growth of a church. What was originally a plan to strengthen finances has developed into definite aids for the whole life of the church. Whatever the program your church wishes to develop—leadership training—friendly visitation—organized men's work—school of missions—increased attendance campaign—evangelistic effort for new converts—it may profit through use of the sound principles employed in the financial enlistment. A few of these salient features are the following:

Challenge

The facing of larger goals led the churches into new victories. Had contentment with last year prevailed, there would have been little advance. In strengthening the spiritual life, church leaders must also prepare a program that will challenge. Perhaps high goals will be set for attendance, for new members, for new group activities, or even more important, for renewed personal concentration. Easy goals lead to degeneration.

Organization

High goals without a workable plan may bring on frustration. Let the minister and his leaders search out plans that have worked elsewhere. It is essential that the leaders not listen to any talk of: "Our church is different." Of course each church is different. So are my five children, but they all get hungry, grow out of their shoes, and need to be loved.

So churches are more similar than different. Most successful plans will work in any size or type of church. There are plans for evangelism and for missionary education, for organizing youth work and for building up attendance. Search out these plans; then use them.

Lay Leadership

The wise minister in his position as leader will not do the work that he can get his laymen to do. Laymen will often do the work far better than the clergyman. But even if some tasks are performed more efficiently by the pastor, the doing of them by the laity strengthens the laymen and often arouses greater concern from the congregation. Use your lay leaders in spiritual activities. If you have no leaders at present, you will develop them as you train and use them. Bring your laity into consultation as you plan new programs. Listen to their ideas. Then use these men in putting their—and your—thoughts into action.

Many Working Together

The most successful financial enlistment is generally that which employs the most persons. The same principle applies to other church programs. If you desire to build up your prayer-meeting attendance, get many persons writing publicity, preparing outlines and maps, sending out mail and making telephone calls. The Rev. Gordon Torgersen, First Baptist Church of Worcester, Massachusetts, will be glad to share with you his plan for stimulating interest in the midweek meeting—a plan that involved putting scores of persons to work and resulted in over one hundred persons attending his midweek study sessions.

Calendar

A set of goals automatically calls for a timetable. Are you to have a five-year plan, a one-year program, or an intensive Lenten emphasis? The calendar will tell when to begin, what to do in the middle, and when to stop. The making of a schedule forces one to organize one's thinking and helps to point out conflicts. During the effort the calendar becomes one's taskmaster, reminding one that today's duties are not to be postponed. Even Jesus had something of a schedule. He went to the synagogue regularly, "as was His custom." He attended every Passover in Jerusalem during His public ministry. For greater spiritual results, make a calendar. Then work according to your schedule.

Publicity

One of the outstanding features of the intensive Every Member Enlistment has been the high quality of publicity, as well as the quantity and variety. Churches have spent more for printed matter in one campaign than they previously spent in five or ten years. It paid off. Members, taking new pride in their churches as they saw attractive folders and posters, were more willing to work for the goals. Let us get professional workmen to assist the church in presenting its claims in the most compelling fashion. Our spiritual objectives deserve the finest, most graphic presentation.

"Almighty and all merciful God, we thank Thee for the bounties of the good earth, for the freedoms of our land, for the fidelity of friends, for the safety and comfort of our homes. Grant us the grace to share our gratitude to Thy church which has kept the light of love and hope burning in our hearts. May the memory of Thy mercies fill us with compassion for those in need and may the gifts of our hands serve the causes of Thy Kingdom: we ask through Jesus Christ our Lord."

Ralph W. Sockman
CHRIST CHURCH, METHODIST
NEW YORK

CHAPTER 12: *What Happens the Second Year?*

*"This is our second campaign of the Every Member
Canvass, and since the beginning we have increased
our giving 185 per cent. We can truthfully say that the
E.M.C. is worth its weight in gold."*

                    EARL E. CAMPBELL
                    JUDSON BAPTIST CHURCH
                    BELLE, WEST VIRGINIA

What happens the second year? Do pledging and giving take a decided drop, or can another increase be expected? How much of the ten-step program should be repeated?

As evidence begins to mount, it is increasingly clear that churches can increase their giving the second year. This is being demonstrated both by churches in repeat sectors and by those working alone.

CHURCHES IN REPEAT SECTORS

In the spring of 1953, seven Baptist churches repeated the sector training program in Rhode Island. Two of the churches reported a slight drop in pledging, while five went ahead a second time. All seven churches declared their financial picture to be healthier the second year. The Central Baptist Church, after a previous increase of $8,600 gained another $3,200. People's Baptist Church of Cranston went ahead an additional $700 in pledges over the preceding year's pledged increase of almost $7,000.

A more complete second-year test was given in the autumn of 1953 when the Springfield (Massachusetts) Council of Churches combined a United Church Canvass with a sector project directed by the American Baptist Convention. Of the thirty-six churches enrolled, twelve had been through a sector experience one year earlier at Holyoke, where the average increase had been 49 per cent. At the end of the second effort, the twenty-four churches enrolled for the first time increased their pledging 56 per cent. The twelve repeat churches reported a 9 per cent increase.

"We were quite hesitant about entering the sector a second year," wrote Rev. Chester E. Miller of the First Christian Church. "It seemed to us that our small group was doing about as well as could be expected following the tremendous increase in 1953. Yet we asked for more, and the folks gave a further increase of 46 per cent. Ninety-two per cent of our people pledged, an average of $1.70 per week."

The First Baptists of Springfield "had the best financial year in history" in 1953. Their 1954 pledging, though less than 1953, was more realistic, thus allowing the same high budget to be maintained. Since this church during the year lost eight large givers by natural causes, Rev. Bryan Archibald concluded it was good that the church followed the intensive program the second year.

This loss of large gifts through death and removals was a common experience. Thus the Old First Congregational Church suffered the loss of one $3,000 gift and one $800 gift, with two retired persons reducing their pledging from $1,500 to $1,000 each. Yet so many persons increased their pledging that the church was able to maintain its enlarged program. Such was also the experience of the Church of the Unity which lost gifts of $1,000 and $500.

The Church of the Good Shepherd, after increasing 44 per cent the first year, advanced an additional 13 per cent the second year. Father George Smith of St. Peter's Episcopal Church (whose church rose from $8,700 to $17,100 in two years) stated that the great advantage the second year was that the church leaders were already convinced of the value of the intensive plan. Their first-year experience further pointed out the need for a closer following of step ten—the collection program.

THE RHODE ISLAND UNITED CHURCH CANVASS, 1953

In 1953 the Rhode Island United Church Canvass offered second-year training to its churches in the ten-step program. All the repeating churches held their advances of the preceding year, while some took another forward step. Calvary Baptist Church, with twenty-eight fewer workers, pledged $2,000 more than the year before. This church reported the amazing figure of 98 per cent collection of pledges. Darlington Congregational Church increased another $2,000, and Pawtucket Congregational went up another $3,000. All three of these churches took significant advances the preceding year.

One of the outstanding results was that of the Mathewson Street Methodist Church in Providence. Increasing $8,000 the first year, this church advanced another $4,600 in its second intensive effort, or an increase of 43 per cent in two years. Dr. Donald G. Wright, the pastor, felt that two factors were of importance the second year: the accumulative effect of the first year's experience and the greater emphasis placed upon advance pledges.

The Phillips Memorial Baptist Church of Cranston, Rhode Island, was one of the three or four churches in the nation which up to the time of writing had followed the ten-step program for three successive years. The minister, Frank Snell, summarized his observations as follows:

1. The first year the church took a magnificent increase of 58 per cent.

2. The second year he found it exceedingly difficult to persuade his leaders to follow the complete program. After doing so, they reported sufficient increase to offset an unusually heavy loss of large gifts through natural causes.

3. The third year the leaders adopted the program without question. Since the church was preparing for a large building campaign within a few months, it aimed only at—and succeeded in—holding its previous operating budget. The church now, declared the pastor, was where he desired it to be—they had found a good system, it worked for three successive years, and they expected to continue that system for the years to come. (Six months later this church pledged $111,000 toward a building goal of $100,000.)

EXPERIENCES OF CHURCHES WORKING ALONE

Churches working alone the second and third years have reported similar results. The Wollaston Baptist Church was one of those in the original Boston sector project. Their record of pledging is as follows:

1951	(before sector)	$15,770
1952		21,220
1953		22,805
1954		24,868

This is one of many churches which has forged ahead despite the payments it is making on a new building.

Roger Williams Baptist Church of Providence, facing the closing of one mill in town and two mills nearby, which would result in much unemployment, collected 92 per cent of their previous high pledging. In their second-year effort, with fewer pledges received, they felt they were in even better position because of the prospect of less shrinkage. "I'm convinced," stated the minister, Frederick Gardner, "that the ten-step plan is *the* way to raise the budget. I'll push for it every year."

In 1951 the Federated Church in Norfolk, Massachusetts, paid its minister $1,400 a year, while he earned another $1,400 as part-time chaplain at the nearby prison colony. Through the Boston pilot project this church was enabled to take on full support of their minister. Two years later the church had so continued to increase their giving that they were paying their pastor $4,500 plus extras.

Another church to follow the ten-step program for three successive years is the First Baptist of Wakefield, Massachusetts. Every year results have been better—both in pledges and in collections. Although this congregation is paying for a new $125,000 building, the church finances are in the healthiest condition in twenty-five years. Their record for local expenses follows:

1951 (prior to sector project)—$12,000, with a growing deficit now totaling
$1,500
1952—$20,000. Books balanced first time in ten years
$3,650 given to missions
1953—$22,350 plus $4,805 for missions. All deficits paid off. Also raised
$16,000 toward new building mortgage
1954—$25,025 plus $4,700 for missions

"The new emphasis on a sound financial program," wrote the Rev. H. Glenn Payne, "has not hampered our important program of evangelism. During my first two years here in Wakefield we took in 250 new members. By the time our fourth year is complete this number will be over 400."

Four years of using most of the ten-step program has been the experience of the First Baptist Church of Monrovia, California. Their record of pledges and collections is as follows:

	Pledged	Envelope collections
1950–1951	$ 8,990	$17,876 (*prior to ten-step program*)
1951–1952	24,500	23,488
1952–1953	27,150	26,111
1953–1954	29,300	28,242
1954–1955	36,100	(46,679 *total budget*)

"I have discovered," wrote Pastor Melvin Pekrul, "the program works with miraculous results as one follows the plan in detail. The fourth effort witnessed 24 per cent increase because we gave greater attention to the many details stressed in the manual. It works in proportion to the amount that you work it."

What happens the second—and the third—year? Churches can—and are—maintaining the forward step taken the first year. They are solidifying their gains through discounting the few irresponsible pledges, making up for losses through death and removals, and improving their collection techniques.

The general feeling of ministers who did not closely follow the program a second year was regret that they had not taken more of the ten steps. Many of these leaders declared that they intended returning to the complete system the third year.

"Last year our thorough Canvass of Every Member netted us the biggest year for Current, Missions, and Building in our history. This year we did not have an Every Member Canvass and the first five weeks of the new year 223 people, who paid for their ride last year, decided to go free this year.

"One thing I have gained out of this experience. Each year henceforth I shall insist that we have *An Every Member Canvass* in which every member will be asked to pay his fare."

Rev. Lee Shane
Calvary Baptist Church
Charleston, West Virginia

Churches can—and are—advancing the second year. Particularly is this the case where churches the first time did not closely follow all the ten steps, or where leadership on the General Committee is strengthened, or where new dramatic challenges are presented to the people. Churches have not yet reached their saturation point in giving.

"O Father-God, of Thy dear Son our Saviour it is written
that though He was rich yet for our sakes became He poor that
we through His poverty might be made rich. Teach us anew the
ancient lesson that it is in giving we ourselves receive, that
he who would save his life shall lose it, and that Thou hast
so established the nature of things that the more we put into
life the more we get out of it. Amen."

James E. Wagner
PRESIDENT
EVANGELICAL AND REFORMED CHURCH

CHAPTER 13: *The Sector Plan and Its Future Possibilities*

"The sector project has deepened the lives of our people spiritually. They have found a new meaning to giving— giving according to their interest in the cause of Christ. They have found that where your treasure is your heart is also."

REV. L. STANLEY MANIERRE
FIRST BAPTIST CHURCH
HANSON, MASSACHUSETTS
NOW OF AMERICAN BAPTIST MISSION
JAPAN

By the winter of 1954–1955 the American Baptist Convention had aided 850 churches through area Every Member Canvass training sessions (known as sector projects) in adding over $4.3 million to their budgets. Fifty-one sectors in less than three years had enabled churches of all sizes and types to increase their programs an average of better than $5,000 apiece. In addition to this impressive total, many more churches had been aided in one-day stands which set forth the essential steps of the plan and presented the helps that were available. Ministers everywhere declared that the spiritual benefits outdistanced the financial gains.

These sectors have been held from Maine to Washington, from California to West Virginia. Large metropolitan churches have been helped. So have small rural churches, congregations in deteriorating neighborhoods, and those in prosperous suburbs. Churches of all sizes and types have taken part. All have been aided—some to a fantastic degree. The plan works everywhere because the laymen in each church make it work. The project is flexible enough to adapt to any local situation.

The sector idea of church financing grew out of the thinking of two men—Dr. Luther Wesley Smith, executive secretary of the American Baptist Board of Education and Publication, and Louis W. Robey, vice-president of Marts and Lundy, Inc., and financial adviser for the promotional department of the American Baptist Convention. It was their belief that the professional techniques used so successfully in our nation's annual philanthropic drives and in college capital-funds campaigns might be adapted to church annual canvasses.

In the autumn of 1951, these two men accepted the invitation of the Massachusetts Baptist Department of Missionary Cooperation to conduct a pilot project in Boston. The director of the department, Othniel A. Pendleton, was aided in supervising this project by Jack Krause of the Northern California Baptist Convention. The preceding spring a group of churches in northern California had sent a team of leaders to spend a week end studying under Krause some of the latest methods in church financing. Krause and Pendleton, working together in the Boston area, enlisted the churches, compiled a manual, devised a calendar, and made up the training agendas. These men, with the cooperation of Isaac Higginbotham and Newton E. Woodbury of the Massachusetts Baptist Convention, conducted the training sessions. Thirty churches, ranging in size from forty members to over one thousand, and embracing all types of congregations, followed this plan. Over a period of eight weeks these churches prepared for the most intensive Every Member Canvass in their history. The minister and a committee of laymen from each church gathered for a series of five training sessions. The result, financially, was an average increase of 56 per cent in pledging (see page 208).

The know-how used in this Boston pilot project has since become, under the leadership of Dr. Ralph M. Johnson, the heart of the American Baptist Convention's Sector Project. Numerous adaptations and improvements have been made, growing out of the experience of conducting three years of these programs. Eleven Baptist field counselors are now giving full time to missionary promotion and to conducting sector projects.

Basic to the sector idea is the desire of the local church to build a greater program for Jesus Christ. The plan is geared not to raise funds so much as to strengthen church programs. Whenever there is divine discontent with past performance (not all churches or ministers have it), the sector moves upon two feet.

The first foot is the use of latest financial and selling techniques. The art of raising money for humanitarian and educational institutions has been so developed that it has become almost a profession. It might even be called a semiscience. Sometimes it seems, as one surveys the annual eleemosynary drives and the occasional capital-funds campaigns, as though every institution knows how to raise funds except the church. The sector project has adapted these professional techniques to fit the annual enlistment of the local church.

The second foot is the training of local leadership to carry the program through to completion. At the heart of the plan is a trained leader whose task it is to train lay leaders to carry on in their own local churches. It is impossible for any denomination to place trained leaders in each church for the period required to carry through an intensive Every Member Enlistment. Thus the sector idea was born—all the churches of a geographical area would be invited to send their lay leaders and ministers into one central location for the training. The training would be given in four sessions, meeting every two weeks. In this way the trained leader could supervise ten to fifty churches at one time. If the local area could in addition provide a trained coordinator with a local office, the field supervisor could the next day travel on to another sector, repeating his training program of the night before. Thus the supervisor could, after some experience, conduct three or four sectors at one time.

There is need that as much uniformity as possible be developed in each sector—and in all sectors. The churches in a sector use the same extensive manual. They follow identical calendars. The printing for each church is done at one time by one printer. All the printed Proposals and pledge cards, though individualized, follow the same pattern. Standardized aids such as training films and turnover charts, are available to every church. All this means that cost is greatly reduced and that all the items on the training session agendas are applicable to all.

Each church sets up its own General Committee, generally five men. These men, together with the minister, attend four training sessions, meeting every other week. At each session reports of progress are filled out by each church, and multiple blank forms are distributed to facilitate the canvass in the local church. At the end of the canvass, the chairman and minister come to a fifth meeting to bring in final reports and to evaluate the sector program.

The Council on Missionary Cooperation of the American Baptist Convention, sponsor of the sector idea, has been developing the concept that its duty is to be a service agency to the local church as well as a promoting agency for the denominational missionary program. So arose this plan to strengthen the finances of every church, both for its local program and its world outreach. In the training sessions, emphasis is placed upon the *total* greater program that the church may draw up. Each church determines its own program and its own desired increase in funds. Once this goal has been arrived at, churches are urged to ask for the same percentage of increase for benevolences as they ask for total expenses. Thus missionary giving tends to increase along with local giving.

The Joint Department of Stewardship and Benevolences of the National Council of the Churches of Christ has followed the sector project with intense interest. The Executive Secretary, Dr. T. K. Thompson, has attended several training sessions and encouraged the formation of the 1953 Springfield Interdenominational Sector which was jointly sponsored by the Springfield Council of Churches and the American Baptist Convention. "This is," he wrote, "the most creative experimentation being done in the field of church finance and stewardship in the United States today. . . . I believe that all the denominations in this country might study the sector-project plan with very great reward. I am hoping that the United Church Canvass can effectively be worked into interdenominational sector projects. . . .

Dr. Ralph M. Johnson, general director of the American Baptist Council on Missionary Cooperation, has been generous in sharing sector experience with other denominations. In 1952, observers from several denominations attended a training session for field supervisors at Green Lake, Wisconsin. In 1953 and 1954, various denominations sent stewardship and promotional leaders to be trained in the Green Lake sessions. The seven interdenominational sectors held under Baptist auspices in New England and New York have demonstrated that any denomination may profit from these techniques, and profit as much as any Baptist church.

The Rt. Rev. W. Appleton Lawrence, Bishop of the Episcopal Diocese of Western Massachusetts, is adapting the sector project for his churches. Thirty-one of these churches have increased pledging by $157,000. Because of this work it is expected that four or five churches, having been struggling missions for thirty or forty years, will become self-supporting parishes within a couple of years.

It is the opinion of many that the sector technique is the next great forward step in the field of church financing. First came the Every Member Canvass. The second advance was the United Church Canvass. Now comes the sector technique which can be, if desired, correlated with the United Church Canvass.

Two interesting developments have been going on in interdenominational circles. In the autumn of 1952, the Baptists of the Holyoke, Massachusetts, area, led by the Rev. Joseph D. Burnett, Newton E. Woodbury, and O. A. Pendleton, invited all neighboring churches to participate in a sector project. Twenty-two churches of eight denominations took part, reporting a total increase of $125,000, or an average of 49 per cent in pledged money (see page 216). So great was the interest aroused by this sector—both among participating and nonparticipating churches—that the Springfield Council of Churches arranged with Dr. Johnson to cosponsor a sector in 1953.

Under the energetic leadership of Harold B. Keir, executive secretary of the Council, and the invaluable assistance of laymen who had been in the previous effort, Springfield enrolled thirty-six churches, twelve of which were in the program for a second year. The training sessions were conducted by Keir, Woodbury, and Pendleton, plus many ministers and laymen. The concern of the Council was to combine the sector project with the United Church Canvass. It was agreed that all newspaper, radio, and television publicity was to be in the form of news stories rather than advertisements. The nearby papers gave splendid cooperation, with the result that a sector story was on the front page each morning after a training session and many times in between. Harold Keir believes that this news was more valuable than paid advertisements. The sector not only brought significant increases to the enrolled churches, it greatly aided the public-relations program of the Springfield Council, and it welded more closely together the various churches of the city. "The project," testified Bryan Archibald, "did more for united Protestantism in Springfield than anything that has happened in the eight years I have been here." (See pages 231, 232 for results.)

At the same time as the Springfield effort, another interdenominational sector project was conducted at Burlington, Vermont, led by Homer C. Bryant and O. A. Pendleton. Fifteen churches of four denominations increased their pledging 50 per cent (see page 232 for results).

The second development of note has been the adoption of some of the sector techniques by United Church Canvasses in various cities. The Rhode Island United Church Canvass, under the leadership of Rev. Earl H. Tomlin, for two years offered their churches four training sessions in the steps used in sector projects. This united canvass combined training with a series of paid advertisements in newspapers and radio. Adaptations of the sector project have been made by the Massachusetts Church Councils in Attleboro, Lawrence, Newton, and New Bedford, and by the Councils in Waterbury, Connecticut, and in Syracuse, New York (see pages 240–248).

What has happened in interdenominational circles in New England can happen anywhere.

"Our heavenly Father, we pray that we may be faithful
in the surrender of ourselves to Thy purposes in the world.
Help us to unselfishly give our time, talent, and treasure
to further the proclamation of the Gospel."

> *Ralph M. Johnson*
> GENERAL DIRECTOR
> COUNCIL ON MISSIONARY COOPERATION
> AMERICAN BAPTIST CONVENTION

How Well Off Are Our People?

Because the cost of living is high and taxes are so heavy, churchmen are inclined to believe that gifts cannot be greatly increased. They fail, however, to consider two factors:

1. The tremendous increase in personal income resulting in greatest liquid assets in United States history
2. The appeal of a vigorous forward-looking Christian program

The first part of this section will deal with official statistics of income and giving. It is designed to help you estimate the potential of your members. The second part will provide forms that have been used successfully in hundreds of churches to stimulate their desire to do better. We believe, rightly used, they will aid your church.

PART 1

Official Statistics: Income and Giving

The United States Federal government, until 1953, used as a norm in its computation of the cost of living the period 1935–1939. Using 1939 as a base year, we may make several interesting comparisons.

1. *Cost of Living*[1]

1939	1954	19 __ (fill in this column, using
100	192	____ latest available figure)

2. *Per Capita Personal Income*[2]

The following table shows the total income divided by the total population:

[1] *Survey of Current Business,* U.S. Department of Commerce, August, 1954, p. S-5.
[2] Each August issue of *Survey of Current Business* contains the per capita income figures for the preceding year. See August issue, 1954, p. 15.

Area	1939	1953	Increase	19 __ (fill in this
United States	$539	$1,709	217%	$ column)
New England	680	1,824		
Middle East	709	1,984		
Southeast	303	1,159		
Southwest	386	1,443		
Central	565	1,884		
Northwest	418	1,535		
Far West	692	1,986		

The per capita personal income figures are also available for each state. Two states are given here as samples:

	1939	1953	Increase	19 __
Massachusetts	$719	$1,812	152%	$
California	741	2,039	175	

In the following blanks place the figures for your state:

	1939	1953	19 __
State of _____	$____	$____	$____

By 1953, United States personal income was up 217 per cent.
By 19__ State of _____ personal income was up ____ %.
                    (your state)

Employment in mid-1954 stood at 62.1 million persons, down only slightly from the record high of 1953.[3]

In 1946 only 10 per cent of all spending units in America had incomes of $5,000 or more. In 1953 almost one-third had such incomes, while an additional third had incomes of $3,000 to $4,999.[4]

Nearly two-thirds of all spending units in the United States in early 1954 owned one or more automobiles, and about one-half owned television sets.[5]

United States average factory weekly earnings in March, 1955, rose to $75.30, a record high.[6]

The American people in 1953, declared *Life* magazine, enjoyed "the best economic year of their lives."[7] The year 1954 was not far behind this record, with indications that 1955 would surpass 1953.

3. *Taxes.* Taxes have, of course, gone up. But still the United States

[3] *Federal Reserve Bulletin,* August, 1954, p. 807.
[4] *Ibid.,* June, 1953, and July, 1954, p. 689.
[5] *Ibid.,* June, 1954, p. 570.
[6] *Ibid.,* April, 1955, p. 370.
[7] January 4, 1954.

personal saving (after taxes and living costs) is the highest since the war years.[8]

	(Billions of dollars)		
	1939	1955	19 __
		(first quarter; seasonally adjusted to annual rates)	
Personal income, total	$72.6	$292.7	$____
Less: Personal tax and related payments	2.4	32.1	
Equals: Disposable personal income	$70.2	$260.6	$
Less: Personal consumption	67.5	242.0	
Equals: personal saving	$ 2.7	$ 18.6	$____

4. *Personal Saving.* Despite the high cost of living, and even higher taxes, the American people continue to build up their liquid assets. From 1939 to December, 1953, the holdings of liquid assets by individuals rose from $49.4 billion to $201.5 billion, a new record.[9] Deposits in mutual savings banks in February, 1955, exceeded $26.6 billion, the highest mark in history.[10] This increase in liquid assets was widely distributed among all income and occupational groups. Home ownership showed a similar upward trend. In 1940, a total of 40 per cent of all homes were owner occupied. In 1953 ownership increased to 57 per cent, approximately half of which were free of mortgages.[11]

The conclusion is obvious. Our people have money. Far more than ever before. It will be tapped by the best salesmen. Should the cause of Jesus Christ "be content with last year"? Or can we keep pace with salesmen of automobiles and television sets, houses and food, in claiming a larger share of America's income? Who will be the better salesmen? Who offers the greater value?

5. *Church Giving.*[12] How does your denomination compare with 1939 and with fifteen other denominations? See the following table.

[8] *Survey of Current Business,* May, 1955, p. 4; "National Income," U.S. Department of Commerce, 1951, p. 151.

[9] *Federal Reserve Bulletin,* July, 1954, p. 710.

[10] *Ibid.,* April, 1955, p. 383.

[11] *Survey of Current Business,* December, 1953, and *Federal Reserve Bulletin,* June, 1954, p. 570.

[12] "United Stewardship Council Statistics," 1939; *Yearbook of American Churches,* 1953, p. 281; and *Statistics of Giving,* November, 1954, National Council of the Churches of Christ.

	1939	1954
1. American Baptist	$13.93	$45.04
2. Southern Baptist	7.39	39.84
3. Church of the Brethren	11.91	43.78
4. Congregational-Christian	18.26	49.91
5. Disciples of Christ	7.93	29.52
6. Evangelical and Reformed	14.82	41.24
7. Evangelical United Brethren:		50.21
United Brethren in Christ	11.93	
Evangelical Church	24.28	
8. United Lutheran	14.62	45.68
9. Methodist:		34.37
Methodist Episcopal	16.70	
Methodist Episcopal, South	10.04	
10. Moravian, Northern Province	11.96	53.26
11. Presbyterian, U.S.	20.85	73.99
12. Presbyterian, U.S.A.	20.64	56.49
13. United Presbyterian	22.09	57.73
14. Protestant Episcopal	22.88	49.02
15. Reformed in America	21.78	68.57
Average of 15 denominations	$13.78	$41.98

(your church)

Lest there be any pride in the above record, let us compare our giving with three small groups:

	1939	1954
Church of the Nazarene	$31.02	$118.33
Free Methodist		194.79
Seventh Day Adventist		173.35

1939 to 1953 church giving to fifteen representative denominations was up 184%

1939 to 19— _____ giving was up _____%
       (your denomination)

1939 to 19— _____ giving was up _____%
       (your local church)

In the above church figures, 1939 included very little for capital expenditure, whereas 1953 included a great deal. Thus if one subtracts the capital expenditures from each year, increased giving to current expenses and benevolences would not amount to 184 per cent. It is possible that giving to current expenses and benevolences will drop as soon as the present heavy wave of building construction and remodeling is finished and paid for.

Two church bodies in Massachusetts (the Baptists and the Episcopalians of the Diocese of Western Massachusetts) reveal that when capital gifts are deleted their current giving has doubled since 1939. In the absence of exact figures, let us assume that these two groups are typical for the nation.

Our picture now reveals (1939–1953):

> Cost of living up 92%
> Personal income up 217%
> Church giving up 100% (exclusive of capital funds)

The giving of our church members has not kept pace with the tremendous upsurge of our personal income. Yet, even if it had, we could and should be giving to the Kingdom of God a greater proportion now than in 1939 when so many Americans were living close to the subsistence level. More money, much more money, is available for Christ's work if we challenge our members.

How does your church rate?

You may wish to fill in the following:

Summary

Since 1939:	1953	19 __
Cost of living is up	92%	____ %
United States per capita personal income is up	217%	____ %
_____ income is up	____ %	____ %
(your state)		
Church giving (exclusive of capital gifts) is up	100%	____ %
_____ giving (exclusive of capital gifts) is up	____ %	____ %
(your denomination)		
_____ giving (exclusive of capital gifts) is up	____ %	____ %
(your local church)		

If our ministers can develop a divine discontent, if our finance committees, vestries, and official boards can develop divine discontents, then the church of Jesus Christ will be on the verge of a magnificent awakening.

PART 2

Can You Use 50 Per Cent Increase?

Claud H. Foster, inventor of the musical automobile horn, invited 110 friends and guests to a dinner party in Cleveland in July, 1952. The seventy-nine-year-old businessman promised them "the surprise of their life." After dining on filet mignon, Mr. Foster arose and handed checks to fifteen charitable institutions and one university. Gifts ranged from $34,486 for the Jones Home to $775,935 for Cleveland's University hospitals—a staggering total of $3,879,680. "Too many institutions," asserted the benefactor, "get their money from dead men. I wanted to see them get it."

Suppose Claud Foster—or anyone—handed you a check amounting to 50 per cent above present income, *could your church use it wisely next year?*

Can you *prove* you could prudently use it?

Hundreds of churches across the country have had their sights lifted by using a check list of present and future possible activities. Such a list, outlining a hundred or more activities or services, gives the church leaders an opportunity to check their present program and to consider which of

THINKING ABOUT OUR CHURCH

This we are doing				1. Worship and Service	This we should be doing		
Good	Fair	Poor	None		Optional	Preferred	Must
				Do you have worshipful music?			
				☐ A competent organist			
				☐ Adequate choir training			
				☐ New music			
				☐ Attractive or new hymnals			
				☐ Attractive choir robes			
				Are your Sunday bulletins properly prepared?			
				☐ Are they mailed to shut-ins, young people in college or in service?			
				Attractive pulpit furniture and communion service			
				A nursery room and helpers			
				Special lighting effects for services			
				Publicity Committee caring for advertising and printing			
				Evangelism Committee, seeking new members			
				A functioning flower committee			
(Larger churches may consider these additional items)							
				A competent Choir Director			
				Able soloists or quartet			
				Hearing aids provided in pews			
				Radio broadcasts of services			
				Regular periodic contacts with non-resident members			
				Public address system— new or in good repair			

FIG. A-1

the other suggestions they may wish to undertake next year. It provides an excellent springboard for building your program.

"Thinking About Our Church," a check list similar to the above, has been developed and successfully used by the American Baptist Convention. With the kind permission of Dr. Ralph M. Johnson I am able to reproduce it. (See Figs. A-1 to A-5.)

Suggestion: Purchase or mimeograph several of these copies of "Thinking About Our Church." Invite your trustees or finance committee to a special meeting at your home. Tell them how you filled out one of these forms and would like them to do likewise. Speak for five minutes on,

THINKING ABOUT OUR CHURCH

This we are doing				2. Pastoral Ministry	This we should be doing		
Good	Fair	Poor	None		Optional	Preferred	Must
				Pastor's salary to match living costs			
				Necessary expenses: allowance for automobile			
				☐ Travel allowance for pastor and wife to state convention			
				☐ Travel allowance for national convention			
				Pension dues provided			
				Parsonage provided and properly maintained			
				Garage for pastor's car			
				Proper equipment for church office, including mimeograph			
				Training books for church officers			
				Missionary magazine for church officers			
				Literature to aid in home visitation			
				Do you provide "new members kits" for new members?			
				Plans for visitation evangelism and or an evangelist			
			(Larger churches may consider these additional items)				
				Pastor's assistant			
				☐ Auto allowance for assistant			
				☐ Housing for assistant			
				Telephone for church office			
				Church visitor			
				Secretarial assistant for pastor			

Fig. A-2

THINKING ABOUT OUR CHURCH

This we are doing				3. Our Church Home	This we should be doing		
Good	Fair	Poor	None		Optional	Preferred	Must
				What are you doing to improve the appearance of your church?			
				Do you have a functioning house committee to watch the needs of your property?			
				Does your building need repairing or painting?			
				☐ Repointing of brick or stone			
				☐ New roof or repairs to the old one			
				☐ New windows or repairs			
				How are the walks?			
				Does your church need landscaping or attention to present shrubbery?			
				Do you have an outdoor picnic area?			
				☐ Outdoor bulletin board			
				☐ Identification signs at nearby intersections			
				☐ Off-the-road parking			
				☐ Flood-lighting			
				Do you need additional Sunday School rooms?			
				A NEW sanctuary or more room in present sanctuary			
				Does the interior of your church need redecorating?			
				☐ Tower chimes			
				☐ New or more adequate lighting fixtures			
				☐ New floors			
				☐ Repairs to pews or new pews			
				☐ New organ or pianos			
				☐ Repairs to present organ or pianos			
				☐ New carpeting			
				☐ Pew racks for hymnals and communion glasses			

FIG. A-3

THINKING ABOUT OUR CHURCH

This we are doing				Our Church Home	This we should be doing		
Good	Fair	Poor	None		Optional	Preferred	Must
				Do you have adequate kitchen and dining-room facilities?			
				☐ Do you need additional chairs or tables?			
				Are there up-to-date rest rooms in the church?			
				Do you need indoor bulletin boards?			
				Does your janitor keep the building neat and clean?			
				Is your janitor properly supervised?			
				Janitor supplies, equipment and tools			
				Do you have adequate cloak-room facilities?			
				Do you need a hallway or foyer at main church entrance?			
				Is there an adequate furnace in good repair?			
				Do you have adequate insurance on all property?			
				How about summer screens for church and parsonage?			

(Larger churches may consider these additional items)

				A new educational unit			
				A parking lot nearby			
				Air conditioning for the sanctuary			

4. Christian Education

				Do you have a functioning Board of Christian Education?			
				Do you provide camp scholarships for deserving young people?			
				Do you need additional Sunday School supplies?			
				☐ Slide projector			
				☐ Motion-picture projector			
				☐ Film-strips or motion pictures for visual education			
				☐ Flannel boards			
				Do you have an up-to-date library of Sunday School literature and teachers' aids?			

Fig. A-4

"Could we wisely use a 50 per cent increase if we had it?" Then allow one hour for the group to discuss and fill in these forms, making sure they talk among themselves. By the time the evening ends, you had better be ready with a plan! It is this idea of a "dream budget" that has been so successfully used in beginning each American Baptist sector project. It does something to church leaders!

When you have finished with these four divisions, you will want to increase your mission giving. The American Baptists have worked out this formula: "After you have determined the percentage of increase you wish for local expense, use at least that same percentage to determine the increase in your benevolence budget." Thus if you wish to increase local expenses 47 per cent, you would also ask for a minimum of 47 per cent increase for missions and benevolences. Each church should strive for a minimum of 20 per cent of the total budget for benevolences. Blessed are those churches which divide their receipts 50 per cent for themselves and 50 per cent for others.

THINKING ABOUT OUR CHURCH

This we are doing				Christian Education	This we should be doing		
Good	Fair	Poor	None		Optional	Preferred	Must
				Do you make available devotional literature?			
				Do you have proper training facilities for teachers?			
				Have you made a survey of community for prospects for Sunday School and church?			
				Do you need to provide a playground?			
				Do you have adequate youth programs, both Sunday and weekday?			
				Do you need a church bus, to reach out into nearby areas?			
				Do you have chairs and tables of proper size for younger groups?			
				Do you have a School of Missions?			
				Is the Board of Missions or Missionary Committee functioning?			
				Do all members receive the State or City DENOMINATIONAL MAGAZINE?			
				(Larger churches may consider these additional items)			
				Director of Christian Education			
				☐ Auto allowance for Director			
				☐ Housing for Director			
				☐ Pension fund dues			

Fig. A-5

Now fill in the following:

5. *Your World Outreach:*
   Your denomination's national goal $___
   Your denomination's state or diocese goal   ___
   Your church's goal   ___
   Denominational institutions   ___
   Other benevolences   ___
   Total for benevolences and missions $___

Having thought about the *advance program* of your church, you are now ready to find out what it will cost. Use pencil on the following form. You may want to erase. Do not be alarmed over the total. This is only preliminary. Step four (Discovering Your Resources) will give you the probable figure for your next campaign.

Preliminary Proposal for ___ ___Church
A PROPOSAL FOR 19__
"Let us rise up and build." Nehemiah 2: 18

Churches differ widely in the division of their funds. To help you get started, however, you might wish to use the following breakdown of the dollar (figures are average of thirty churches):

1. The church home   30¢
2. Pastoral ministry   25
3. Worship and service   20
4. Christian education   5
5. Missions and benevolences   20
                              _____
   Total $1.00

1. *Your Church Home*
   Repairs and improvements $___
   Fuel   ___
   Insurance   ___
   Services and supplies   ___
   Sexton   ___
   Utilities   ___
   Telephone   ___
   Miscellaneous   ___
      Total $___ $___
2. *Your Pastoral Ministry*
   Salary $___
   Pension   ___
   Travel   ___
   Pulpit supply   ___
   Conventions   ___
   Parsonage   ___
      (Fuel and upkeep)   ___
   Other   ___
      Total $___ $___

3. *Your Worship and Service*
   Office secretary $____
   Office supplies   ____
   Printing and stationery   ____
   Postage   ____
   Organist and director   ____
   Music   ____
   Flowers   ____
   Entertainments   ____
   Advertising   ____
   Radio and television   ____
   Every Member Canvass   ____
   Other   ____
      Total $____ $____
4. *Your Educational Ministry*
   Pastor's assistant $____
   Church school   ____
   Youth groups   ____
   Travel for assistant   ____
   Equipment   ____
   Camp scholarships   ____
   Miscellaneous   ____
   _____   ____
   _____   ____
   _____   ____
      Total $____
   Total, local expenses $____
5. *Your World Outreach*
   Your denomination's national goal $____
   Your denomination's state or diocese goal ____
   Your church's goal   ____
   Denominational institutions   ____
   Other benevolences   ____
      Total for benevolences and missions $____
Grand total, local expenses and missions $____

What Is the Saturation Point?

We have a tendency to compare our present standing with last year. If this reveals progress, we find satisfaction. If we can point out a steady advance for five years, we are tempted to take some ease in Zion. Then arises the question: "Has not our saturation point been reached?"

Suppose your church, not being in a rapidly growing community, has annually taken a 15 or 20 per cent increase in giving for several years. Can it go ahead further, particularly if the last year showed a leveling off? Perhaps you are in a major capital-funds program. Would not this prevent any significant increase, at least for the time being?

Working with several hundred churches has convinced me that it is extremely dangerous—if not impossible—to determine a church's saturation point.

Take this matter of a large building program. The experiences of two churches might help us.

Washington Park Methodist Church, Providence, Rhode Island

"Perhaps you could have called Washington Park Methodist a play-boy church," declared Pastor Harvey K. Mousley. "At least up until three years ago. For you see everything had been built around our gym. Ever since 1916 our athletic program was the big thing—going to church was not important. Then I began putting the challenge right up to my people."

It worked, too. For in 1951 these Methodists in Providence, spurred on by their energetic pastor, dedicated their lovely new church sanctuary. Beginning with $49,000 in hand, they raised an additional $160,000 in four years for the building. The church, in an old residential section of the city, has no members of wealth. The largest building contribution was $1,500.

The church now faced a problem. With their building campaign pledges expiring in six months, and a large outstanding mortgage, what would be the best financing plan? The official board finally decided to see if they could pay for the structure in ten years by putting $8,000 annually into the regular budget for debt reduction. Then they would join the United Church Canvass of Rhode Island which was promising each church detailed training in the ten-step financial method.

"We were," stated Pastor Mousley, "as near war-weary over finances as anyone could be, because of our building fund. Yet we went far ahead this year." Under the chairmanship of Marshall Allen, the pastor enjoyed, he later said, more freedom than he had ever had in a campaign. The General Committee requested the congregation to help build the proposed budget. "We even had the unmitigated gall," said the pastor with a twinkle, "to suggest to some people that four dollars a week was not too much to give to church. Now these people are attending church better. I guess they want to see where their money is going."

Results? Washington Park Methodists increased their pledging 67 per cent, including an additional thousand dollars to missions. The $8,000 for mortgage reduction was underwritten. All salaries were raised. And now for the first time the Sunday School had extra funds to buy new equipment and to make needed expansion.

"This effort," concluded Mr. Mousley, "has solidified our whole financial level. This is the high level of giving we think we can maintain year after year."

Calvary Baptist Church, Lowell, Massachusetts

Early on the morning of January 6, 1948, Rev. Victor Scalise awoke to the wail of fire sirens. His church across the street was ablaze, and by daybreak it was a total loss. But before dawn the trustees had met in the parsonage and resolved to rebuild Calvary Baptist Church on the same site in Lowell. Two problems now faced the leaders. Would disheartened members drift to other nearby churches? Would prospects of the gigantic rebuilding operation discourage all givers?

Fire insurance on the loss totaled only $56,500. A new structure would be apt to cost $400,000. Meanwhile the church worshipped in the state armory. For over three years Victor Scalise preached to his people in the bleak drill hall, his chancel a portable platform, his backdrop a large cannon.

On April 8, 1951, the congregation held their first worship service in the new sanctuary. One of the most attractive small churches in New England, the brick colonial structure cost less than $250,000. By early 1951 these folks had paid $138,000 toward the building, leaving a mortgage of $50,000. Meanwhile they had *increased* their giving both to local expenses and to missions.

The question now before the board of trustees was whether the building pledges (soon to expire) could be renewed as part of the local expense budget without damaging either current operations or building amortization. Under the chairmanship of Walter Clement, a committee of aggressive laymen agreed to make the effort. Most of the ten steps were followed. The result was an increase from $8,700 to $16,900 in the local budget, from $1,500 to $2,900 in missions. There was now $4,000 extra for a new youth worker, a raise in salaries, and a higher missionary goal, in addition to $6,900 for amortization and interest. "We shall never lose sight of the fact," wrote Walter Clement, "that had we at any time faltered in our Faith, this could not have been accomplished."

Some denominations, practicing a high stewardship, have trained their members to give well. Whereas the average per capita gift for all Protestants in 1953 was $45.64, the Seventh Day Adventists contributed $173.35 and the Church of the Nazarene, $118.33.[1] Such high giving by whole denominations, and by other individual churches scattered across the country, testifies that the so-called saturation point—if there is any— is a good deal higher than we normally think.

Churches which have had successful enlistments for a number of years are still able to get significant increases by using all the ten steps. Twenty years ago when Dr. Charles Stanley Jones became pastor of the First Congregational Church in Burlington, Vermont, the church was in debt $75,000. The debt was gradually paid off, and each year there was an increase in current giving, brought about by consistent stewardship preaching and the use of Every Member Canvasses. Yet the use of the full ten steps in 1953 resulted in 25 per cent increase (despite the loss by death of one gift of twenty-five dollars a week), enabling the church to install a new heating system, repair and reupholster the pews, add an assistant to the pastoral staff, and increase salaries.

In Waterville, Maine, the First Baptist Church in 1948 had a total budget of $8,000 and an outstanding mortgage of $15,000. The first task was the retirement of the mortgage. Then another campaign to renovate the building raised $65,000. Following that, a $20,000 parsonage was purchased. By 1952, the budget reached $18,000. Then the church entered the Waterville sector project and pledged $23,000, an increase of 72 per cent above envelope receipts of 1952. One year later, the Rev. Richard Keach reported, the church pledged $25,030 in a second "ten-step" effort.

In ten years the budget of the Park Place Congregational Church in Pawtucket, Rhode Island, doubled. Since the canvass of 1951 had produced a glorious 69 per cent increase, there was a feeling that the limit had been reached. Yet as part of the Rhode Island United Church Canvass in 1952, this church took another 22 per cent increase.

The Rev. A. King Wise, minister of the First Baptist Church in Glens

[1] "Statistics of Giving," 1954, National Council of Churches, New York.

Falls, New York, drove 200 miles one day to tell his story to a group of Vermont churches. For a number of years this church had conducted excellent canvasses. In addition the members were giving $12,000 a year toward a renovation project. Then in the 1953 Glens Falls sector this church advanced another 25 per cent, raising their giving from $14,000 to $36,000 in three years.

Sometimes a large endowment fund cripples the spiritual life of a church people. Wise administration of such funds, however, will prevent their freezing the level of the members' giving. Much to the astonishment of everyone in the First Baptist Church of Pittsfield, Massachusetts, they read in the newspaper one day in 1939 of a bequest for over $332,000 left them by a deceased member, Nelson J. Lawton. Before the money was available, the church, advised by the pastor, Rev. Paul L. Sturges, and the trustees, agreed to place in the bylaws an article that would ensure forever that at least one-half of the income must be used for Kingdom Extension (missions and benevolences). Since then the per capita giving to both local expenses and missions has continued to increase (having doubled since 1939) under the pastoral leadership of Christian B. Jensen. In 1946 and 1947 the church members gave more to Kingdom Extension than they did to the local church.

When does a church reach its saturation point? Perhaps when the people are given no new vision. Perhaps it is better never to raise this question but to keep pressing on to do ever more to win the world for Christ.

APPENDIX C: *A Sales Hint to Ministers*

The steps outlined in this manual make up an intensive program. Whereas a few churches will be quick to see the possibilities and eager to enter into the plan, most churches will hesitate. Such hesitation is apt to build up around the work called for, the costs involved ("Will we get our expenses back?"), or the opinion that such-and-such a step will not work in this congregation ("Our church is different, you know").

Someone has said that every American is a salesman. If he is not selling a gadget or a commodity, he is selling an idea. The idea may be a business one or purely social or civic. Perhaps it is the community of which he is so proud, or his child's school, or the American way of life. Certainly most of us are constantly selling ourselves—trying to make favorable impressions upon others.

Salesmanship is the art of planting one's idea into someone else's mind. But this process is not an easy one. Students of psychology inform us that the human mind has two parts—the conscious and the subconscious, separated by a threshold. The conscious mind tells us that we are hungry or sleepy or that we want to listen to opera or to popular music. The subconscious mind is, however, the more important, for it determines our character and personality. To get an idea into the conscious mind, we need but state or print it. But to get that idea into the subconscious mind where it will serve to motivate the man is far more difficult. For that threshold acts, as the English clergyman Leslie Weatherhead has said, as a policeman whose duty it is to ward off all attempts to cross it.

The preacher delivers his sermon, hoping that his idea will take root in some mind, that it will enter the subconscious. But each member says at the dinner hour: "Wasn't that a good sermon for Mr. X?" There is, however, a way to crack this threshold. *Constant repetition* will finally force an entry past the policeman into the subconscious. Hitler's lieutenants knew this to be a truth when they stated: "It does not matter how big a lie you tell. If you keep repeating it, men will come to believe it." At the opposite pole of humanity stood our Saviour who also illustrated the power of repetition. Over and over again, in parables or miracles or sermons He repeated those truths that were so fundamental. Peter did not understand until after the Resurrection, but by the Day of Pentecost the truth of Jesus had cracked the threshold of his inner self. Henceforth he was a new man. Christ within Peter, as Christ within Paul, caused "old things to pass away, all things to become new."

So it is in this program of rejuvenating the church through a magnified budget. The pastor must begin "selling" and keep on "selling." He should use the same tact and persistence, coupled with enthusiasm, that Paul reveals in II Corinthians, Chapters 8 and 9, when he is "selling" these Christians on taking up an offering for the poor of Jerusalem. Sold himself on the merits of his plan for a revitalized church, the pastor must sell his finance committee the general idea. Later he must sell the idea of a resources committee.

The minister-salesman will need but one argument and one tool. The argument is simply: "Others have done it. We can do it, too." His facts he will find in Chapter A and in the tables in Appendixes E and F. Somewhat similar results are possible for your church, *if you follow the plan* outlined in the preceding chapters. No matter what the objection, the answer always should be, "Do we want a more vital program? Could we wisely use more money?" Once this premise is granted, the minister replies: "These churches obtained their larger program. They did it by following the ten-step plan. We can, also."

Some church leaders do not see the need of raising more funds. Often this attitude results from their skepticism of the workability of the plan. Perhaps in the back of their minds is the thought: "We tried an Every Member Canvass once. It didn't work very well then. I know it won't work now." To help sell these leaders, a tool is provided. It is the check list presented in Appendix A.

I have seen use of the check list cast an almost magical spell over the participants. Men who walked into the first meeting indifferent or even slightly hostile began to change as they pored with pencils over an ideal budget for their church. As men from the same church worked together, freed for once from the need of wondering where the money was coming from, and concerned only with the pure delight of drawing on paper those projects they had long desired for their church, these financial officers within the space of one hour sold themselves on the plan.

Ministers and trustees need not—in fact should not—take this ten-step plan to the church for its approval. Such action is unnecessary, since the church has already given authority to the board to raise funds. This particular plan is only one of many methods the trustees might choose to engage. Since they are charged with the duty of raising funds, it is their right to choose whatever method they desire. Later in the program the church will be given the opportunity to vote on the actual *goal* of the campaign.

Bringing this matter before the church at this time is also dangerous. Since the plan is involved, and there may be many questions which cannot be answered at that meeting, the congregation may vote the plan down.

The church members will be sold, not all at once, but step by step, as they advance into the project. The two primary sales points are the leadership (in whom the church has confidence) and the proposed new program (which the people help to formulate).

Evil men are laboring to win the world for themselves. Long ago Jesus Christ paid the cost for redeeming mankind. The world belongs to Him—we churchmen need but claim it for Him. But our efforts, our plans, our devotion of yesterday have not been sufficient. We need wiser strategy, more aggressive action, greater fearlessness.

We have a magnificent Christ. We need to become better salesmen for Him.

APPENDIX D: *The United Church Canvass Works*[1]

The United Church Canvass idea was born almost simultaneously in three widely separated communities: Council Bluffs, Iowa; Medina, Ohio; and Newton, Massachusetts. It was in the early 1930s when the depression was at its worst that these communities discovered that churches prospered by having their financial campaigns simultaneously with community-wide publicity. From these three centers the movement spread until in January 1, 1953, the United Church Canvass became a part of the National Council of Churches.

The number of communities having a United Church Canvass in recent sample years is as follows:

1942	31
1944	73
1947	35
1950	44
1953	71

It is interesting to note that during the war years the number of United Church Canvasses increased sharply. This was due to the influence of united campaigns for the USO, united war funds, and similar other community-wide financial campaigns.

While the United Church Canvass is strongest in the New England area, it has good representative strength across the country. Some of the strong United Church Canvass communities are as follows: Bismarck, North Dakota; Evanston, Illinois; Springfield, Massachusetts; Keene, New Hampshire; Hackensack, New Jersey; Worcester, Massachusetts; Attleboro, Massachusetts; New Haven, Connecticut; Hartford, Connecticut; Beloit, Wisconsin; Auburn, New York. Many of these communities have

[1] This appendix was contributed by T. K. Thompson, Executive Director, Joint Department of Stewardship and Benevolence, National Council of the Churches of Christ in the United States of America.

conducted United Church Canvasses for ten years or more because they have found many advantages to the plan.

Publicity is a difficult problem for the churches because the average community has many churches, and newspaper and radio cannot give very much publicity to any one church. However, when the churches band together in a great community-wide effort, public media of information are delighted to give space and time to the effort. This has been especially true since 1949 when the Advertising Council gave a major allocation to "Religion in American Life," a movement designed to publicize the place of religious institutions in the life of the nation. Newspapers, radio, TV, billboards, car cards, and many other media are used to emphasize the spiritual foundations of our nation.

The second great advantage of the United Church Canvass is the increased fellowship among laymen in the churches. By the very nature of the case, the financial leadership of the churches must be borne by the laymen. Many men of outstanding skills in sales and advertising are willing to give their time to train visitors and organize canvasses, and many of the weaker churches can call upon the leadership of stronger churches through the local sponsoring committee. Most United Church Canvasses include a great community-wide canvasser inspiration meeting with a prominent speaker. Between 1,500 and 2,000 laymen gather each year for such a laymen's stewardship rally in the communities in the North Shore of the Boston area.

A third advantage of the United Church Canvass is increased income. Over the years, churches participating in these joint efforts usually show about a 10 per cent gain in income over the previous year. Much larger gains are possible where churches carefully organize a thorough Every Member Canvass in their local parishes.

During recent years, interest in United Church Canvass has accelerated rapidly because of a number of new developments. In a number of communities in New England, the United Church Canvass has been combined with the "sector plan" of the American Baptist Convention, described by Dr. O. A. Pendleton in this book. When the churches plan their Every Member Canvasses carefully in accordance with this outline and have community-wide training meetings and use the best materials, gains oftentimes up to 100 per cent have been achieved. Extensive use of the sector plan has been made in Holyoke, Springfield, and Attleboro, Massachusetts; Burlington, Vermont; and Providence, Rhode Island. The use of the sector plan in connection with the United Church Canvass will be increasing across the nation in the years just ahead.

January 1, 1954, Dr. Arthur O. Rinden of Attleboro, Massachusetts, was called to become Associate Executive Director of the Joint Department of Stewardship and Benevolence with special responsibilities for the

United Church Canvass. Dr. Rinden, out of long experience as a missionary in China, as Director of audio-visual aids for the Missions Council of the Congregational Christian Churches, and as Executive of the Attleboro Council of Churches is splendidly prepared to give leadership to the United Church Canvass movement. This department of the National Council of Churches has a speakers' bureau of outstanding laymen who have had success in leadership in the United Church Canvass and who are willing to interpret the idea to other interested communities. The cost is only for the travel expenses involved. A new United Church Canvass Manual has been published and is available from the Joint Department of Stewardship and Benevolence, 297 Fourth Avenue, New York.

APPENDIX E: *Statistics of American Baptist Sectors,*
1951–1954

The American Baptist Council on Missionary Cooperation conducted fifty sectors embracing 800 churches between September, 1951, and December, 1954. These projects, scattered from Bangor, Maine, to Santa Ana, California, included every conceivable type of Baptist church. Seven of the sectors, all in New England but one, were interdenominational. The results were the same regardless of size, location, or denomination of church.

Figures include both local expenses and benevolences, but do not include major building or debt items. Comparison is made between *envelope receipts* of the preceding year and *pledges* for the new year. Comparison of pledges with pledges was not possible since in virtually every sector there were a few churches which did not take pledges the year before. In every case, total budgets will be higher than the envelope receipts or pledges listed here.

1. *Boston Pilot Project, Autumn, 1951*

This was the test sector from which arose all succeeding sectors.

Directors: Jack Krause and O. A. Pendleton

Church	Minister	1951 envelope receipts	1952 pledges	Per cent increase
1. Arlington, First	N. W. Wood	$ 24,173	$ 35,028	44
2. Attleboro, First	R. H. Seguine	7,202	15,058	110
3. Belmont, First	J. G. Beveridge	5,362	10,232	91
4. Cambridge, First	H. C. Eatough	12,833	17,526	37
5. Chelmsford, Central	L. N. Selfridge	3,929	7,345	87
6. Chelsea, Horace Memorial	J. L. Ice	1,510	5,811	285
7. Everett, Glendale	F. C. Zagunis	5,394	8,745	62
8. Fitchburg, First	T. M. Thompson	12,250	14,065	14
9. Framingham, Park Street	R. B. Hardy	17,647	28,672	63
10. Franklin, Federated	Jordan Cole	4,317	11,872	175
11. South Hanson	L. S. Manierre	1,460	6,144	321
12. Haverhill, First	Clarence Gilbert	26,128	30,749	14
13. Hyde Park, First	H. B. Higgins	5,809	7,750	33
14. Medfield, First	Hugh Smith	2,188	4,614	111
15. Milford, First	A. H. Melanson	5,567	7,357	32
16. Milton, First	D. W. Geary	7,154	16,392	129
17. Newton Centre	R. H. Bishop	29,545	34,086	15
18. Norfolk, Federated	Arthur Samuelson	3,736	9,776	161
19. North Hanover	R. F. Bishop	3,011	5,513	82
20. Norwood, First	O. W. Olsen, Jr.	8,500	10,680	25
21. Reading, First	H. C. Mathews	8,464	12,594	49
22. Rock Village	G. N. C. Mott	1,350	2,142	50
23. Roslindale, First	A. Z. Arnold	7,322	10,683	46
24. Somerville, Grace	W. D. Callender	7,581	11,126	47
25. Somerville, Union Square	G. J. Kirk	6,232	9,801	57
26. Wakefield, First	H. G. Payne	11,923	25,410	113
27. West Acton	D. W. Thompson	2,947	6,400	117
28. Weston, First	F. F. Peterson	6,550	10,325	57
29. Winchester, First	W. L. Bailey	11,975	13,960	18
30. Wollaston, First	H. O. Tatum	15,740	21,220	35
Total		$267,883	$407,165	52

2. *Newark, New Jersey, Sector, Spring, 1952*

Directors: Harold G. Stoddard and Norman Booth

Church	Minister	1951–1952 envelope receipts	1952–1953 pledges	Per cent increase
1. Baptistown	M. E. Wetzel	$ 2,825	$ 5,085	80
2. East Orange, Central	G. F. Kurtz	7,315	10,644	46
3. Carlstadt	Otto Brenner	3,796	5,711	50
4. Demarest	M. A. Thornton	8,100	8,800	9
5. Elizabeth, Central	V. G. Higgs	8,833	10,320	17
6. Elizabeth, First	R. O. Seeley	8,056	15,382	91
7. Flemington	E. C. Dunbar	10,511	15,052	43
8. Glenwood	Walter Rice		2,626	
9. Highland Park	A. A. Dickson	6,351	7,250	14
10. Irvington	G. S. Miller	9,492	13,706	44
11. Lambertville	J. Y. Elliott	3,764	6,435	71
12. Matawan	L. R. Bailey	7,251	12,400	71
13. Metuchen	T. J. Bell	3,660	7,415	103
14. Morristown	R. B. Barbour	11,485	14,585	27
15. Newark, Peddie Memorial	W. F. Davison	28,800	34,468	20
16. Newark, Walnut Street	Lenox Palin	5,807	9,735	67
17. New Brunswick, First	R. E. Dowdy	14,783	19,500	31
18. New Brunswick, Livingston Ave.	P. B. Henderson	16,500	24,250	47
19. Paterson, First	Fred MacArthur	17,723	26,320	48
20. Paterson, Union Avenue	R. A. Broyles	9,883	16,200	63
21. Perth Amboy, First	Peter Kowalchuk	7,788	10,135	29
22. Rahway	E. A. Goldsworthy	14,200	25,120	77
23. Scotch Plains	E. E. Peterson	10,550	16,069	52
24. South Amboy	W. H. Blackley		4,125	
25. South Plainfield	E. J. Kocsis	3,800	4,800	26
26. Stelton	L. A. Williams	7,685	13,800	79
27. Sussex	A. G. Graham, Jr.	1,860	3,652	96
28. Trenton, Calvary	R. G. Martin	11,046	16,000	45
29. Union, First	K. A. Dalton	6,000	11,500	91
30. Westfield	E. E. Gates, Jr.	23,445	27,600	17
Total		$271,309	$398,685	47

3. *Denver, Colorado, Sector, Spring, 1952*

Directors: M. E. Bratcher and R. J. Hanson

Church	Minister	1951–1952 envelope receipts	1952–1953 pledges	Per cent increase
1. Brighton	J. L. Losh	$ 2,360	$ 7,405	214
2. Denver, Berkeley	A. W. Schuessler	4,164	4,295	3
3. Denver, Bonnie Brae	A. R. Smith	3,975	8,153	105
4. Denver, Broadway	James Macpherson	10,581	19,002	80
5. Denver, Calvary	H. G. Smith	33,646	49,959	48
6. Denver, Chaffee	———	889	5,928	566
7. Denver, City Park	B. B. Fordham	17,691	27,868	58
8. Denver, Curtis Park	R. J. Kuechmann	120	350	192
9. Denver, Grace	W. E. Simmons	6,909	9,726	41
10. Denver, Montclair	H. H. Bailey	5,998	9,270	55
11. Denver, W. Alameda	H. D. Johns	2,272	6,215	174
12. Littleton	W. C. Barclay	2,924	8,345	185
13. Greeley	H. B. Lundgren	12,317	18,454	50
14. Loveland	F. K. Lauseman	10,375	18,336	77
Total		$114,200	$193,296	69

4. *Nebraska-Iowa Sector, Spring, 1952*

Directors: R. J. Hanson and W. E. Hayler

Church	Minister	1951–1952 envelope receipts	1952–1953 pledges	Per cent increase
1. Omaha, Benson	W. H. Dickinson	$ 6,700	$ 10,300	53
2. Omaha, Calvary	W. J. Niven	20,500	26,552	29
3. Omaha, First	V. I. Olson	51,564	58,000	12
4. Omaha, Immanuel	Roger Wickstrand	9,190	13,180	34
5. Omaha, McKinley Park	C. H. Shanklin	4,693	6,937	48
6. Omaha, Olivet	J. M. Elving	9,470	12,823	35
7. Omaha, Park Side	Willard Ballard	4,137	5,447	31
8. Omaha, Trinity	E. F. Edmonds	10,254	15,336	50
9. Valley, Federated	Dale Kamrath	4,882	9,440	93
10. Lincoln, First	G. H. Schroeder	26,024	31,484	21
11. Lincoln, Second	E. E. Smith	13,551	21,299	57
12. Peru	G. W. T. Boyd	2,706	3,000	11
13. Grand Island	W. A. Dalton	7,233	24,047	232
14. Council Bluffs, Iowa	A. L. Farrell	15,655	26,928	72
15. Red Oak, Iowa	Asa Popp	3,984	9,826	147
Total		$190,543	$274,599	43

5. *Rhode Island Sector, Spring, 1952*

Directors: O. A. Pendleton and P. R. Shaub

Church	Minister	1951–1952 envelope receipts	1952–1953 pledges	Per cent increase
1. Central Falls, Broad Street	Frank Barber	$ 3,077	$ 6,158	100
2. Cranston, Arlington	D. G. Cook	2,876	7,506	161
3. Cranston, Pawtuxet	W. H. Herman	6,800	11,981	77
4. Cranston, People's	L. F. Kenney	16,649	23,375	40
5. Cranston, Phillips Memorial	F. H. Snell	22,730	34,881	53
6. Georgiaville	D. W. Passage	4,785	8,147	72
7. Lonsdale	W. B. Drolette	5,860	8,205	40
8. Mount Vernon Parish	B. O. Waterman	356	690	89
9. Natick, First	Adolph Johnson	3,238	4,644	43
10. Pawtucket, Bethany	H. H. Powell	4,191	9,100	117
11. Pawtucket, First	E. C. Prime	17,833	23,991	35
12. Providence, Central	P. L. Sturges	20,600	29,234	41
13. Providence, Emmanuel	E. L. Saabye	4,700	7,076	51
14. Providence, Federal Hill	Anthony Collea	4,792	6,796	41
15. Providence, Fourth	J. E. Ring	16,660	20,459	22
16. Providence, Pond Street	E. E. Crawford	3,960	12,862	224
17. Providence, Roger Williams	F. E. Gardner	8,268	14,048	70
18. Providence, South	M. T. Wiant	3,700	8,425	127
19. Providence, Trinity	H. H. Graichen	3,208	6,851	114
20. Providence, Union	A. J. Rodrigues	1,467	2,524	71
21. Tiverton, Central	E. R. Sherblom	6,396	9,642	50
22. Wakefield	R. H. Lightbody	6,924	12,365	79
23. Warwick, Central	F. L. Parsons	6,100	10,882	79
24. Warwick, Shawomet	L. H. Barr	7,448	10,184	36
25. Warwick, Spring Green	K. S. Dannenhauer	2,306	3,678	60
26. Wickford, First	S. D. Crabtree	2,640	8,660	229
27. Woonsocket, First	A. R. Sanborn	7,023	9,849	40
Total		$194,387	$312,219	60

6. Watertown, Massachusetts, Sector, Spring, 1952

Directors: O. A. Pendleton and N. E. Woodbury

Church	Minister	1951–1952 envelope receipts	1952–1953 pledges	Per cent increase
1. Boston, Immanuel	Robert Willett	$ 3,194	$ 6,601	106
2. Boston, White Street	L. R. Beckwith	1,680	4,930	193
3. Braintree, First	S. J. Riggs	11,045	15,400	39
4. Charlestown, First	I. I. Sears	5,400	8,700	61
5. Medford, First	Alexander Henderson	32,344	34,788	8
6. Milton, Mattapan	R. L. Weaver	10,720	15,300	43
7. North Abington	R. W. Hill	5,658	13,246	133
8. Rockland, First	H. W. Rogers	9,612	14,165	47
9. Watertown, Belmont Street	W. B. McGinnis	9,027	12,233	36
10. Watertown, First	J. W. Sillen	13,142	18,237	38
11. West Medford, Shiloh	O. G. Phillips	2,400	5,811	141
12. Whitman, First	A. R. Freeman	7,140	10,300	45
13. Worcester, Pleasant Street	H. A. Spinney	11,330	21,000	85
Total		$122,692	$180,711	47

7. Northern California Sector, Spring, 1952

Directors: W. P. Halbert and Jack Krause

Church	Minister	1951–1952 envelope receipts	1952–1953 pledges	Per cent increase
1. Carmichael	J. M. Hestenes	$ 3,650	$ 7,478	105
2. Broderick	Louis Mitchell	795	1,420	80
3. Marysville, First	J. R. Moy	3,800	9,845	159
4. Menlo Park	F. E. Eden	9,410	11,598	23
5. Merced, First	H. B. Transchel	9,500	16,613	75
6. Redwood City	W. B. Smith	18,626	23,000	23
7. Rio Vista	Harold Jackson	4,700	9,683	106
8. San Anselmo	W. R. Gorsage	9,000	11,905	32
9. San Lorenzo	Gerald Moyer	11,385	20,329	79
10. Willows	B. M. Franklin	5,564	13,855	149
11. Sacramento, First	Wilbur Christians	55,924	64,152	15
12. Sparks, Nevada	H. A. Eaton	3,812	10,123	166
13. Palo Alto	Guy Wimmer	25,650	28,000	9
Total		$161,816	$228,001	40

8. *Southern California Sector, Spring, 1952*

Directors: J. A. Ramsay and Jack Krause

Church	Minister	1951–1952 envelope receipts	1952–1953 pledges	Per cent increase
1. Alhambra	W. L. Prigger, Jr.	$ 46,186	$ 72,968	58
2. Bella Vista	W. C. Morrison	4,398	11,531	161
3. Brea, First	R. C. McFadden	4,576	8,863	93
4. Corona, First	Earl Robertson	16,128	23,000	44
5. La Jolla, First	C. I. Reid	10,664	15,600	46
6. Los Angeles, El Segundo	Jesse Powers	4,806	11,500	139
7. Los Angeles, Rosewood Park	G. M. Merrifield	2,200	4,478	104
8. Los Angeles, Wilshire	M. O. Brininstool	5,680	11,543	103
9. Maywood, First	L. H. Coker	40,916	52,000	27
10. Monrovia, First	M. A. Pekrul	23,488	27,150	15
11. Orange, First	C. W. Sanders	12,314	15,000	22
12. Pasadena, First	George Hill	60,744	66,612	10
13. Pomona, First	H. L. Fickett, Jr.	70,638	101,000	43
14. San Bernardino, Calvary	Boyce Van Osdel	29,483	44,968	52
15. Santa Monica, Trinity	F. M. Judson	28,000	66,000	136
16. Temple City, First	E. A. Williams	21,538	26,231	22
Total		$381,759	$558,444	46

9. *Pittsburgh, Pennsylvania, Sector, Spring, 1952*

Directors: H. E. MacCombie and P. K. Shelford

Church	Minister	1951–1952 envelope receipts	1952–1953 pledges	Per cent increase
1. Aliquippa	E. C. Poole	$ 5,087	$ 19,020	274
2. Ambridge	J. A. Millard	6,135	8,183	33
3. Canonsburg	J. E. Fosnight	7,300	15,935	118
4. Carnegie	E. F. Pruden	8,472	14,597	72
5. Coraopolis, First	G. W. Whitney	8,700	19,282	121
6. Coraopolis, Mooncrest	G. E. Kirkwood	4,400	9,030	105
7. Donora, Emmanuel	R. A. Unger	6,731	13,234	96
8. Ford City	S. W. Stewart	11,313	18,741	66
9. Greensburg	R. H. Williams	9,773	18,500	89
10. Homestead	D. R. Beecher	17,125	24,390	42
11. McKeesport, First	F. B. Long	28,400	31,937	12
12. McKeesport, Park	W. J. Clawson	12,003	18,000	50
13. New Kensington	Wilfred Noble	18,365	27,256	48
14. North Hills	D. W. Cazer	2,350	3,926	67
15. Pittsburgh, Bellevue	W. H. Willkens	15,120	23,000	52
16. Pittsburgh, Crafton	R. A. Selby	8,130	11,540	42
17. Pittsburgh, East End	A. H. Ryan	18,537	22,939	24
18. Pittsburgh, Emmanuel	A. A. Blake	3,000	5,240	75
19. Pittsburgh, First	L. B. Moseley	47,970	56,320	17
20. Pittsburgh, Homewood	J. F. Sparks	8,253	11,520	40
21. Pittsburgh, Knoxville	R. J. Schmidt	4,540	7,349	62
22. Pittsburgh, Lorenz Avenue	R. A. Selby	2,788	5,962	114
23. Pittsburgh, Wilkinsburg	E. R. Sidler, II	28,601	32,762	15
24. Rochester	G. D. Younger	9,000	13,591	51
25. Tarentum	O. C. Metzger	13,000	18,053	39
26. Washington, First	E. C. Gross	16,800	25,949	54
27. Brownsville	H. V. Layhew	6,600	14,000	112
28. Ellwood City	Ralph Newell	17,500	30,322	73
Total		$345,993	$520,578	50

10. *Waterville, Maine, Sector, Autumn, 1952*

Directors: T. L. Brindley and O. A. Pendleton

Church	Minister	1952 envelope receipts	1953 pledges	Per cent increase
1. Auburn, Court Street	S. J. Holt	$10,700	$ 15,013	40
2. Augusta, Penney Memorial	M. E. Golding	10,008	13,025	30
3. Bangor, Columbia Street	A. W. Geary	18,700	29,638	58
4. Bangor, First	W. L. Cook	11,101	12,464	12
5. Bath, First	C. R. Simms	2,843	5,396	90
6. Bath, Corliss Street	Harold Allen	3,074	6,744	118
7. Burnham	Mrs. Nellie Lane	1,520	5,137	238
8. Damariscotta	Hartley Johnston	2,413	4,690	94
9. Livermore Falls	F. S. Kinley	4,660	7,541	62
10. Pittsfield	G. S. Johnston	2,560	6,100	135
11. Thomaston	John Fitzpatrick	3,180	11,201	252
12. Waterville, First	R. L. Keach	13,334	22,981	71
13. Waterville, Second	Sterling Helmer	2,529	4,437	75
Total		$86,622	$144,567	67

11. *New Hampshire Sector, Autumn, 1952*

Directors: E. W. Parsons and O. A. Pendleton

Church	Minister	1952 envelope receipts	1953 pledges	Per cent increase
1. Ashland	W. S. Norman	$ 3,778	$ 5,741	52
2. Concord United	M. E. Levy	7,574	14,052	86
3. Exeter	E. H. Shuman	5,724	11,026	92
4. Manchester, First	W. J. Setzer	9,548	16,042	68
5. Milford	E. M. Jones	3,891	7,586	95
6. Nashua	W. H. Porter	15,212	25,762	69
7. Penacook	O. C. Northcott	4,000	6,925	73
8. Portsmouth, Middle Street	R. F. Smith	8,139	10,760	32
9. Whitefield	R. S. Cummings	2,854	5,295	85
Total		$60,720	$103,189	70

12. *Holyoke, Massachusetts, Sector, Interdenominational, Autumn, 1952*

Directors: J. D. Burnett, N. E. Woodbury, O. A. Pendleton

Church	Minister	1952 envelope receipts	1953 pledges	Per cent increase
BAPTIST				
1. Holyoke, Second	J. D. Burnett	$ 17,700	$ 22,000	24
2. Northampton	A. W. Whitmarsh	4,751	7,701	63
3. Palmer	J. K. Banks	3,340	6,300	88
4. Springfield, First	B. F. Archibald	32,819	50,196	53
5. Springfield, Harvey St.	Mrs. F. A. Mac-Donald	3,015	4,937	64
6. Springfield, Park Memorial	W. A. Aschenbach	20,041	29,000	45
7. W. Springfield, First	E. L. Wallace	7,185	11,574	65
CONGREGATIONAL				
8. Greenfield, First	H. W. Curtis	9,100	11,828	30
9. Greenfield, Robbins Memorial	Albert Baller	4,000	5,575	39
10. Ludlow	A. W. Kennan	6,863	11,350	65
11. Springfield, Old First	J. E. Wallace	39,900	63,000	58
12. Springfield, Wachogue	H. B. Keir	5,548	8,540	54
13. W. Springfield, First	Pierre Vuilleumier	20,597	27,000	31
14. W. Springfield, Mittineague	C. G. King	14,450	19,250	33
METHODIST				
15. Springfield, Wesley	L. H. Johnson	24,890	36,989	48
16. W. Springfield, First	G. W. Stump	2,069	7,191	248
EPISCOPAL				
17. Springfield, St. Peter's	G. W. Smith	8,677	16,212	86
18. W. Springfield, Good Shepherd	R. W. D. Smith	7,200	10,366	44
OTHERS				
19. St. Andrews E. & R. Holyoke	Carl Nugent	4,308	5,805	35
20. First Christian, Springfield	C. E. Miller	1,570	2,675	70
21. First Presbyterian, Springfield	L. B. Bearse	6,000	8,210	37
22. Unity, Springfield	E. H. Sommerfeld	9,500	13,000	37
Total		$253,523	$378,699	49

Total   22 churches
        8 denominations

13. *Connecticut Sector, Autumn, 1952*

Directors: R. I. Madsen and F. T. Hoadley

Church	Minister	1952 envelope receipts	1953 pledges	Per cent increase
1. Bridgeport, Second	W. W. Sullivan	$ 3,716	$ 7,381	98
2. Bristol	F. T. Hoadley	8,147	15,248	87
3. Hartford, Asylum Ave.*	R. P. Bartlett	18,000	18,873	5
4. Hartford, Blue Hills	————	7,778	9,147	18
5. Hartford, Central	K. L. Maxwell	42,229	48,564	15
6. Hartford, Memorial	M. L. Johnson	11,696	17,514	50
7. Meriden, Italian	Luigi Turco	2,272	6,228	174
8. Meriden, Main St.	W. V. Allen	3,585	6,044	69
9. Middletown, First	A. D. Johnson	8,420	11,003	30
10. Mystic, Union	L. F. Emery	3,089	9,083	194
11. New Haven, First	E. A. Sherwood	13,650	16,329	20
12. New London, First	M. H. Mason	8,082	19,370	139
13. Noank	G. A. Knauer	9,062	12,661	39
14. Norwich, First	O. F. Gracey	6,521	10,152	55
15. Old Mystic	D. C. Tuttle	2,204	5,134	133
16. Shelton, First	W. G. Keucher	7,791	12,787	64
17. Stonington, United	C. E. Worcester	3,225	8,250	156
18. West Haven, First	William Meyers	5,925	9,775	65
Total		$165,392	$233,543	45

* Partial participation.

14. *Boston, Massachusetts, Sector II, Fall, 1952*

Directors: N. E. Woodbury and O. A. Pendleton

Church	Minister	1952 envelope receipts	1953 pledges	Per cent increase
1. Beverly, First	G. E. Bigelow	$ 21,443	$ 33,279	55
2. Boston, Center St.	S. J. Fletcher	3,607	5,696	58
3. Brockton, First	J. A. Davidson	17,976	26,800	49
4. Brookline	K. L. Garrison	11,301	24,647	118
5. Grafton, First	Albert Grady	3,062	5,027	64
6. Holden, First	H. T. Grandin	13,074	20,087	54
7. Marlboro, First	F. M. Keech	3,057	9,324	204
8. Natick, First	A. R. Phillips	7,943	11,317	42
9. Norwood, First*	O. W. Olsen, Jr.	10,039	10,133	1
10. Salem, First	W. L. Loomis	6,970	11,536	65
11. West Acton*	R. H. Noble	6,591	7,710	17
12. Winthrop, First	R. B. Watson	5,310	10,400	96
Total		$110,373	$175,956	59

* Indicates church in sector project a second time.

15. *Northern New Jersey Sector, Fall, 1952*

Directors: H. B. Stoddard and P. K. Shelford

Church	Minister	1952 envelope receipts	1953 pledges	Per cent increase
1. Arlington, First	D. T. Erickson	$ 9,612	$ 19,460	101
2. Bergenfield	S. W. Robinson	6,563	7,732	18
3. E. Orange, First	R. W. Pratt	25,220	35,287	40
4. Freehold	R. B. Rose	12,279	17,874	45
5. Georges Road	Clifford Lofgren	5,205	9,221	77
6. Jersey City, First	A. B. Drummond	15,577	18,240	17
7. Leonardo	R. P. Young	3,260	6,263	90
8. Millington	H. B. Morris	5,505	8,699	58
9. Newark, Park Ave.	——	1,581	3,947	149
10. Newark, Roseville	C. F. Bleakney	5,576	9,773	75
11. Northfield	D. M. Weeden	5,729	9,443	65
12. Orange, North	S. T. Hardin	23,480	30,425	29
13. Orange, Washington St.	A. T. Mercer	6,306	9,506	51
14. Piscatawaytown	J. H. Bubar	2,386	5,361	124
15. Red Bank, First	W. C. Powers	13,760	20,000	45
16. Roselle, First	A. A. Gordanier	9,943	16,077	61
Total		$151,982	$227,312	49

16. *Buffalo, New York, Sector, Spring, 1953*

Directors: C. E. Lawson and P. K. Shelford

Church	Minister	1952–1953 envelope receipts	1953–1954 pledges	Per cent increase
1. Buffalo, Central Park	E. H. Drew	$ 11,510	$ 15,425	34
2. Buffalo, Dearborn St.	W. I. Greenawalt	6,200	8,807	42
3. Buffalo, Delevan Ave.	W. F. Nowlan	7,243	12,966	78
4. Buffalo, Delaware Ave.	Robert Zearfoss	38,000	44,000	16
5. Buffalo, Edison St.	A. P. Goodwin	9,037	12,071	34
6. Buffalo, Emmanuel	A. J. McKinney	5,376	6,915	28
7. Buffalo, Masten Park	M. H. Dallman	12,390	16,215	30
8. Buffalo, South Park	J. R. Davie	12,905	15,688	21
9. Chaffee	J. R. Riley	3,300	4,765	44
10. East Aurora	R. H. Emmons	9,500	12,562	32
11. Lancaster	Arthur Ventura	1,745	3,692	111
12. Kenmore	Franklin Crutchlow	31,469	33,155	5
13. Tonawanda, Broad St.	P. G. Smithson	7,000	9,424	34
14. Batavia, Emmanuel	K. L. Sniffen	6,425	8,874	37
15. Bethany Center	E. W. Harris	1,944	5,974	236
16. Bliss	H. G. Burlingame	1,700	5,314	212
17. Oakfield, Alabama	Charles Capper	4,050	6,806	68
18. Fredonia	C. A. Russell	14,040	21,062	50
19. Jamestown, First	G. H. Tolley	34,000	46,500	37
20. Ripley	Richard Ashley	2,000	2,997	50
21. Busti	G. H. Munger	5,740	5,725	0
22. Falconer	L. H. Wiemer	10,100	10,228	0
23. Clarence	E. W. Harris	2,499	7,275	191
24. Sanborn	Glenn Faucett	5,700	9,975	75
25. Akron	T. B. Light	4,373	9,005	106
26. Lockport	Harleigh Rosenberger	23,000	29,642	29
27. Niagara Falls, First	H. V. Kane	29,000	35,338	22
Total		$300,246	$400,400	33

17. *Rochester, New York, Sector, Spring, 1953*

Directors: A. R. DeMott and P. K. Shelford

Church	Minister	1952–1953 envelope receipts	1953–1954 pledges	Per cent increase
1. Rochester, Atlantic Ave.	W. E. Schmitt	$ 1,769	$ 3,277	84
2. Rochester, Baptist Temple	Kyle Hazeldon	32,662	41,720	27
3. Rochester, Calvary	George Middleton	28,100	39,686	41
4. Rochester, Church of the Master	C. O. Harding	22,000	28,260	28
5. Rochester, Genesee	R. C. Johnson	23,185	26,903	16
6. Rochester, Immanuel	O. H. McDonald	25,665	28,200	10
7. Rochester, Mt. Olivet	C. E. Boddie	7,816	14,210	82
8. Rochester, Parsells Ave.	Clarence Gilbert	21,100	29,229	38
9. Rochester, South Ave.	D. E. Haglund	13,622	20,500	51
10. Rochester, Waring	J. R. Nichols	3,508	5,096	46
11. Brockport	G. D. Manson	7,562	13,950	83
12. Chili Center	K. E. Hardy	3,700	4,636	24
13. East Rochester	Arthur Lacey	9,561	11,478	20
14. Fairport, First	J. E. Dahlen	8,560	11,578	36
15. Fairport, Raymond	E. L. Clendenning	9,158	11,642	26
16. Greece	F. E. Dean	24,750	36,550	47
17. Mumford, Second	Paul McDaniel	5,135	8,602	69
18. Le Roy, First	W. R. Spence	5,748	7,564	31
19. Ontario	Kent Kiser	7,900	11,800	49
20. Palmyra	H. J. Stephanz	5,436	9,289	70
21. Walworth	——	4,300	5,352	25
22. Wolcott	R. G. Gordon	5,829	8,300	43
Total		$277,066	$377,822	36

18. *Albany, New York, Sector, Spring, 1953*

Directors: J. R. Raker, Jr., and R. I. Madsen

Church	Minister	1952–1953 envelope receipts	1953–1954 pledges	Per cent increase
1. Albany, Emmanuel	A. F. Jennings	$ 19,600	$ 27,276	39
2. Albany, Hope	A. C. Davison	7,443	10,270	38
3. Albany, Madison Avenue	Kermit Lawton	11,100	16,378	47
4. Albany, Temple	E. W. Eldridge	12,700	17,895	41
5. Amsterdam	Derwood Smith	9,988	12,786	28
6. Burnt Hills	Thomas Hunter	1,106	5,251	374
7. Clifton Park	Earl Blansfield	5,015	7,511	50
8. Cohoes	G. F. McElvein	4,700	9,980	112
9. Gloversville	C. C. Hustead	10,707	15,929	49
10. Mechanicville	E. D. Wooddell	9,900	15,728	59
11. Preston Hollow	H. E. Kemp	2,400	4,722	96
12. Schenectady, Calvary	Benjamin Profio	6,116	7,919	29
13. Schenectady First	W. F. Nowlan	9,302	13,896	49
14. Schenectady Tabernacle	H. S. Jones	9,400	13,800	44
15. Scotia	W. R. Rogers	8,928	18,096	102
16. Troy, First	R. J. Bertholf	16,225	26,207	61
17. Troy, Millis Memorial	J. M. Wubbenhorst	2,699	5,215	93
18. Waterford	Fred Blue, Jr.	1,800	7,730	329
19. W. Hoosick	H. E. Hammer	4,074	5,722	40
Total		$153,205	$242,312	58

19. *Glens Falls, New York, Sector, Spring, 1953*

Directors: J. R. Raker, Jr., and E. R. Hughes

Church	Minister	1952–1953 envelope receipts	1953–1954 pledges	Per cent increase
1. Ballston Spa	J. B. Freestone	$ 7,692	$ 10,300	34
2. Bolton Landing	A. W. Curren	1,213	2,950	143
3. Cambridge	G. J. Knepka	1,359	3,155	132
4. E. Poultney, Vermont	W. C. Arbo	1,484	3,280	127
5. Fair Haven, Vermont	A. C. Wentworth	3,278	5,234	63
6. Glens Falls, First	A. K. Wise	19,931	27,759	38
7. Bottskill	L. N. Powell	4,917	9,284	89
8. Hartford	O. C. Corbett	1,167	4,331	271
9. Hudson Falls	LaRue Loughhead	13,300	18,046	36
10. Minerva	H. E. Hinton	2,100	3,896	86
11. North Creek	H. E. Hinton	2,023	4,002	98
12. Poultney, Vermont	Miss M. T. Borden	2,655	5,357	102
13. Rutland, Vermont	H. G. Ford	9,039	13,389	48
14. Saratoga Springs	L. J. Beynon, Jr.	13,250	21,585	62
15. Westport, Federated	J. E. Donovan	6,159	8,762	42
16. Whitehall	A. H. Ganoung	3,492	5,350	53
Total		$93,064	$146,684	61

20. *New York, New York, Sector, Spring, 1953*

Directors: M. M. Lewis and R. I. Madsen

Church	Minister	1952–1953 envelope receipts	1953–1954 pledges	Per cent increase
1. Central Park	E. F. Weston	$ 2,986	$ 4,432	48
2. Chambers Memorial	Harry Stevenson	2,738	3,583	31
3. Elmhurst	C. E. Kite	10,091	13,700	36
4. Emmanuel, Brooklyn	T. E. Miller	21,780	23,226	7
5. Garden City, L.I.	E. J. Shearman	18,402	19,622	7
6. Hollis Woods, L.I.	H. R. Johnson	7,665	11,990	56
7. Jamaica	J. N. Ziegler	13,064	14,632	12
8. Lefferts Park	B. T. Dahlberg	6,078	9,000	48
9. Lenox Road	G. H. Baker	8,622	11,856	38
10. Madison Avenue	Ralph Walker	6,349	11,051	74
11. Mt. Vernon	D. H. Miller	33,212	44,221	33
12. Parkchester	M. W. Carrico	7,703	12,327	60
13. Park, Port Richmond	A. C. Porteous	15,065	16,500	10
14. Queens	J. C. Robbins	19,870	31,040	56
15. Redeemer, Brooklyn	M. J. S. Ford	15,491	25,133	62
16. Rockville Center, L.I.	C. C. McLaughlan	14,266	16,747	17
Total		$203,389	$269,062	32

21. *Camden, New Jersey, Sector, Spring, 1953*

Directors: H. F. Stoddard and G. W. Swope

Church	Minister	1952–1953 envelope receipts	1953–1954 pledges	Per cent increase
1. Bordentown	C. R. Pedersen	$ 6,856	$ 12,189	77
2. Beverly	J. A. Swetnam	5,898	5,941	0
3. Camden, Fairview	J. A. Dillon	7,742	13,530	75
4. Camden, Parkside	C. E. Garrett	6,500	7,422	14
5. Chesterfield	A. V. Allen	1,325	5,089	284
6. Jacobstown	A. V. Allen	1,324	3,537	167
7. Collingswood	Stanley Nodder	19,124	30,515	60
8. Erlton	——	12,374	21,138	70
9. Haddonfield	R. G. Middleton	24,000	36,100	50
10. Hightstown	Leland Higginbotham	9,500	23,146	157
11. Hornerstown	Gordon Schweitzer	462	1,208	161
12. Mt. Holly	W. G. Hackler	13,216	16,617	25
13. Mt. Royal, Berkley	Albutt Gardner, Jr.	2,208	4,607	108
14. Oaklyn	J. H. Allen	12,020	17,007	41
15. Pennsauken, Calvary	J. R. Hawley	8,552	13,650	52
16. Pennsauken, Highland Community	——	3,465	8,452	145
17. Pitman	R. A. Mahoney	8,102	10,964	34
18. Salem, Memorial	Garrett Detweiler	6,846	14,334	109
19. Trenton, First	J. B. Peterson	12,405	14,700	18
20. Trenton, Memorial	F. H. West	5,019	8,282	65
21. Trenton, Olivet	F. V. Hanley, Jr.	6,815	10,810	72
22. Trenton, St. Johns	Joseph Bolognese	2,403	4,640	93
23. Woodbury, Central	W. R. McNutt	12,010	22,300	86
24. Woodstown	Eric Osterle	8,792	12,790	42
Total		$196,958	$318,968	61

22. *Charleston, West Virginia, Sector, Spring, 1953*

Directors: C. R. Osborn and R. I. Madsen

Church	Minister	1952–1953 envelope receipts	1953–1954 pledges	Per cent increase
1. Chelyan	R. B. Nelson	$ 9,183	$ 16,104	75
2. Clendenin	J. R. Gillespie	4,547	9,720	113
3. Emmanuel, Charleston	W. G. Farmar	21,816	24,000	10
4. Gauley Bridge	P. E. Vandercoy	5,934	6,650	12
5. Hampton	B. W. Griffith	3,621	5,950	64
6. Highlawn, St. Albans	L. M. Keeney	11,861	18,072	52
7. Hurricane	B. H. Grubb	11,203	24,000	114
8. Judson, Belle	G. R. Pauley	7,752	16,915	118
9. Kanawha City	C. T. Hensley	7,310	6,000	−17
10. Madison	H. E. Waltz	9,667	14,928	54
11. Montgomery	J. M. Fogg	10,593	8,545	−19
12. Nitro	W. B. Moyer	15,000	16,110	7
13. St. Albans	J. L. Emery	43,839	55,092	25
14. South Charleston	H. L. Parkinson	21,620	41,000	89
15. Starcher	T. H. Kingston	12,549	17,980	43
Total		$196,495	$281,066	43

23. *Columbus, Ohio, Sector, Spring, 1953*

Directors: H. E. MacCombie and C. A. Pepper

Church	Minister	1952–1953 envelope receipts	1953–1954 pledges	Per cent increase
1. Columbus, First	R. L. Bailey	$ 36,281	$ 48,782	34
2. Columbus, Maynard Ave.	B. V. Arthur	3,492	7,423	113
3. Columbus, South High	N. H. Sanders	7,400	9,934	34
4. Columbus, Tenth Ave.	E. L. Hill	14,670	18,636	27
5. Delaware	J. B. Stephenson	3,028	4,705	55
6. Marion, Fite Memorial	N. D. Renn	11,641	18,204	56
7. Marion, Trinity	J. B. Holloway	22,878	27,248	17
8. Newark, First	C. M. Pomeroy	16,395	23,028	40
Total		$115,785	$157,960	36

24. Indianapolis, Indiana, Sector, Spring, 1953

Directors: J. F. Knight and H. E. MacCombie

Church	Minister	1952–1953 envelope receipts	1953–1954 pledges	Per cent increase
1. Cumberland	C. E. Williams	$ 8,776	$ 13,243	51
2. Indianapolis, Emerson Ave.	R. E. Halls	19,599	25,000	26
3. Indianapolis, First	O. D. Pruett	66,400	71,587	8
4. Indianapolis, Franklin Road	J. W. Kinnett	5,449	17,582	223
5. Indianapolis, Garfield Park	Walter Laetsch	18,200	39,468	117
6. Indianapolis, Memorial	G. G. Kimsey	9,500	13,221	38
7. Indianapolis, New Bethel	P. T. Rushford	9,824	11,870	21
8. Indianapolis, North	W. R. Jewell	1,673	2,626	57
9. Indianapolis, Tabernacle	C. C. Moman	11,500	20,000	74
10. Indianapolis, Woodland	W. A. Hull	7,265	14,830	104
11. Indianapolis, Woodruff Place	W. R. Hand	27,100	40,190	48
12. Alexandria	George Calhoun	12,600	17,600	34
13. Anderson, First	K. P. Losh	28,745	52,278	82
14. Anderson, Meadowbrook	Phillip Philbrook	11,155	23,300	109
15. Columbus	S. E. Mugridge	20,262	33,128	63
16. Franklin	Walter Marchand	19,660	30,287	54
17. Hope	Miles Raisor	6,365	8,018	26
18. Shelbyville	Melvin Phillips	13,162	17,178	31
19. Southport	R. H. Lindstrom	19,250	37,676	95
20. Waldron	K. Neuenschwander	4,000	9,567	139
Total		$320,485	$498,649	55

25. Detroit, Michigan, Sector, Spring, 1953

Directors: R. J. Hanson and A. L. Farrell

Church	Minister	1952–1953 envelope receipts	1953–1954 pledges	Per cent increase
1. Covenant, Detroit	W. R. Cole	$122,713	$135,090	10
2. Dearborn, Calvary	W. J. Montgomery	24,100	31,125	29
3. East Detroit	W. H. Schobert	8,300	13,075	58
4. Ferndale, First	C. F. Hamilton	20,242	22,055	9
5. First, Detroit	G. H. Grotey	37,436	45,500	22
6. Garden City, First	I. F. Rose	7,301	10,101	38
7. Hurlbut Ave., Detroit	C. J. Pearse	7,300	11,502	58
8. Immanuel, Detroit	Harlan Stenger	15,570	22,118	49
9. Jefferson Ave., Detroit	H. J. Armstrong	36,509	50,899	39
10. Northwestern, Detroit	Hale Thornberry	43,744	52,195	19
11. Norwayne, Detroit	H. E. Secord	5,506	9,171	67
12. Plymouth	D. L. Rieder	7,250	19,542	169
13. Redford, Detroit	R. S. Shahbaz	17,732	28,000	58
14. Royal Oak, First	W. W. Clark	57,866	72,144	25
15. Woodward Ave., Detroit	W. J. Washer	19,746	24,970	26
16. Wyandotte, First	Robert Lietz	13,819	16,700	21
Total		$450,114	$570,759	27

26. *Lansing, Michigan, Sector, Spring, 1953*

Directors: R. J. Hanson and A. L. Farrell

Church	Minister	1952–1953 envelope receipts	1953–1954 pledges	Per cent increase
1. Alma	J. L. Lewis	$ 4,576	$ 5,662	24
2. Ann Arbor	C. H. Loucks	24,107	31,391	30
3. Bath	R. E. Briggs	4,438	8,081	82
4. Battle Creek, First	H. K. Shafer	19,508	25,756	32
5. Battle Creek, Lakeview	G. D. Seifert	8,800	15,646	78
6. Belding	P. D. Warford	8,560	14,643	71
7. Grand Rapids, Burton Hghts.	C. A. Lawton	11,960	17,554	47
8. Gregory	W. T. Cochran	3,933	6,800	75
9. Harbor Beach	James Burgess	7,346	11,051	50
10. Howell	M. R. Meeden	13,322	20,000	50
11. Ionia	W. W. Pixley	5,547	7,687	39
12. Jackson, First	R. L. Pobst	20,400	26,000	27
13. Kalamazoo, First	T. T. Wylie	39,075	51,856	33
14. Kalamazoo, Portage St.	C. R. Hulbert	8,120	16,733	106
15. Lansing, First	Julius Fischbach	42,338	50,827	20
16. Lansing, Judson	G. A. Miles	13,228	15,829	20
17. Lansing, Olivet	H. E. Harfst	11,410	17,215	51
18. Lansing, Penn. Ave.	L. W. Boyd	9,660	14,762	53
19. Marshall	Peter Bissett	7,436	11,836	59
20. Mason	L. G. Caraway	5,900	8,056	37
21. Mayville	Robert Hewitt	5,950	9,344	57
22. Midland	R. D. Hotelling	17,034	28,240	66
23. Millington	D. E. Glasgow	4,420	6,284	42
24. Monroe	H. C. Carnell	18,438	22,437	22
25. Niles	R. L. McCoy	11,820	18,397	56
26. Owosso	E. F. Norton	10,668	13,880	30
27. Ovid	R. E. Briggs	4,715	5,543	18
28. Pontiac, Bethany	F. R. Tiffany	24,838	33,796	36
29. Saginaw, Michigan Ave.	H. C. Hall	14,239	19,300	36
30. Shelton Park	Keith Goss	3,091	5,138	66
31. South Haven	Eugene Burgess	3,516	6,617	88
32. Walled Lake	Wendall Maloch	6,000	7,038	17
33. Willow Run	——	2,760	5,525	100
Total		$397,153	$558,924	47

27. *Alton, Illinois, Sector, Spring, 1953*

Directors: R. J. Hanson and R. W. Sorensen

Church	Minister	1952–1953 envelope receipts	1953–1954 pledges	Per cent increase
1. Alton, Cherry St.	W. F. Privett	$ 21,089	$ 26,209	24
2. Alton, First	R. E. Turnbull	23,219	27,282	17
3. Upper Alton	La Rue Jensen	19,731	24,714	24
4. Alton, Main St.	Horton Presley	5,497	9,100	65
5. Alton, Twing Memorial	J. F. Glock	2,153	2,285	6
6. Cottage Hills	J. B. Head	6,293	21,831	246
7. East Alton, First	W. F. Bohn	15,498	20,000	29
8. Wood River	E. J. White	17,700	21,039	18
9. East St. Louis	Rayburn Dunbar	21,875	23,445	7
10. Belleville	S. B. Janssen	14,960	17,037	13
11. Kane	William Sealock	6,050	7,727	27
12. Highland	Jack Brown	5,626	6,200	10
13. Hillsboro	J. H. Scheibe	2,200	5,264	139
14. Jerseyville, First	LaVerne Poole	19,600	21,099	7
15. Edwardsville	L. C. Boergadine	10,400	16,840	61
Total		$191,891	$250,072	30

28. *Milwaukee, Wisconsin, Sector, Spring, 1953*

Directors: H. A. Schlink and Jack Krause

Church	Minister	1952–1953 envelope receipts	1953–1954 pledges	Per cent increase
1. Milwaukee, Blue Mound	W. A. Peebles	$ 3,461	$ 4,820	39
2. Milwaukee, First*	B. W. Kinlaw	18,485	20,296	9
3. Milwaukee, Grace	Wayne Christensen	7,612	9,846	29
4. Milwaukee, Roundy Memorial	Carl McAllister	12,508	18,175	45
5. Milwaukee, Tabernacle	C. E. Fretz	16,271	18,293	12
6. Oconomowoc	C. W. Bloedow	4,956	5,813	17
7. Kenosha, First	J. K. Huyck	13,802	14,782	7
8. Fond du Lac	F. M. Morse	20,804	22,700	10
Total		$97,899	$114,725	17

* Second year in using sector techniques.

29. *Beloit, Wisconsin, Sector, Spring, 1953*

Directors: H. A. Schlink and R. W. Sorensen

Church	Minister	1952–1953 envelope receipts	1953–1954 pledges	Per cent increase
1. Beloit, First	W. O. Macoskey	$13,793	$ 25,080	82
2. Janesville, First	W. A. Dalton	16,322	22,261	36
3. Delavan	E. M. Wegner	6,404	10,181	59
4. Elkhorn	R. C. Werner	4,735	5,668	20
5. Marengo, Illinois	J. J. Garver	8,551	10,560	23
6. Rockford, State St.	N. L. Godbey	14,426	26,918	87
7. Belvidere, Illinois	S. L. Buchanan	6,600	7,732	17
Total		$70,831	$108,400	53

30. *Twin Cities, Minnesota, Sector, Spring, 1953*

Directors: W. E. Hayler and J. I. Chapman

Church	Minister	1952–1953 envelope receipts	1953–1954 pledges	Per cent increase
1. Hopkins	Robert Wheatley	$ 1,964	$ 4,548	128
2. Minneapolis, Calvary	O. L. Ice	23,433	30,284	29
3. Minneapolis, Judson Mem.	A. J. Jeffries	21,816	38,678	77
4. Minneapolis, Temple	C. A. Thunn	22,065	26,759	22
5. Minneapolis, University	J. S. Bone	11,292	17,341	54
6. St. Paul, First	Pieter Smit	26,702	35,153	25
7. St. Paul, Lake Park	J. H. Beyer	2,769	5,526	101
8. St. Paul, Pilgrim	Floyd Massey, Jr.	14,750	19,232	30
Total		$124,791	$177,523	42

31. *Sioux Falls, South Dakota, Sector, Spring, 1953*

Directors: W. E. Hayler and Otto Nallinger

Church	Minister	1952–1953 envelope receipts	1953–1954 pledges	Per cent increase
1. Brookings	E. E. Klein	$11,000	$ 13,230	20
2. Dell Rapids	H. J. Smith	3,100	4,885	58
3. Mitchell	G. W. Hendrixson	5,978	11,157	88
4. Sioux Falls, Emmanuel	H. S. McMullen	7,850	11,460	46
5. Sioux Falls, First	A. M. Hintz	49,047	56,132	14
6. Trent	S. G. Cleveland	3,950	5,837	46
Total		$80,925	$102,701	27

32. Seattle, Washington, Sector, Spring, 1953

Directors: R. M. Rushton and Jack Krause

Church	Minister	1952–1953 envelope receipts	1953–1954 pledges	Per cent increase
1. Everett, First	C. E. Shikles	$ 32,300	$ 37,605	16
2. Everett, Delta	J. E. H. Nelson	5,850	6,295	8
3. Everett, Memorial	F. H. Fahringer	2,457	4,397	80
4. Marysville, First	Peter Stroem	5,250	7,639	45
5. Seattle, Calvary	J. L. Ross	8,928	10,670	19
6. Seattle, Columbia	J. W. Bowles	5,580	7,016	25
7. Seattle, First	H. V. Jensen	81,768	94,195	15
8. Seattle, Japanese	M. Wada	3,850	5,372	40
9. Seattle, Oak Lake	Wellington Chew	6,700	9,200	37
10. Seattle, Ridgecrest	A. H. Plummer	6,107	8,457	38
11. Seattle, University	A. S. MacNair	23,544	28,601	21
12. Seattle, Washington Pk.	David Hungerford	2,700	3,800	41
13. Seattle, West Side	R. E. Best	11,432	20,889	83
14. Tacoma, 6th Ave.	V. A. McKee	23,329	26,000	11
15. Tacoma, Grace	Aubrey Splawn	5,454	4,834	−11
Total		$225,249	$274,970	22

33. Southern California Sector, Spring, 1953

Directors: J. A. Ramsay and Melvin A. Pekrul

Church	Minister	1952–1953 envelope receipts	1953–1954 pledges	Per cent increase
1. Anaheim, First	Robert Kevorkian	$ 15,168	$ 24,950	64
2. Arcadia, First	C. B. Flint	7,189	11,184	55
3. Blythe, First	R. R. Pulliam	11,132	29,133	162
4. Inglewood, First	Herman Rice	27,463	55,191	101
5. Long Beach, University*	G. W. Fussell	827	8,400	
6. Los Angeles, Southside Bethany	C. S. Maddox	14,063	16,808	19
7. Los Angeles, Wilshire	M. O. Brininstool	11,305	15,042	33
8. Monrovia, First	M. A. Pekrul	26,111	29,300	12
9. Pasadena, Tremont	F. A. Robertson	18,153	28,125	54
10. Sunland, First	J. F. Lane	15,750	21,157	34
11. Temple City, First	E. A. Williams	26,719	33,227	24
12. Santa Monica, Trinity	F. M. Judson	55,305	82,255	48
13. West Covina	C. H. Mazouch	1,105	3,977	262
14. West Hollywood	S. P. Cornils	16,171	17,847	10
15. Woodland Hills	Grant Yeatman	3,237	7,619	135
Total		$249,698	$384,215	54

* Since this church was organized six months before the campaign, it is impossible to give a true comparison with the preceding year.

34. *Berkshire, Massachusetts, Sector, Spring, 1953*

Directors: O. A. Pendleton and N. E. Woodbury

Church	Minister	1952–1953 envelope receipts	1953–1954 pledges	Per cent increase
1. Adams, First	A. E. Darby	$ 4,138	$ 6,237	51
2. Becket, Federated	W. K. Price	2,092	5,585	166
3. Florida, First	C. I. Osterhout	1,275	3,076	141
4. Lanesboro, Federated	F. C. Peters	2,056	5,733	178
5. North Adams, First	R. K. Adams	27,152	35,385	30
6. Pittsfield, First*	C. B. Jensen	33,959	39,109	15
7. Pittsfield, Morningside*	P. D. Chamberlain	22,900	27,919	21
8. Pownal Parishes	Richard Hall	7,000	10,200	46
9. Stamford, Vermont	J. H. Fletcher	960	2,857	198
Total		$101,532	$136,101	35

* Followed the sector techniques the year before.

35. *Rhode Island, Sector II, Spring, 1953*

Directors: P. R. Shaub and O. A. Pendleton

Church	Minister	1952–1953 envelope receipts	1953–1954 pledges	Per cent increase
FIRST-TIME CHURCHES				
1. East Providence, Second	——	$ 5,237	$ 12,503	119
2. Pascoag	H. R. Collins	3,935	9,033	129
3. Pawtucket, Memorial	E. R. Ramsdell	5,862	9,090	59
4. Pawtucket, Woodlawn	N. J. Smith	16,505	22,515	37
5. Westerly, Central	J. W. Elliott	20,310	24,759	21
Total		$ 51,849	$ 77,900	50
REPEAT CHURCHES (second year in a sector)				
6. Cranston, People's	L. F. Kenney	20,401	24,055	18
7. Pawtucket, Bethany	H. H. Powell	7,530	8,348	10
8. Providence, Central	P. L. Sturges	29,750	32,400	9
9. Providence, Roger Williams	F. E. Gardner	12,329	11,685	−5
10. Warwick, Spring Green	K. S. Dannenhauer	3,975	5,034	26
11. Warwick, Central	F. L. Parsons	11,741	10,389	−13
Total		$ 85,726	$ 91,911	7
Grand Total		$137,575	$169,811	23

36. *Springfield, Massachusetts, Sector, Interdenominational, Autumn, 1953*

Directors: O. A. Pendleton and H. B. Keir

Church	Minister	1953 envelope receipts	1954 pledges	Per cent increase
First-time Churches				
BAPTIST				
1. Agawam*	B. T. Lockhart	$ 11,500	$ 11,365	−1
2. Westfield, Central	R. L. Wallace	7,259	12,812	76
CONGREGATIONAL				
3. Agawam	E. T. Chapman	9,198	20,500	123
4. Chicopee Falls	Philip Kelsey	5,087	6,950	28
5. Holyoke, First	Walter Telfer	21,700	25,000	15
6. Holyoke, Second	J. W. Trexler	48,842	59,023	21
7. Northampton, First	B. R. Andrews, Jr.	15,028	22,328	49
8. North Wilbraham	J. K. Moorehead	3,400	5,850	72
9. South Hadley	J. L. Lancaster	17,221	22,000	28
10. Springfield, Emmanuel	A. J. Stanton	18,550	34,593	87
11. Springfield, Union	C. S. Lantz	7,000	10,954	56
12. Westfield, Second	E. W. Brown	8,638	17,924	107
EPISCOPAL				
13. Chicopee, Grace	R. H. Cummings	5,200	11,978	131
14. Longmeadow, St. Andrews	Charles Havens, Jr.	13,284	23,450	77
15. N. Agawam, St. David's	R. B. Lane	2,693	6,289	133
16. Springfield, Christ Cathedral	M. F. Williams	29,000	33,350	15
17. Springfield, St. Barnabas	G. P. Donelly	8,397	17,862	113
18. Springfield, St. Luke's	E. J. H. Nichols	6,100	15,315	150
19. Westfield, Atonement	P. T. Shultz, Jr.	8,500	18,500	117
METHODIST				
20. Chicopee Falls	E. F. Redfern	6,307	10,573	70
21. Springfield, St. James	G. D. Glazier	5,900	12,926	118
22. Westfield, First	H. N. Clay	12,329	23,684	93
23. W. Springfield, Mittineague	Ralph Norsworthy	8,350	12,715	52
FEDERATED				
24. Hampden	Arthur Sanders	7,128	13,750	93
Total (first-time Churches)		$286,611	$449,691	56
Repeat Churches (second year in a sector)				
BAPTIST				
25. Holyoke, Second	J. D. Burnett	$ 19,077	$ 20,977	10
26. Springfield, First	B. F. Archibald	41,825	44,112	6
27. Springfield, Park Memorial	W. A. Aschenbach	26,000	28,265	10
CONGREGATIONAL				
28. Ludlow	E. L. Wallace	11,405	12,715	11
29. Springfield, First	J. E. Wallace	60,164	60,000	0
30. Springfield, Wachogue	Howard Munson	7,441	9,305	25
EPISCOPAL				
31. Springfield, St. Peter's	G. W. Smith, Jr.	12,182	17,096	40
32. W. Springfield, Good Shepherd	R. W. D. Smith	9,416	11,856	26

Repeat Churches (second year in a sector) (*continued*)

Church	Minister	1953 envelope receipts	1954 pledges	Per cent increase
METHODIST				
33. Springfield, Wesley	L. W. Johnson	32,196	36,494	13
34. West Springfield, First	Prescott Grout	5,649	6,300	11
OTHER				
35. Springfield, First Christian	C. E. Miller	2,518	3,643	44
36. Church of Unity	E. H. Sommerfeld	15,200	14,296	−6
Total (repeat churches)		$243,073	$265,059	9
Grand total (36 churches)		$529,684	$714,750	35

* Followed the sector technique the year before.

37. *Burlington, Vermont, Sector, Interdenominational, Autumn, 1953*

Directors: O. A. Pendleton and H. C. Bryant

Church	Minister	1953 envelope receipts	1954 pledges	Per cent increase
BAPTIST				
1. Bristol, First	H. B. Van Vliet	$ 3,838	$ 6,239	62
2. Burlington, First*	R. L. Johnson	14,545	17,573	21
3. Richford, First	G. M. Miller	4,100	7,521	83
BAPTIST AND CONGREGATIONAL				
4. Charlotte, Federated	R. A. Frye	3,000	4,211	40
5. Colchester, United	E. G. Bucklin	3,252	6,283	96
CONGREGATIONAL				
6. Barre	R. J. Divine	11,440	19,517	67
7. Burlington, College St.	L. L. Gilbert	11,562	17,413	51
8. Burlington, First	C. S. Jones	42,149	59,776	40
9. East Barre	C. J. Parsley	2,486	8,700	240
10. Essex Junction	R. A. Snelling	6,745	11,331	49
11. Lyndonville	W. R. Mayhew	7,900	11,246	63
CONGREGATIONAL AND METHODIST				
12. Milton, United	P. E. Barnes	5,241	6,315	21
13. Northfield, United	D. W. Morgan	2,447	7,607	211
METHODIST				
14. Burlington, First	H. F. Goewey	25,946	31,453	21
UNITARIAN				
15. Burlington	R. S. Miller	8,274	14,320	73
Total		$152,925	$229,505	50

* Second year in using sector techniques.

38. *Boise, Idaho, Sector, Spring, 1954*

Directors: D. S. Dodson and M. E. Bratcher

Church	Minister	1953–1954 envelope receipts	1954–1955 pledges	Per cent increase
1. Boise, First	H. E. Coulter	$31,528	$46,787	38
2. Boise Valley	M. Y. Miller	2,473	6,173	149
3. Gooding	G. W. Goddard	4,542	9,415	107
4. Nampa	Frank McCray	9,168	10,695	16
5. Payette	B. R. Iddins	10,040	13,860	38
Total		$57,751	$86,930	50

39. *Portland, Oregon, Sector, Spring, 1954*

Directors: E. C. Adams and M. E. Bratcher

Church	Minister	1953–1954 envelope receipts	1954–1955 pledges	Per cent increase
1. Aloha	Erling Monnes	$ 3,311	$ 7,656	131
2. Camas, Wash.	Lyndall Logee	5,834	7,428	27
3. Gresham	J. E. McDowell	7,019	13,197	88
4. McMinnville	E. E. Smith	13,209	21,831	65
5. Oceanlake	Phil Kinkel	739	3,160	327
6. Portland, Arleta	Walfred Erickson	7,051	7,479	6
7. Portland, Calvary	J. S. Congdon	2,042	5,301	159
8. Portland, Canyon Road	———	2,348	4,185	78
9. Portland, Fellowship	James Bennett	1,206	4,317	259
10. Portland, Glenhaven	C. M. Strong	1,183	2,820	138
11. Portland, Grace	E. W. Roberts	12,558	13,000	3
12. Portland, Grant Park	S. P. Benson	13,863	17,934	29
13. Portland, Highland	D. F. Thomas	13,543	15,701	15
14. Portland, Mount Olive	J. J. Clow	10,276	12,913	24
15. Portland, Pleasant Valley	Marvin Skidmore	1,999	4,200	110
16. Salem, Calvary	H. I. Fox	24,524	30,818	25
17. Stayton	Nick Neufeld	1,442	5,446	285
Total		$122,147	$177,386	45

40. *Akron, Ohio, Sector, Spring, 1954*

Directors: H. E. MacCombie and W. T. Packer

Church	Minister	1953–1954 envelope receipts	1954–1955 pledges	Per cent increase
1. Akron, Arlington St.	G. W. Terjung	$ 28,000	$ 39,645	40
2. Akron, Calvary	H. S. Wilson	24,480	36,300	49
3. Akron, Goodyear Heights	G. W. Weber	27,900	37,750	35
4. Akron, West Hills	Roy Evans	30,680	38,700	27
5. Alliance	Walter Loomis	15,250	19,193	26
6. Barberton, First	O. W. Tibbets	23,300	44,920	93
7. Campbell, First	J. D. Michael	4,589	11,807	157
8. Cuyahoga Falls	J. R. Pennington	8,000	13,807	72
9. Darrowville	A. L. Derry	3,500	7,638	118
10. Hubbard	C. A. Weed	14,500	23,046	58
11. Warren, First	C. H. French	17,998	26,000	44
12. Youngstown, Calvary	John Krier	20,747	27,470	32
13. Youngstown, Immanuel	Joseph Westcott	11,600	20,438	76
Total		$230,544	$346,714	50

41. *Marion, Indiana, Sector, Spring, 1954*

Directors: H. E. MacCombie and J. F. Knight

Church	Minister	1953–1954 envelope receipts	1954–1955 pledges	Per cent increase
1. Alexandria (Ohio)	L. J. Day	$ 18,500	$ 19,000	3
2. Anderson, First	K. P. Losh	48,200	49,000	2
3. Decatur	Eugene McAlister	9,500	15,221	60
4. Elwood	R. W. Sage	9,366	15,587	66
5. Frankfort	C. H. Wallace	15,000	26,010	73
6. Indianapolis, Central	Harm Weber	10,966	21,185	93
7. Indianapolis, Immanuel	F. F. Smith	7,680	13,225	72
8. Liberty Center	Raymond King	6,401	7,890	23
9. Logansport	M. L. Robinson	18,534	30,680	66
10. Marion, First	Harry Mattingly	17,584	23,570	34
11. Muncie, First	R. C. Johnson	41,345	56,000	35
12. Rochester	H. G. Hyde	8,531	12,281	43
13. Salem, Second	Raymond Riley	2,300	5,000	117
Total		$213,907	$294,649	38

42. *Cleveland, Ohio, Sector, Spring, 1954*

Directors: H. E. MacCombie and A. C. Hull, Jr.

Church	Minister	1953–1954 envelope receipts	1954–1955 pledges	Per cent increase
1. Broadview	R. G. Van Court	$ 5,600	$ 10,514	89
2. Cleveland, Antioch	W. H. McKinney	58,500	82,100	40
3. Cleveland, Chesterland	Allan McGaw	4,444	11,439	157
4. Cleveland, Church of the Master	R. C. Newell	16,500	23,891	44
5. Cleveland, Columbia	G. K. Tuttle	5,800	9,180	58
6. Cleveland, East	W. E. Towner	24,000	33,400	39
7. Cleveland, Euclid Ave.	J. J. Wilkes	13,500	20,008	48
8. Cleveland, Euclid Immanuel	E. J. Dreisinger	15,770	20,610	30
9. Cleveland, Fairview	S. H. Cassell, Jr.	31,000	41,307	33
10. Cleveland, Fidelity	R. D. Short	5,487	9,438	72
11. Cleveland, First	H. C. Phillips	105,000	132,000	25
12. Cleveland, Garfield, Trinity	H. B. Parrott	21,965	31,956	45
13. Cleveland, Lakewood	L. H. Lomas	46,000	55,832	17
14. Cleveland, Lee Road	D. L. Wright	6,201	12,870	107
15. Cleveland, Lyndhurst	Harrison Williams	14,280	21,018	47
16. Cleveland, Roumanian	Danila Pascu	2,434	2,970	22
17. Cleveland, South Hills	Grant McMichael	15,000	17,000	14
18. Cleveland, West Shore	J. S. Conover	4,400	8,839	100
19. Lorain, First	Floyd Buckland	7,000	14,607	108
Total		$402,881	$558,979	38

43. *Decatur, Illinois, Sector, Spring, 1954*

Directors: J. F. Scott and C. R. Osborn

Church	Minister	1953–1954 envelope receipts	1954–1955 pledges	Per cent increase
1. Arthur	Kenneth Tyler	$ 6,074	$ 7,729	27
2. Bloomington	Rudolph Loidolt	19,482	22,122	12
3. Champaign, First	Paul Goodwin	19,112	23,328	22
4. Charleston	——	7,019	9,804	40
5. Lincoln	E. H. Eckstein	5,755	9,369	63
6. Mattoon, First	M. M. Dice	17,181	32,506	88
7. Moweaqua	Ray Smith, Jr.	6,706	8,000	20
8. Springfield, Fairview	Ransom Hines	1,529	2,524	65
9. Tuscola	Wayne Brackett	1,810	3,285	82
10. Urbana	Carleton Goodwin	13,927	15,891	14
Total		$98,595	$134,558	36

44. *Wichita, Kansas, Sector, Spring, 1954*

Directors: C. C. Browne and W. E. Hayler

Church	Minister	1953–1954 envelope receipts	1954–1955 pledges	Per cent increase
1. Derby	H. A. Low	$ 5,324	$ 8,924	67
2. McPherson	R. M. Wood	24,862	34,346	38
3. Newton	C. J. Mustain	25,836	29,876	16
4. Pratt	J. H. Cochrane	12,326	26,948	118
5. Valley Center	Frank Bentley	12,175	13,146	9
6. Wichita, Old Manor	J. J. Zier	14,353	25,662	78
7. Wichita, Trinity	J. L. Robbins	13,260	15,960	19
8. Wichita, West Side	B. E. Mills	23,383	26,036	11
Total		$131,519	$180,898	37

45. *Syracuse, New York, Sector, Spring, 1954*

Directors: J. R. Raker, Jr., R. I. Madsen and O. A. Pendleton

Church	Minister	1953–1954 envelope receipts	1954–1955 pledges	Per cent increase
1. Auburn	R. D. Ross	$ 9,232	$ 18,073	96
2. Baldwinsville	Walter Anderson	6,130	14,157	131
3. Camillus	Earl Abel	8,723	13,167	51
4. Cazenovia Village	F. N. Darling	8,000	11,995	50
5. Fabius	G. J. Smith	3,150	7,575	140
6. Fulton	W. A. Van Arsdale	12,215	21,178	74
7. Groton	J. H. Rood	5,565	8,740	57
8. Meridian	R. S. Komp	2,210	5,395	144
9. Oneida	E. W. Fetter	6,945	9,367	35
10. Oswego, First	L. C. Jackman	3,115	6,795	118
11. Oswego, West	A. S. Lowrie	8,511	12,555	47
12. Phoenix	C. Bammesberger	3,000	7,939	165
13. Syracuse, Bethany	L. R. Murphy	9,000	17,953	99
14. Syracuse, Calvary	George Middleton	10,000	14,506	45
15. Syracuse, Delaware St.	C. M. Thompson, Jr.	26,832	36,990	38
16. Syracuse, Eastwood	Nicholas Titus	43,000	51,800	20
17. Syracuse, Fairmount Union	Edward Gunther	14,800	23,800	61
18. Syracuse, Lowell Ave.	William George	4,100	7,353	79
19. Syracuse, Tabernacle	Samuel Fehl	11,198	20,888	87
20. Syracuse, Immanuel	C. C. Walker	5,709	8,750	53
Total		$201,435	$318,976	58

46. Binghamton, New York, Sector, Spring, 1954

Directors: J. R. Raker, Jr., R. I. Madsen and O. A. Pendleton

Church	Minister	1953–1954 envelope receipts	1954–1955 pledges	Per cent increase
1. Athens, Pennsylvania	W. S. Hammond	$ 6,400	$ 9,505	49
2. Binghamton, Conklin Ave.	————	23,000	35,700	55
3. Binghamton, Main Street	C. G. Brownville	23,000	28,413	23
4. Binghamton, Port Dickinson	Norman Lawton	7,800	18,800	141
5. Endicott, Vestal	F. E. Oerth	5,600	8,438	51
6. Oxford	A. L. Anderson	8,273	11,279	36
7. Sayre, Pennsylvania	Edward Cuthbert	5,625	11,892	111
Total		$79,698	$124,027	55

47. Milford, Massachusetts, Sector, Interdenominational, Autumn, 1954

Directors: N. E. Woodbury and O. A. Pendleton

Church	Minister	1954 envelope receipts	1955 pledges	Per cent increase
1. Hudson, Federated	E. M. Hand	$ 5,893	$10,059	71
2. Manchaug, Baptist	Jarle Brörs	600	1,742	190
3. Mendon, Baptist	W. C. Nelson	2,355	6,750	193
4. Milford, Congregational	D. G. DeBoer	6,574	11,087	70
5. Milford, First Methodist	Floyd Duren	8,114	11,500	32
6. West Sutton, Baptist	Jarle Brörs	1,700	4,048	139
7. Westwood, First Baptist*	L. L. Maxfield	7,000	13,000	86
8. Woodville, Baptist	Thomas.Elliott	1,800	6,350	356
Total		$34,036	$64,536	90

* Did not follow complete ten-step program.

48. *Reading, Massachusetts, Sector, Interdenominational, Autumn, 1954*

Directors: N. E. Woodbury and O. A. Pendleton

Church	Minister	1954 envelope receipts	1955 pledges	Per cent increase
1. Arlington Heights Methodist	N. S. Booth	$ 8,995	$ 13,520	50
2. Lynn, East Baptist	J. M. Greer	17,155	26,980	49
3. Lynn, First Baptist	H. W. Buker	13,960	16,800	20
4. Medford, First Methodist	W. J. Cook	9,000	23,000	155
5. Medford, St. John's Methodist	J. L. Christian	3,415	7,100	108
6. Medford Hillside Methodist	J. S. Leslie	9,155	12,000	25
7. Reading, First Baptist*	H. C. Mathews	12,514	16,625	33
8. Somerville, Broadway Congregational	W. T. Howe	8,220	9,496	16
9. Stoneham, First Baptist*	F. W. Hensley	15,457	17,575	13
10. West Medford, Trinity Methodist	S. M. Seminerio	8,313	12,904	55
11. Weston, First Baptist*	Joseph O'Donnell	10,511	13,550	29
Total		$116,649	$169,550	45

* Second year in using sector techniques.

49. *Bangor, Maine, Sector, Interdenominational, Autumn, 1954*

Directors: T. L. Brindley and O. A. Pendleton

Church	Minister	1954 envelope receipts	1955 pledges	Per cent increase
BAPTIST				
1. Bangor, Columbia St.*	A. W. Geary	$28,014	$ 42,675	54
2. Bangor, Essex St.	C. A. Marstaller	5,996	12,328	105
3. Bar Harbor†	V. W. Dyer	3,650	4,256	17
4. Ellsworth	Paul Keirstead	6,250	9,520	52
5. Bradley	A. M. Kilpatrick	2,102	4,153	98
6. Milo	L. A. Perry	4,925	10,636	120
7. Millinocket	Donald Thompson	8,000	17,764	122
OTHER				
8. Millinocket, Congregational		8,000	12,300	52
9. Millinocket, Episcopal		5,390	7,660	42
Total		$72,327	$121,292	68

* This church previously increased 58 per cent in Waterville sector two years earlier.
† Did not follow complete ten-step program.

50. *Syracuse, New York, Sector, Interdenominational, Autumn, 1954*

Directors: J. R. Raker, Jr., and James Bennett

Church	Minister	1954 envelope receipts	1955 pledges	Per cent increase
BAPTIST (and Baptist related)				
1. Canastota	Arthur Wentworth	$ 4,071	$ 9,460	131
2. Elbridge Community	Ellis Eaton	9,527	15,354	61
3. New Woodstock	Cortland Bryant	5,212	8,365	59
4. Fayetteville, United	Evor Roberts	25,940	35,280	36
EPISCOPAL				
5. Church of the Saviour	A. B. Merriman	11,090	18,000	62
6. Trinity	C. H. Leyfield	20,764	29,000	40
METHODIST				
7. Asbury	James Bennett	4,270	7,400	73
8. East Syracuse	J. D. Wilcox	5,723	11,242	96
9. James Street	Leonard Basford	15,500	26,884	73
10. Lafayette Avenue	W. F. Clark	34,000	39,097	15
11. Christ Community	James Bennett	500	3,092	518
12. Rockwell	C. J. Luther	3,390	10,490	209
13. Freeman Avenue	R. H. Jones	3,536	7,752	120
OTHERS				
14. Geddes Congregational	Albert Hotchkiss	3,346	5,744	71
15. Plainville Christian	H. S. Tigner	3,400	4,842	41
16. Howlett Hill United Presbyterian	D. T. Kauffman	1,462	5,600	281
17. Valley Presbyterian	R. W. Firth	17,641	27,209	54
18. Friedens Evangelical and Reformed	R. L. Redman	8,553	14,483	69
Total		$177,925	$279,294	57

APPENDIX F: *Statistical Tables of Churches Which Used All or Most of the Ten Steps Outlined, but Which Were Not in American Baptist Sectors*

COUNCILS OF CHURCHES WHICH PROVIDED TRAINING SESSIONS

1. *Rhode Island Council of Churches, Providence, Rhode Island, Autumn, 1952*

United Church Canvass Chairman: Harold B. Semple
Executive Secretary: Rev. Earl H. Tomlin
Director: O. A. Pendleton

Church	Minister	1952 envelope receipts	1953 pledges	Per cent increase
BAPTIST				
1. Cranston, Meshanticut Park	J. C. Zuber	$ 9,600	$ 11,800	23
2. Cranston, Phillips Memorial*	F. H. Snell	34,511	35,723	3
3. East Providence, First	W. S. Pratt	8,490	14,020	64
4. Lakewood†	C. J. Armstrong	9,504	10,388	8
5. Norwood, Norwood Union†	H. W. McIntire	9,540	10,880	14
6. Oak Lawn	C. R. Andrews	6,966	10,243	47
7. Phenix	H. V. Howlett	4,147	5,041	22
8. Providence, Calvary	J. G. Koehler	28,795	38,112	32
9. Providence, First	A. C. Thomas	12,400	18,574	50
10. Providence, Mount Pleasant	A. W. Swift	9,000	12,586	39
11. Providence, Cranston St. Roger Williams	S. A. Bennett	8,750	16,989	94
CONGREGATIONAL				
12. Central Falls	M. L. Clough	4,960	7,946	60
13. East Providence, Newman†	Frank Crook	14,634	19,594	34
14. Pawtucket Congregational	A. P. Colbourn	23,583	26,974	14
15. Pawtucket, Park Place	C. A. Glover	17,700	21,400	21
16. Providence, Beneficent†	A. E. Wilson	18,231	18,762	3
17. Providence, Darlington	J. L. Udall, Jr.	9,254	15,506	66
18. Providence, Plymouth Union	J. W. Prince	8,490	9,735	14
19. Providence, United	N. J. Wert	6,300	7,100	13

240

Church	Minister	1952 envelope receipts	1953 pledges	Per cent increase
METHODIST				
20. Arnolds Mills	H. O. Bennett	$ 2,900	$ 3,755	29
21. Centreville†	——	5,200	5,289	
22. Central Falls, Embury	H. A. Clark	4,878	7,500	53
23. Coventry, Washington†	Wesley Hodge	6,421	7,488	17
24. East Greenwich	R. G. Colby	5,800	10,716	84
25. East Providence, Haven	R. H. Chrystie	10,227	17,627	74
26. Gaspee Plateau, Asbury	G. A. Dahlquist	12,140	18,458	50
27. Pawtucket, Epworth	L. F. Almond	4,819	9,500	98
28. Pawtucket, First	O. L. Monson	6,000	7,434	24
29. Pawtucket, Thomson	T. W. Bomar	4,542	7,532	70
30. Providence, Mathewson St.	D. G. Wright	29,000	37,000	27
31. Providence, Trinity Union	H. G. Metzner	15,482	28,137	75
32. Washington Park	H. E. Mousley	14,850	24,604	66
33. Woonsocket, First	J. M. Harrell	4,000	5,500	37
PRESBYTERIAN				
34. Central Falls, First United	C. R. Cheeks	8,513	12,498	47
35. Providence, Second	D. B. De Rogatis	8,491	10,899	28
UNITARIAN				
36. Providence, First†	R. H. Schade, Jr.	17,378	19,588	13
Total		$405,496	$544,898	34

* Six months earlier this church took 53 per cent increase in a Rhode Island Baptist sector project.

† Did not follow complete ten-step program.

2. *Worcester Convocation of the Episcopal Diocese of Western Massachusetts, Autumn, 1953*

Bishop: Rt. Rev. W. Appleton Lawrence
Business Manager: Robert W. Boyer
Directors: Rev. George W. Smith, Jr., and O. A. Pendleton

Church	Rector	1953 envelope receipts	1954 pledges	Per cent increase
1. Athol, St. John's	Archer Torrey	$ 6,825	$ 12,060	76
2. Auburn, St. Thomas'	Thaddeus Clapp	2,686	5,154	92
3. Clinton, Good Shepherd	E. I. Swanson	6,725	10,610	58
4. Fitchburg, Good Shepherd	A. B. Parson	5,095	10,093	98
5. Gardner, St. Paul's	J. H. Payne, Jr.	7,734	11,105	44
6. Holden, St. Francis'	———	6,324	9,209	46
7. Leominster, St. Mark's	G. St. J. Rathbun	6,880	12,459	81
8. Milford, Trinity	J. L. O'Dell	6,782	11,043	62
9. Millville, St. John's	H. E. Taylor	2,574	5,130	99
10. N. Brookfield, Christ	D. L. VanMeter	2,780	4,337	56
11. N. Grafton, St. Andrew's	H. E. Buck	4,786	9,008	88
12. Oxford, Grace	R. E. Davis	3,508	4,053	16
13. South Barre, Christ	D. L. VanMeter	3,190	7,368	131
14. Southbridge, Holy Trinity	N. L. Kellett	9,666	13,774	42
15. Webster, Reconciliation	R. E. Davis	7,241	13,698	89
16. Westboro, St. Stephen's	E. L. Sanford	6,032	9,533	58
17. Whalom, All Saints'	R. H. Gurley	6,546	8,970	37
18. Whitinsville, Trinity	H. E. Taylor	7,066	11,500	64
19. Worcester, St. John's	E. R. Walker	9,015	12,603	40
20. Worcester, St. Mark's	Thaddeus Clapp	5,212	9,266	78
21. Worcester, St. Matthew's	J. V. McKenzie	23,179	27,909	20
22. Worcester, St. Michael's*	R. H. Throop	14,723	30,482	107
Total		$154,510	$249,364	61

* Its building destroyed in 1953 tornado, this church combined a building campaign with its annual budget.

3. The Council of Churches, Attleboro, Massachusetts, Autumn, 1953

United Church Canvass Chairman: Lester P. Brown
Executive Secretary: Rev. Arthur O. Rinden
Director: O. A. Pendleton

Church	Minister	1953 envelope receipts	1954 pledges	Per cent increase
BAPTIST				
1. Attleboro, First*	Ralph Seguine	$ 9,354	$ 10,155	9
2. North Seekonk, Hebron†	D. W. Beebe	4,800	4,992	4
CONGREGATIONAL				
3. Attleboro Falls, Central	E. E. Craig	5,231	8,391	60
4. Attleboro, Second	Russell Richardson	21,485	26,340	23
5. Wrentham, Original	Lionel Whiston	12,276‡	21,640	76
EPISCOPAL				
6. Attleboro, All Saints†	Walter Sheppard	15,810	17,700	12
7. North Attleboro, Grace	E. D. Romig	12,500	19,000	52
METHODIST				
8. Attleboro, Centenary	P. M. Spurrier	10,434	16,024	54
9. Chartley	Wesley Allen	2,866	7,252	152
10. Hebron	Shibley Malouf	2,887	4,600	58
11. North Rehoboth	Wesley Allen	1,100	2,800	154
12. North Attleboro, First	F. T. Bertram	5,063	6,880	36
LUTHERAN				
13. Attleboro, Immanuel	Walter Pearson	8,000	10,033	25
14. CHRISTIAN UNION, Attleboro	R. B. Davis	464	875	88
Total		$112,270	$156,682	40

* Used sector techniques two years earlier in Boston pilot project.
† Did not follow complete ten-step program.
‡ In addition raised $7,850 toward new parish house in separate campaign. In 1954 both were combined into one local expense budget.

4. *Greater Lawrence Council of Churches, Lawrence, Massachusetts, Autumn,*
1953

United Church Canvass Chairman: Rev. Ralph D. York .
Executive Secretary: Rev. George A. Ackerly
Director: O. A. Pendleton

Church	Minister	1953 envelope receipts	1954 pledges	Per cent increase
BAPTIST				
1. Haverhill, Portland St.	E. J. Woodbury	$ 6,901	$ 14,925	116
CONGREGATIONAL				
2. Lawrence, Lawrence Street	W. F. Knox	8,900	11,725	31
3. Lawrence, Riverside	A. R. McAllister	3,200	5,710	79
4. Lawrence, South	Stanley Gould	5,300	7,500	41
EPISCOPAL				
5. Lawrence, Grace*	Harold Deacon	30,211	34,337	13
6. Methuen, St. Andrew's	George Argyle	5,177	8,387	62
7. North Andover, St. Paul's	A. S. Twombly	10,100	11,200	10
EVANGELICAL LUTHERAN				
8. Lawrence, Redeemer*	F. P. Nissen	*c.* 4,000	*c.* 5,000	25
METHODIST				
9. Lawrence, Central	W. S. Holliday	10,000	14,910	49
10. Lawrence, St. Mark's	N. W. Smith	4,583	7,003	53
11. Lawrence, St. Paul's	John Torosian	4,100	9,010	119
12. Lawrence, Vine Street	Fay Gemmell	4,637	5,304	14
13. Methuen, First	Robert Drew	6,286	7,451	18
14. North Andover, First	R. D. York	6,700	9,100	36
15. Salem, New Hampshire	G. W. Douglass	1,100	3,123	183
PRESBYTERIAN				
16. Lawrence, Christ*	Hans Sidon	19,611	20,883	6
UNIVERSALIST				
17. Lawrence, Good Shepherd	K. C. Hawkes	3,000	5,566	85
Total		$133,806	$181,123	35

* Did not follow complete ten-step program.

5. Newton Council of Churches, Newton, Massachusetts, Autumn, 1954

United Church Canvass Chairman: Chester E. Borden
Executive Secretary: Rev. Sydney Adams
Director: O. A. Pendleton

Church	Minister	1954 envelope receipts	1955 pledges	Per cent increase
CONGREGATIONAL				
1. Auburndale	C. E. Blossom	$ 17,644	$ 24,039	41
2. Newton Center, First	N. M. Guptill	36,104	45,915	29
3. Newton Highlands	F. Groetsema	22,924	30,750	39
4. West Newton, Second	Ross Cannon	52,094	60,548	16
EPISCOPAL				
5. Newton Highlands, St. Paul's	J. M. Balcom	10,000	12,262	23
6. Newton Lower Falls, St. Mary's	W. G. Berndt	21,177	24,688	16
7. Newtonville, St. John's	W. J. Kingwill	12,850	19,826	54
8. West Newton, Church of Messiah	F. W. Rapp	15,431	23,300	51
METHODIST				
9. Auburndale, Centenary	Sydney Adams	9,000	13,540	50
10. Newton Lower Falls	E. J. Helms	2,494	4,268	71
11. Newton Upper Falls, First	H. Beukelman	6,652	11,195	46
12. Newtonville	H. M. Gifford	23,940	32,178	34
Total		$230,310	$302,509	31
13. Newton, Grace Episcopal*	R. W. Woodroofe	$26,476	$28,235	6
14. Waban, Union Church*	J. C. MacDonald	32,100	37,109	15

* Did not follow complete ten-step program.

6. *The Council of Churches, Attleboro, Massachusetts, Autumn, 1954*

Second year of following ten-step program

United Church Canvass Chairman: Harold Cash, Jr.
Executive Secretary: Rev. Robert Ryder
Director: O. A. Pendleton

Church	Minister	1954 envelope receipts	1955 pledges	Per cent increase
BAPTIST				
1. Attleboro, First*	Ralph Seguine, Jr.	$ 11,538	$ 13,483	17
CONGREGATIONAL				
2. Attleboro, Second	Russell Richardson	23,450	24,800	5
3. Foxboro, Bethany	M. V. B. Sargent	12,274	17,355	40
4. Wrentham, Original	Lionel Whiston	20,372	21,400	5
EPISCOPAL				
5. Attleboro, All Saints	Walter Sheppard	18,351	23,602	28
LATTER DAY SAINTS				
6. Attleboro	Ralph Power	1,950	4,082	109
LUTHERAN				
7. Attleboro, Immanuel*	E. M. Olson	10,200	10,200	
METHODIST				
8. Attleboro, Centenary	P. M. Spurrier	16,445	17,787	8
9. Hebron	Shibley Malouf	4,050	6,220	53
UNITARIAN				
10. Norton	G. C. Whitney	1,345	4,220	213
Total		$119,975	$143,149	19

* Did not follow complete ten-step program.

7. *Worcester Convocation of the Episcopal Diocese of Western Massachusetts, Autumn, 1954*

Second year of following ten-step program

Bishop: Rt. Rev. W. Appleton Lawrence
Business Manager: Robert W. Boyer
Directors: Rev. Charles Havens, Jr., and O. A. Pendleton
 The following figures show the increase for a two-year period.

Church	Rector	1953 envelope receipts	1955 pledges	Per cent increase
1. Athol, St. John's	R. A. Torrey	$ 7,336	$ 12,687	73
2. Auburn, St. Thomas'	Stanley Nelson	2,780	5,156	85
3. Fitchburg, Good Shepherd	A. B. Parson	4,630	9,630	108
4. Gardner, St. Paul's	J. H. Payne, Jr.	7,493	12,007	60
5. Holden, St. Francis'	H. B. Boughey	5,780	10,842	88
6. Leominster, St. Mark's	G. St. J. Rathbun	5,680	14,031	147
7. Millville, St. John's	D. O. G. Gauclair	2,369	5,300	124
8. No. Brookfield, Christ Memorial	D. L. VanMeter	2,820	4,811	71
9. No. Grafton, St. Andrew's	H. E. Buck	4,786	9,075	90
10. Rochdale, Christ Church	Stanley Nelson	2,169	5,518	154
11. Shrewsbury, Trinity*	S. D. Hart		9,540	
12. South Barre, Christ Church	D. L. VanMeter	2,731	6,500	138
13. Southbridge, Holy Trinity	N. L. Kellett	10,470	15,328	46
14. Westboro, St. Stephen's	E. L. Sanford	6,031	11,100	84
15. Whitinsville, Trinity	H. E. Taylor	7,955	13,700	72
16. Worcester, All Saints*	R. C. Preston	60,942	71,500	17
17. Worcester, St. Mark's	Thaddeus Clapp	5,043	9,194	82
18. Worcester, St. Matthew's	J. V. MacKenzie	23,166	31,040	34
19. Worcester, St. Michael's	R. H. Throop	13,810	33,026	138
Total		$176,002	$289,985	64

* First-year churches. All others participated the preceding year.

8. *New Bedford Council of Churches, New Bedford, Massachusetts, Autumn, 1954*

Executive Secretary: Rev. William Cate
Director: O. A. Pendleton

Church	Minister	1954 envelope receipts	1955 pledges	Per cent increase
BAPTIST				
1. New Bedford, First	E. D. Dolloff	$ 20,000	$ 27,000	35
2. New Bedford, North	George Pike	4,400	7,654	74
CONGREGATIONAL				
3. Fairhaven	J. H. Maddaford	10,500	17,376	66
4. Marion	George Robinson	6,600	10,600	60
5. New Bedford, North	J. T. Powell	9,851	15,107	53
6. New Bedford, Pilgrim	Charles Hodges	6,612	8,902	35
7. Smith Mills	Harold Worster	1,358	4,870	269
EPISCOPAL				
8. New Bedford, Grace*	Howard Lowell	35,000	37,841	8
9. New Bedford, St. Andrew's	Richard Peters	5,565	11,966	114
10. New Bedford, St. Martin's	Ralph Tucker	11,368	17,666	55
METHODIST				
11. Acushnet	John Dunham	2,912	6,577	127
12. New Bedford, St. Paul's	Edgar Smith	11,050	15,000	36
13. New Bedford, Trinity	G. H. Parker	10,050	14,177	40
14. New Bedford, Wesley*	Domenic Volturno	3,800	6,000	58
FRIENDS				
15. Smith's Neck	Joseph Weber		2,800	
Total		$139,066	$203,646	46

* Did not follow complete ten-step program.

RESULTS OF CHURCHES WHICH USED TECHNIQUES OF SECTOR PROJECT, BUT WHICH WORKED ALONE IN THEIR ENLISTMENT

Many hundreds of churches have successfully used all, or most, of the steps of the sector project without being in a sector. Perhaps the minister attended some sector training sessions, perhaps the Finance Committee attended a one-day Planning and Action Conference which outlined the major steps, or perhaps the church merely obtained copies of the Every Member Canvass Manual from the Council on Missionary Cooperation of the American Baptist Convention. These churches have reported noteworthy gains made through these efforts. The following typical cases are but a few of the many that have come to my attention.

Church	Minister	Preceding year envelope receipts or pledges	New pledges	Per cent increase
National Memorial Baptist (1953) Washington, D.C.	E. B. Willingham	$52,106	$102,000	96
First Baptist (1953) Hampton Falls, N.H.	E. R. Scruton	3,998	6,856	71
Central Square Baptist (1953) Portland, Maine	H. C. Bonell	13,657	18,778	38
First Baptist (1952) Plaistow, N.H.	J. R. Wood	4,644	6,912	48
First Baptist (1952) Bridgeport, Conn.	M. R. Wilkes	24,427 (1951)	29,254 (1952) 30,300 (1953)	20
First Baptist (1952) Claremont, N.H.	H. S. Campbell	6,807	10,338	51
First Baptist (1953) Keene, N.H.	L. M. Blackmer	10,171	13,117	29
United Baptist (1953) Saco, Maine	D. B. Howe	11,246	23,100	104
Calvary Baptist (1952) Lowell, Mass.	V. F. Scalise	8,700	16,900	94
Tremont Temple (1952) Boston, Mass.	S. W. Powell	73,226	94,726	29
First Baptist (1953) Steubenville, Ohio	J. O. White	2,945	10,345	251
First Baptist (1951) Lowell, Mass.	O. R. Loverude	34,217	48,246	41
First Baptist (1953) Stoneham, Mass.	F. W. Hensley	12,253	18,741	53
Second Baptist (1953) North Grafton, Mass.	T. E. Roth	4,621	8,900	93
Wesley Methodist (1953) Worcester, Mass.	J. R. Uhlinger	62,816	78,592	25
First Baptist (1953) Middletown, Ohio	J. I. Parr	31,000	56,500	82

The following Augustana Evangelical Lutheran Churches, all in Minnesota, followed the ten-step program under the supervision of Martin E. Carlson, Director of Stewardship and Finance for his denomination.

Church	Minister	Pledges 1953	1954
Edina, Normandale	Donald Carlson	$14,115*	$20,565*
Forrest Lake, Faith	L. K. Anderson	13,000	24,956
Minneapolis, Lebanon	Grant Olson	10,100	15,004
Minneapolis, Messiah	Leonard Kendall	48,500	65,000
St. Peter, First	Millard Ahlstrom	16,500	23,000

* Included a capital-funds project.

INDEX

Numbers that are preceded by the letter "K" refer to pages in the Canvass Kit section immediately following the index.

A

CANVASS KIT

1. FORMS
2. AGENDAS
3. LETTERS
4. ANALYSES OF RESULTS
5. CALENDARS

1. FORMS

Before mimeographing, fill in actual months and days below.

_____ _____ CHURCH

Every Member Enlistment, 19—

GUIDING PRINCIPLES

1. The advance program for which we are working is the result of the thinking of many of our church members.

2. Many persons will be working together to bring this program to success.

3. Each worker will be assigned a definite duty, which will not be done unless that person does it.

4. The enlistment calendar (see dates below) must be rigidly followed.

5. There is a right and a wrong way to perform every task in this enlistment. Be informed of the right way. Do your job the right way.

6. Be informed of our program and goals.

7. Attend *both* visitors' training conferences.

IMPORTANT DATES

Tuesday, Week 2	7:30 P.M.	General Committee meets
Sunday, Week 4	3:00 P.M.	Resources Committee meets
Friday, Week 4	7:30 P.M.	Telephone squad meets
Monday, Week 5	7:30 P.M.	Church council meets
	8:30 P.M.	Captains and division leaders meet
Wednesday, Week 5	6:30 P.M.	CONGREGATIONAL DINNER MEETING
Sunday, Week 6	3:00 P.M.	Advance Pledge Committee meets
Sunday, Week 7	3:00 P.M.	Advance Pledge Committee meets
Sunday, Week 8	3:00 P.M.	FIRST WORKERS' TRAINING CONFERENCE
Friday, Week 8	6:30 P.M.	SECOND WORKERS' TRAINING CONFERENCE
Sunday, Week 9	11:00 A.M.	Dedication Service
	12:30 P.M.	Workers' Dinner
	6:00 P.M.	First Report Meeting
Wednesday, Week 9	6:30 P.M.	Second Report Meeting
Friday, Week 9	6:30 P.M.	Third Report Meeting
Sunday, Week 10	6:30 P.M.	Fourth Report Meeting
Wednesday, Week 10	6:30 P.M.	Victory Report Meeting

Name of Group:			Date:	
Services to be performed	Estimated cost	Check one of the following		
		Optional	Preferred	Must

(Courtesy of American Baptist Convention)

For use of this form, see pages 40–42.

COMPOSITE PROPOSAL (Preliminary)				
Services to be performed	(1) Optional	(2) Preferred	(3) Must	(4) Proposed budget

(Courtesy of American Baptist Convention)

For use of this form, see page 42.

To be prepared by the Publicity chairman on WEDNESDAY, Week 2, for use by the Resources Committee on SUNDAY, Week 4.

FORM D

No.	Name	Address	Member or nonmember	Phone	Would he or she make a good:		Estimated giving potential
					Leader	Worker	
Resource appraisal sheet							Page No. 1

(Courtesy of American Baptist Convention)

The first five columns are to be filled in when the form is prepared. The remaining columns will be completed by the Resources Committee at its meeting, SUNDAY, Week 4. Provide one copy of the entire list for each member of the Resources Committee plus an extra twenty for use in other ways. Cut each stencil as above. But do not put on mimeograph machine until names, addresses, and telephone numbers are cut in.

SUMMARY APPRAISAL SHEET

(For use of Resources chairman and Resources Review Committee)

Date   Sheet

(1) Name and address	(2) List of individual appraisals	(3) Total of appraisals	(4) Number of appraisals	(5) Average appraisal	(6) Revised appraisal
Here paste column of names and addresses clipped from an appraisal sheet.	This sheet should be at least 14 inches wide, giving column 2 all the extra width				
Total names				Total of revised appraisals	$

For use of this form, see pages 58–61.

K-9

FORM F

MASTER LIST

Date: _____   Chairman: _____

Number (1)	A.P. or worker (2)	Name (3)	Address (4)	Member or nonmember (5)	Assigned to (6)	Present pledges			Suggested appraisal (10)	New pledges			Comments (14)
						Local (7)	Missions (8)	Total (9)		Local (11)	Missions (12)	Total (13)	
TOTALS													

Note on use of master list:

1. Make one copy only, for use of General chairman.

2. Check carefully spelling of names and correct addresses.

3. Number each name in column 1. This will later correspond with number on pledge card.

4. If name is advance pledge prospect, write A.P. in column 2. If worker in E.M.E. organization, write W.

5. In column 5, write M if member, N if nonmember.

6. List prospects by incomes, rather than by individuals or families.

For use of this form, see page 79.

K-11

PROPOSAL FORM

This is a guide for your Proposal Committee in preparing copy for the printed Proposal in Week 5. The subheadings are only suggested and you may change them to suit your need, but do not exceed six lines of copy under each section. After you have filled out this form, make a duplicate copy and give it to the printer on THURSDAY, Week 5. Please use ink. Double-check all additions and spellings.

Name of Church————————————————————————
City———————————————State————————————

For Our Church Home

Repairs and improvements	$————
Insurance	————
Custodian	————
Utilities and fuel	————
Service and supplies	————
Miscellaneous	————
Total	$————

For Our Pastoral Ministry

Salary	$————
Travel (including car upkeep)	————
Honoraria for supply preachers	————
Parsonage upkeep, fuel, etc.	————
Convention expenses	————
Minister's pension	————
Total	$————

For Benevolences and Our World Mission

Our share of denominational missionary budget	$————
Our denominational institutions	————
Other benevolences	————
Total	$————

For Our Worship and Service

Choir director	$————
Organist	————
Music and supplies	————
Office secretary	————
Office supplies	————
Total	$————

(see over)

For Our Christian Education Work

Church school $_____

Youth groups   _____

Equipment   _____

Materials   _____

Special projects   _____

Total $_____

Total Amount of Proposal $_____

MINISTER'S PICTURE CAPTION

(Print name)_____, pastor

(*Chairman's letter*)

Dear Friends:

The above Proposal represents our hope for next year. It is a hope we can realize, if we truly wish it. With such a program our church will be able to give a stronger witness to Jesus Christ at home and around the world.

Will you pray that this Proposal may become a reality? Will you also pray about your share in it? Soon some friend from the church will call upon you to discuss this matter. Be ready to ask questions.

Very sincerely yours,

(*Print name*)_____

General Chairman
Every Member Enlistment
Committee

Resources chairman gives FORM H-1 and FORM H-2 (see below and following page) to Publicity chairman, THURSDAY, Week 4.

Publicity chairman gives FORM H-1 and FORM H-2 to printer not later than THURSDAY, Week 5.

FORM H-1 is to be filled in by Resources and Publicity chairmen to provide completed copy for the printer.

FORM H-2 will show printer the format and wording of the pledge card.

It is important that these forms reach the printer not later than THURSDAY, Week 5. If these forms are given to the printer earlier, it will mean that the Publicity Committee will have additional time for typing names and addresses.

....CHURCH

Make any correction desired in the following:

GIVING PLAN PER WEEK

Local expenses	$........................
Benevolences	$........................
(Any other)	$........................
TOTAL	$........................

These Commitments Will Underwrite Our Church Proposal

___at $_____ per week
___at $_____ per week
___at $_____ .per week
___at $_____ per week
___at $._____ per week
___at $_____ per week
___at $_____ per week
___at $_____ per week
___at $_____ per week
___at $1.00 per week

Youth Pledges
___at $_____ per week
___at $_____ per week

Total
Proposal $_____
per year

The Committee believed you would want to be in the group checked.

FORM H-1

Name.............

Address.............

Card No.............

NAME OF CHURCH, CITY, STATE

MY PERSONAL COMMITMENT

In recognition of my time, talent and treasure as gifts from God, I am happy to join with others in the following commitment.

GIVING PLAN PER WEEK

Local Expenses	$.............
Benevolences	$.............
(Any other)	$.............
Total	$.............

Signature:.............

This pledge may be increased, decreased, or canceled by notifying the treasurer or financial secretary.

FORM H-2

These Commitments Will Underwrite Our Church Proposal

The Committee believed you would like to be in the group checked.

Team No.............

This card taken by.............

This form for use by General chairmen in churches of more than 500 members.

Date...

ALL THAT I AM
BELONGS TO GOD

EVERY MEMBER CANVASS ORGANIZATION

The Enlistment of Division Leaders

I desire to strengthen the work of my church and will strive for its advancement through the coming Every Member Canvass. I agree to serve as a DIVISION LEADER, and will:

1. Enlist four Captains for my division by (Monday, Week 4)
2. Meet with my four Captains on (Monday, Week 5) and help them select their prospective Visitors and encourage them to complete their teams by (Thursday, Week 6)
3. Attend the first Training Session on (Sunday, Week 8) and encourage my Captains to do likewise
4. Secure the pledges of my Captains, in so far as possible, by (Tuesday, Week 8)
5. Attend the second Training Conference on (Friday, Week 8), and encourage my Captains to do likewise
6. Attend, in so far as possible, *all* report meetings and encourage my Captains to do likewise

"I will pray for the success of the Canvass."

Signature of Division Leader	Address	Business Phone	Home Phone
1.			
2.			
3.			
4.			

(There should be a space on this form for each division leader in your organization)

(*Adapted from a form of the American Baptist Convention*)

(In churches of 500 members or more, supply one of these to each Division Leader. In churches of 100 to 499 members, General chairman uses this form.)

Division Leader..

Date...

ALL THAT I AM
BELONGS TO GOD

EVERY MEMBER CANVASS ORGANIZATION

The Enlistment of Captains

I desire to strengthen the work of my church and will strive for its advancement through the coming Every Member Canvass. I agree to serve as a CAPTAIN, and will:

1. Meet on (Monday, Week 5) to select the names of prospective Visitors and enlist four Visitors by (Thursday, Week 6)
2. Attend and encourage my four Visitors to attend the first Training Conference on (Sunday, Week 8)
3. Secure the pledges of my Visitors, in so far as possible, by (Friday, Week 8)
4. Attend the second Training Conference on (Friday, Week 8) and encourage my Visitors to do likewise
5. Train all my Visitors who miss either Training Conference
6. Attend, in so far as possible, *all* report meetings and encourage my Visitors to do likewise

"I will pray for the success of the Canvass."

	Signature of Captain	Address	Business Phone	Home Phone
1.				
2.				
3.				
4.				

(*Adapted from a form of the American Baptist Convention*)

K-21

Supply one of these to each Captain.

Captain..

Date ....

ALL THAT I AM
BELONGS TO GOD

EVERY MEMBER CANVASS ORGANIZATION

The Enlistment of Visitors

I desire to strengthen the work of my church and will strive for its advancement through the coming Every Member Canvass. I hereby agree to serve as a VISITOR, and will:

1. Attend the first Workers' Training Conference on (Sunday, Week 8) at _____ P.M.
2. Make my own pledge before the second Workers' Training Session
3. Attend the second Workers' Training Conference on (Friday, Week 8 at _____ P.M.), and select the prospects whom I will visit in person as soon after (Sunday, Week 9) as it is possible for me to do so
4. Attend Dedication Service on (Sunday, Week 9 at _____ A.M.)
5. Attend, in so far as possible, *all* report meetings, turning in *at least* one completed card at each report

"I will pray for the success of the Canvass."

	Signature	Address	Business Phone	Home Phone
1.				
2.				
3.				
4.				

(*Adapted from a form of the American Baptist Convention*)

K-23

WORKERS' ORGANIZATION CHART

_____ _____ Church
John Doe, General Chairman
Richard Roe, Organization Chairman

DIVISION I
David Smith, leader
Captains

A. Joseph Jones	B. Thomas Stephens	C. _____	D. _____
1. John Williams	5. _____	9. _____	13. _____
2. James Neal	6. _____	10. _____	14. _____
3. _____	7. _____	11. _____	15. _____
4. _____	8. _____	12. _____	16. _____

DIVISION II
Samuel Brown, leader
Captains

E. _____	F. _____	G. _____	H. _____
17. _____	21. _____	25. _____	29. _____
18. _____	22. _____	26. _____	30. _____
19. _____	23. _____	27. _____	31. _____
20. _____	24. _____	28. _____	32. _____

Note: Enlarge this chart as needed. Place on larger sheet of paper. Make several copies, posting one on bulletin board, and giving one to each division leader and captain.

2. AGENDAS

AGENDA
General Committee Meeting
MONDAY, WEEK 2

Presiding: GENERAL CHAIRMAN

Prayer for the Success of the Canvass

MINISTER

(*5 min.*) Our Hopes for Next Year   MINISTER
The Needs and Opportunities Facing Us

(*15 min.*) General Plan of Procedure

GENERAL CHAIRMAN

The Ten Steps
The Number of Committees
The Function of Committees
Proposal
Resources
Publicity
Advance Pledge
Organization

(*10 min.*) Highlights of the Time Schedule

PUBLICITY CHAIRMAN

(*5 min.*) Number of Visitors Needed

ORGANIZATION CHAIRMAN

(*5 min.*) How Visitors Are Enlisted and Trained

ORGANIZATION CHAIRMAN

(*5 min.*) Materials Needed for Campaign

PUBLICITY CHAIRMAN

(*5 min.*) Importance of Following the Plan and
Keeping on Schedule   GENERAL CHAIRMAN
Prayer and Adjournment

K-27

AGENDA
Resources Committee Meeting
SUNDAY, WEEK 4

Presiding: RESOURCES COMMITTEE CHAIRMAN

3:00 Scripture: II Corinthians 8:8–15

3:03 Prayer   MINISTER

3:05 Opening Statement   MINISTER
    "We are instruments of the Holy Spirit, and
    we ought to be willing to be used. . . . "

3:10 Our Hopes for Next Year   PROPOSAL CHAIRMAN

3:15 What Others Have Done, We Can Do
                         GENERAL CHAIRMAN

3:20 The Task before Us   RESOURCES CHAIRMAN
    A. We are to discover three facts:
        1. Who our leaders and workers will be
        2. A total goal for our church
        3. A suggested amount for each person to
           consider giving
    B. We shall follow three principles (see page 56)
    C. How to discover our resources (see page 57)
        Read aloud the sixteen points
        Answer briefly any questions

3:35 Discovering Our Resources
    The committee scatters about the room
    Each one has his own list
    Each begins working

SUGGESTED AGENDA
*For Congregational Meetings
In Local Churches*
(WEDNESDAY, WEEK 5)

6:30 Invocation and Dinner

7:20 Hymn

7:25 Scripture and Prayer

7:30 What Are the Needs of Our Church and Christ's
Kingdom?   PROPOSAL CHAIRMAN
(Equipment, repairs, expansion, personnel for a
greater program)

7:40 Presentation of Our World Mission   MINISTER
(A brief missionary film or filmstrip may be shown
here)

7:55 How Can These Needs Be Provided For?
RESOURCES CHAIRMAN
(Resources exist. The goal is within reach)

8:00 Telling the Story   PUBLICITY CHAIRMAN
(When our members know the need, they will
want to have a part)

8:05 Do We Give All We Should to Our Church?
ADVANCE PLEDGE CHAIRMAN
(From 1939 to 19__ United States personal in-
come rose __% while giving to our church rose
__%. Reports from other church campaigns)

8:10 We Are Proposing a Plan of Achievement
(5 min.—Briefly outline major steps in organization)   GENERAL CHAIRMAN
(5 min.—We shall need visitors to call in every
home)   ORGANIZATION CHAIRMAN
(5 min.—Present budget proposal giving only
major items and total cost)
PROPOSAL CHAIRMAN

8:25 "We Can, If We Will"   MINISTER

8:35 A Motion to Place Matter before the Meeting
Discussion of Values of the Plan
Action on the Plan
Adjournment

NOTE: Items in parentheses should not be mimeographed.
They are suggestions for the speakers.

AGENDA
Advance Pledge Committee Meeting No. 1
SUNDAY, WEEK 6
(This may be a luncheon meeting if desired)

Presiding Officer: ADVANCE PLEDGE CHAIRMAN

1. Opening Prayer
2. Quick Review of Every Member Enlistment Organization   GENERAL CHAIRMAN
   a. Proposal for next year (*Proposal Committee*)
   b. Analysis of resources (*Resources Committee*)
   c. The time schedule
   d. Publicity and aids
   e. Advance pledges (*Monday, Week 7—Friday, Week 8*)
   f. General solicitation (*Sunday, Week 9 ff.*)
3. Why We Have a High Goal   PROPOSAL CHAIRMAN
   Needs
   Opportunities
4. How We Can Reach Our Goal   RESOURCES CHAIRMAN
   The appraisal figure
   Ten per cent of members will be called on early
   All workers will be called on early
   Need for all to increase giving
5. Why We Have Advance Pledging (see pages 85 to 87)   ADVANCE PLEDGE CHAIRMAN
6. How to Use the Turnover Chart (or Making the Turnover Chart)
7. Reading of Worker's Information Booklet
8. Showing of Training Film
9. Discussion of Film
10. Advance Pledge Calendar
    Sunday, Week 7—Cards selected
    Monday, Week 7—First calls made
    Friday, Week 7—First Report Meeting
    Friday, Week 8—Final Advance Pledge Report Meeting
11. Adjournment

NOTE: Pastor and General chairman should make their pledges *today*. General chairman should obtain pledges in home of Advance Pledge chairman on *Monday. Rest of week*, Advance Pledge chairman obtains pledges of all advance pledge workers.

K-33

AGENDA

Advance Pledge Committee Meeting No. 2

SUNDAY, WEEK 7

Presiding Officer: ADVANCE PLEDGE CHAIRMAN

1. Opening Prayer   MINISTER
2. Report of Progress to Date
                                ADVANCE PLEDGE CHAIRMAN
3. Second Reading of Worker's Information Booklet
                                      PUBLICITY CHAIRMAN
4. How to Use the Turnover Chart   GENERAL CHAIRMAN
5. How to Introduce the Appraisal Figure
                                ADVANCE PLEDGE CHAIRMAN
   Tell story of committee of thirty
   Strive to get prospect to ask the question
   Show special pledge card
6. Second Showing of Training Film
7. Importance of Report Meetings
                                ADVANCE PLEDGE CHAIRMAN
   First Report—Friday, Week 7
   Final Report—Friday, Week 8 (*at Second Workers'
      Training Conference*)
8. Selection of Prospect Cards
9. Adjournment

SUGGESTED AGENDA
First Workers' Training Conference
(SUNDAY, WEEK 8)

Presiding: GENERAL CHAIRMAN

3:00 An Enlarged Program to Meet the Needs of Our Church and Christ's Kingdom   MINISTER

3:15 Showing of a denominational missionary filmstrip if available

3:30 How We Shall Accomplish Our Program (Our Organization and Timetable)   GENERAL CHAIRMAN

3:45 The Share of Each Worker in This Program: work and pledge   MINISTER

3:55 Report of Progress: amount pledged to date
ADVANCE PLEDGE CHAIRMAN

4:00 The Importance of Making Our Pledges before Calling on Others   ORGANIZATION CHAIRMAN

4:10 Training film, such as the American Baptist sound filmstrip, "Thy Mission High Fulfilling"

4:25 Demonstration of Turnover Chart
GENERAL CHAIRMAN

4:45 Brief Summary of Worker's Booklet
ORGANIZATION CHAIRMAN

4:50 What Happens at Our Meeting Friday
GENERAL CHAIRMAN

4:55 Questions

5:00 Prayer and Adjournment
Distribution of Turnover Charts and Workers' Booklets

NOTE: If this is a noon dinner meeting, move the time suggested here forward 1½ or 2 hours.

Be sure to use several leaders as suggested above.

Do not have one person speak longer than 15 minutes at any one time.

Beware of using any lengthy motion picture. Your workers are not here to be entertained.

Churches making their own turnover charts may devote the first forty-five minutes to having each visitor copy his chart from a master chart. Charts should seldom be over twenty pages, never over twenty-five.

SUGGESTED AGENDA
Second Workers' Training Session
(FRIDAY, WEEK 8)

Presiding: GENERAL CHAIRMAN

6:30 Invocation and Dinner

7:30 Restatement of the Needs of our Church and Christ's
Kingdom   MINISTER

7:35 The Canvass Goal   PROPOSAL CHAIRMAN

7:40 The Steps Already Taken   GENERAL CHAIRMAN

7:45 Report of Progress   ADVANCE PLEDGE CHAIRMAN
(After the Advance Pledge chairman reports the
total received by his committee, have each division leader or captain stand and announce total
received from his workers. Add these totals to advance pledge totals.)

7:55 The Steps Ahead   ORGANIZATION CHAIRMAN
Making the Calls
The Report Meetings

8:05 Another Look at the Training Film

8:25 The Turnover Chart Demonstration
     GENERAL OR PUBLICITY CHAIRMAN

8:40 The Workers' Booklet   ORGANIZATION CHAIRMAN

9:00 The Pledge Card   PUBLICITY CHAIRMAN

9:10 The Call in the Home   GENERAL CHAIRMAN
     1. How to get into the house
     2. Showing the turnover chart
     3. Introducing the suggested figure
     4. Presenting the pledge card
     5. How to make an exit

9:40 The Minister's Final Word

9:50 Selecting the Pledge Cards

(SUGGESTION: If you are using a training film, it is good
technique to train as the film is being shown. Stop the
film and record to interpolate wherever you wish to emphasize some point. If you do, rearrange the above
agenda, allowing 45 minutes for use of film.)

A QUIZ FOR INQUISITIVE VISITORS

(Instructions: The leader will ask each visitor to write the answer to question 1 without conferring with anyone. Then he will ask for volunteer answers from the floor. All will write in necessary corrections. The leader will then follow the same procedure for question 2, and on to the end. Questionnaires should be taken home by each visitor.)

1. What is our total goal? _____
2. What is local expense goal? _____ Benevolence goal? _____
3. What are the new items in Proposal?
4. Why is _____ in Proposal?
5. Why is _____ in Proposal?
6. Why is _____ in Proposal?
7. Why is missions increased?
8. How can we reach our goal?
9. Is any visitor going to tell anyone how much he must give? _____
10. Will each visitor be prepared to make a suggestion? _____
11. How is the suggested figure introduced?
12. Will visitor leave pledge card if prospect asks him? _____
13. What should visitor do with card if prospect is not at home for first two calls?
14. What are the three duties for each visitor?
    (1) To attend two training sessions
    (2)
    (3)

K-41

SUGGESTED ORDER OF WORSHIP
Dedication Sunday
(SUNDAY, WEEK 9)

ORGAN PRELUDE

PROCESSIONAL HYMN "The Church's One Foundation"

SALUTATION

Minister: "As the mountains are round about Jerusalem, so the Lord is round about His people."

People: "I was glad when they said unto me, Let us go into the house of the Lord."

Minister: "Unto thee do I lift up mine eyes, O thou that dwellest in the heavens."

People: "Let thine hand help me; for I have chosen thy precepts."

INVOCATION AND LORD'S PRAYER

RESPONSIVE SELECTION (To include references to the Lord's house or the Lord's work)

GLORIA PATRI

SCRIPTURE LESSON Psalm 27: 1–8

PASTORAL PRAYER

ANTHEM

CHILDREN'S STORY SERMON (Here the minister should identify the children with the program)

HYMN "I love Thy Kingdom, Lord" (Here the children may leave for their classes)

PARISH ANNOUNCEMENTS

OFFERTORY ANTHEM

DOXOLOGY AND DEDICATION OF THE OFFERING

SERMON "Except the Lord Build the House" (Except the Lord build the house, they labor in vain that build it. Psalm 127: 1)

LITANY OF DEDICATION

Minister: "On this Dedication Sunday we, the members and friends of this church, now enter upon a campaign to enlarge our program for next year, that we might better serve Almighty God. At this hour of morning worship we dedicate ourselves, through sacrifice and service, to this great task which we here and now inaugurate to the glory of God, to the honor

K-43

of His Son, Jesus Christ, our Lord, and to the enrichment of the spiritual lives of all our people.

"Members of the Campaign Organization (here the said members will stand): In full realization of the plans undertaken, do you individually reaffirm the acceptance of the office to which you have been called, and do you covenant to discharge its duties faithfully in the love of God and in the service of your fellow men?"

Members of the Campaign Organization: "By the help of God, we will."

Minister: "Will you, as parishioners of this church *(here the congregation will stand)*, receive these, your fellow parishioners, as servants of God, welcome them with cordial generosity, earnestly consider their appeal, and gladly do your part in this great undertaking according to your fullest ability?"

Congregation: "By the help of God, we will."

In Unison: "We, the members and friends of this church, grateful for our heritage and remembering the sacrifices of those who have gone before us, do dedicate ourselves anew to the service of God and to the building of a program which will give praise to God, bear Christian witness to men around the world, turn our community toward paths of righteousness, and strengthen our homes and loved ones. To this end we promise and pledge to do our part as God hath prospered us."

PRAYER OF DEDICATION (by the minister)

"Almighty God, our heavenly Father, who delightest in the assembling of Thy people and who hast promised to be with them as they so gather: look with loving favor upon us this day as we seek to undergird Thy work by firm financial foundations, adequate for the work we would do for Thee. Bless these people who will go forth to tell the story of Thy church. We thank Thee for them and pray that as they open the doors of opportunity for sharing they may find such a response that this church may do that which is well-pleasing in Thy sight. Through Jesus Christ our Lord. Amen.

RECESSIONAL HYMN "God of Grace and God of Glory"

BENEDICTION

ORGAN POSTLUDE

Prepared by the Rev. Frank H. Snell
Phillips Memorial Baptist Church
Cranston, R.I.

K-44

3. LETTERS

These letters have been prepared to help your church raise more money. Almost identical letters have been used with great success by other churches. Use them as is, if at all possible. Their use will save valuable time and make it possible to have secretarial work done well in advance.

Personally typed letters with handwritten signatures prove of great value; mimeographing should be avoided where possible. If sufficient volunteer typists are recruited far enough ahead, all letters for any size church can be individually typed.

Although the majority of these letters are signed by the minister and General chairman, it is the duty of the Publicity chairman and his committee to prepare them. Each of them should be ready for signature approximately one week before mailing. Since preparation dates are not included in the Publicity chairman's chapter of this book, he will want to refer to this section frequently to see that the letters are prepared well ahead of time.

Time schedule dates (SUNDAY, Week 3; THURSDAY, Week 5; etc.) should be changed into the proper calendar dates before each letter is typed.

While it may appear that many letters are being used, only four basic letters are mailed to members of the congregation. They are as follows:

Letter B—General chairman's letter inviting members to attend the Congregational Dinner

Letter H—General chairman's letter to the prospects enclosing a copy of the Proposal

Letter K—Minister's letter to the prospects asking them to give in a spirit of prayer

Letter M—General chairman's acknowledgment of pledges

Letters have also been prepared to be mailed on different dates to the advance pledge prospects and nonresident members. Two letters are suggested for the nonresident members: the first to include the Proposal and the second to enclose a pledge card. The other letters are for members of the organization.

Most church letters are too wordy. Keep yours short and concise. Use these tested letters.

To ensure thirty members being present at Resources Committee meeting, send this letter to sixty persons.

(*Smaller* churches may use committee of twenty members.)

Personally signed by minister.

Tuesday, Week 3

Dear Friend:

    Our church is planning a great forward step for next year. To aid us in doing so, we are forming a large Resources Committee to give us counsel. This group will meet only once, this Sunday afternoon, (month and date), at 3:00 P.M.

    You will help our church a great deal if you will be present.

Very sincerely,

Minister

To all members and friends of the church.
Use General chairman's personal letterhead.

                              Wednesday, Week 3

     Dear ____:

          On (Wednesday, Week 5), our church
     will meet in business session to discuss
     ideas for an enlarged ministry for the
     coming year. You will be thrilled to
     hear our plans to strengthen our church.
          Come and share your views. Kindly
     return the enclosed card for your dinner
     reservation. Dinner will be served at
     6:30 P.M.

                         Sincerely yours,

                         General Chairman
     Enclosure

     (Note: Enclose return postal card for
     dinner reservation.)

To all prospective members of the General Organization.
Type individually on church letterhead.

Friday, Week 4

Dear _____:

This year we are planning an unusually fine Every Member Enlistment. It will be done much more thoroughly than ever before and with the highest goal we have ever attempted. In order to assure the success of this challenging program, we need outstanding members of our congregation to give it leadership.

This year every home in our church will be visited. This will be possible only as we enlist a sufficient number of workers.

Last week a committee met and reviewed the entire membership list of our church. This committee has recommended your name as one who could add strength to this program. If called upon, I hope that you will find it possible to serve.

Sincerely yours,

Minister

To advance gift prospects and members of the General Organization selected thus far.

(Workers, who have not been chosen yet, should be mailed their copies of this letter and the printed Proposal by SATURDAY, Week 7.)

Type individually on General chairman's letterhead.

Saturday, Week 6

Dear ___:

Do you not agree that the enclosed Proposal for our church sets forth a program of which we can be proud? We believe we can do this job with the help of you and everyone.

The Finance Committee of our church is interested in making this one of our most significant years. The tools for doing this work will be supplied by our giving. You will want to have a real part in this worthy project.

A few of our homes will be visited between (Monday, Week 7 and Saturday, Week 8), in advance of our general solicitation. I know you will be giving thought to your share in this enlarged program. Your gift not only means the bringing of hope to many others at home and abroad, it also means an enriching of your own life.

Sincerely yours,

General Chairman

Enclosure:

(Note: Include a copy of the printed Proposal.)

To all advance pledge prospects and members of the General Organization.

                              Tuesday, Week 7

        Dear Friend:

            You and I--and the rest of our
        church members--are joined together in a
        wonderful fellowship. Ours is the privi-
        lege of worshipping God together, of
        holding up one another in sorrow and
        trial, of aiding others in our commu-
        nity. To a world enmeshed in fear and
        near-war we present the only everlasting
        hope for peace. A privilege and an op-
        portunity are ours as church members.
            We are now facing the future. Being
        dissatisfied with the past, we are de-
        termined to go out into larger fields of
        service. With your help--and the aid of
        all our members--we can realize our pro-
        posed new program. Your time, your pray-
        ers, your gifts are all essential.
            I pray that you may give in propor-
        tion to the great need and your ability.
        Our church desires to strengthen our
        witness for Christ in our community and
        around the world. With your help, we
        shall do so.

                          In His service,

                          Minister

        (Note: Enclose a tract on stewardship or
        missions in each letter.)

To all captains.

Churches using division leaders may adapt this letter to them, mailing it MONDAY, Week 4.

Thursday, Week 4

Dear ____:

    Thank you for agreeing to serve as a Captain in our forthcoming Every Member Enlistment. Yours is an important task, . involving

    1. The selection of four visitors to work under your supervision

    2. Seeing that these visitors attend the two training sessions

    3. Calling upon these four for their pledges

    4. Making certain that they complete all calls assigned to them

Your duty is not so much to make calls as to see that calls are made.

    I greatly appreciate your help.

Sincerely,

General Chairman

(see over)

K-57

P.S.

You will want to keep in mind these important dates:

(MONDAY, Week 5)--Captains meet at _____ _____ at ____ P.M. to select visitors

(WEDNESDAY, Week 5)--CONGREGATIONAL DINNER MEETING

(THURSDAY, Week 6)--Deadline for securing visitors

(SUNDAY, Week 8)--First visitors' training conference

(FRIDAY, Week 8)--Second visitors' training conference

(SUNDAY, Week 9)--11:00 Dedication Service

12:30 Luncheon and final instructions

2:30 Begin visitation

7:30 First report meeting

(WEDNESDAY, Week 9)--Second report meeting

(FRIDAY, Week 9)--Third report meeting

(SUNDAY, Week 10)--Fourth report meeting

(WEDNESDAY, Week 10)--Victory report meeting

To all visitors.

Wednesday, Week 7

Dear ___:

I am very happy to hear that you have agreed to serve as a visitor in our Every Member Enlistment. As you know, we are planning to have one of the most thorough visitations in the history of our church. Because the achievement of our goal will depend upon the leaders of our canvass, it is encouraging to know that you will be joining with us.

You will want to keep in mind the dates listed below. Your attendance at these meetings is very important.

Sincerely yours,

General Chairman

(SUNDAY, Week 8)--First visitors' training conference
(FRIDAY, Week 8)--Second visitors' training conference
(SUNDAY, Week 9)--11:00 Dedication Service
                12:30 Luncheon and final instructions
                2:30 Begin solicitation
                7:30 First report meeting
(WEDNESDAY, Week 9)--Second report meeting
(FRIDAY, Week 9)--Third report meeting
(SUNDAY, Week 10)--Fourth report meeting
(WEDNESDAY, Week 10)--Victory report meeting

K-59

To all prospects, omitting those who received Letters D and J.

Visitors who were not selected at the time Letter D was sent should receive their printed Proposals and copies of Letter D at the same time this letter is mailed to general prospects.

Type individually on General chairman's letterhead.

Saturday, Week 7

Dear ____:

On (SUNDAY, Week 9) we will take an important forward step as a church. In a spirit of consecration and worship we will dedicate ourselves to greater service for Christ during the coming year.

We hope that you will be present to join with us in this simple service. Although no financial commitments will be taken at that time, the occasion will inaugurate our Every Member Enlistment. This year our church has adopted two objectives:

  1. Every member pledging to local expenses and benevolences
  2. Every pledge increased

I am enclosing a copy of the proposed budget. It sets forth both needs and opportunities.

During the week starting (SUNDAY, Week 9), church visitors will call upon all members and friends to discuss our plans for the coming year. We invite you to consider prayerfully and earnestly your part in this enlarged program. Plan to be with us on Dedication Sunday. Let us together face the challenge which lies before our church.

Cordially yours,

General Chairman
Every Member Enlistment Committee

Enclosure

(Note: Enclose copy of printed Proposal.)

K-61

To all nonresident members.

Saturday, Week 7

Dear ____:

On (SUNDAY, Week 9), we are taking an important step forward as a church. In a spirit of consecration and worship we will dedicate ourselves to greater service for Christ during the coming year.
We wish it were possible for you to join with us in this inspiring service. If distance or travel prevents your being present, I hope you will remember your church in your prayers on that date. Although no financial commitments will be taken at that time, the occasion will inaugurate our Every Member Enlistment.
I am enclosing a copy of our proposed program for next year. We invite you to consider prayerfully and earnestly the part you will want to have in this enlarged work. At a later date we shall send you a pledge card. We covet your prayers as we enter this forward program.

Yours in Christ,

Minister

Enclosure

(Note: Enclose copy of printed Proposal.)

To all prospective givers, omitting those who received Letters E and L. Enclose a stewardship or missionary leaflet.

Wednesday, Week 8

Dear Friend:

After careful study by our church, we have undertaken a greatly increased program of service for the year ahead. We need to become stronger in our personal faith. We wish to make our Christian witness more effective. We desire more aggressive action against the ills in America and the world.

You can help us achieve our goal. It is my ardent hope that you will first pray and then that you will give in proportion to the need and to the extent of your ability. Your gift will help us build a more vital program for Jesus Christ.

A visitor from the church will shortly go into every home to discuss this matter with each one.

In His service,

Minister

Enclosure: Stewardship folder.

P.S. It is my earnest desire that each one will make a pledge both to local expenses and to benevolences.

To nonresident members.
Type individually on General chairman's letterhead.

Wednesday, Week 8

Dear _____:

I know that you will want to have a part in the Kingdom-building program which your church is planning for the coming year. The achievement of the goal set forth in our Proposal will mean increased service for Jesus Christ. We are proud that it represents both vision and faith.

This year, we have set for ourselves two goals:

1. Every member pledging to local expenses and benevolences
2. Every pledge increased

A pledge card and a self-addressed stamped envelope are enclosed for your use. Several weeks ago a group of representative members were asked to study independently the entire membership. Privately they wrote opposite each name what they thought that person might like to give in order to reach our high objective. The Resources chairman later calculated the average of those figures for each name. The total of the average figures is being used as the goal for our enlarged program.

Although some will not be in a position to give the suggested amount, others will want to do more. We feel you would appreciate securing this confidential information to guide you in thinking about your pledge. In your case the suggested amount averaged $_____ per week. Of course, what you wish to pledge

K-67

is entirely between you and God.

Thank you for your continued interest in our church. Thank you for your pledge.

Cordially yours,

General Chairman

Enclosures: Stewardship folder
Pledge card
Stamped envelope

P.S. If there is a church near your home in which you could become more active, we would be happy to forward your letter of transfer.

To all those who made pledges.
Type individually, using the church letterhead.

Friday, Week 10

Dear ____:

This is an expression of appreciation for your pledge in our Every Member Enlistment. You will be pleased to
know that our pledges will provide a
budget of $____. This will make possible
new avenues of service for God and man.
Ours will be a stronger church because
of your giving.

As chairman of our church enlistment, I should like to thank you for
your fine cooperation and for your gift,
which, according to our records, amounts
to:

$____ per week to local expenses
$____ per week to benevolences

If these figures are incorrect, please
notify me or the financial secretary.

With sincere appreciation,

General Chairman

Dear Member of _____ Church:

The last month has been a rich one in the life of our church. Because of the new interest aroused by our Every Member Enlistment we have made several forward steps.

A new men's club has been organized.

We now have a new youth leader who is spending each week end with us to guide our young people's work.

Four new members have been received.

Work has begun on our organ, and we have let contracts to remodel and paint the kitchen.

As soon as funds are available, we shall begin to transform the old storage room into a modern nursery.

Thank you for your part in all this advance.

                      Sincerely yours,

                      Minister

P.S. We are enclosing a statement to each member. If there is any error, kindly notify our financial secretary.

Collection letter 2

Dear Fellow Member:

Pleasant Street Church is on the march! Everywhere there is a new spirit evident.

Our morning congregations are the largest in years, and Sunday School attendance is up. The new men's club is planning a full year's activities.

Have you heard our organ since it was overhauled? Our choir is larger. The music is inspiring.

Soon our kitchen will be ready for use. And within two weeks we shall begin work on our new nursery.

Our members have given well. Thank you for your part.

Sincerely,

General Chairman

P.S. Our books read as follows for your giving record. If incorrect, kindly notify me:

    Amount pledged for two months $_____
    Amount paid for two months $_____

Collection letter 3

Dear Member:

    We are indeed grateful for the way
God is blessing our church.

    Last Sunday, despite the heavy rain,
there were _____ persons present at our
worship service. Because of increased
Sunday School attendance we have added
two new teachers to our Junior Department. They are Viola and Gordon Lee.

    Next Wednesday we shall hold our
monthly parish supper and family night.
Return the enclosed postal for your
reservation. There will be a surprise
feature!

    The visitors who called during our
Every Member Enlistment have asked that
they be allowed to do some friendly
visiting. So beginning next Monday they
will visit every home urging all members
to attend church during the next six
weeks.

    Our new nursery opened last Sunday.
Five babies were present. This is our
fastest growing department.

                Cordially yours,

                Minister

P.S. **Our financial** secretary will fill
out **the next two lines.** If incorrect,
kindly **notify** _____.
    Amount pledged for _____ weeks $____
    Amount received for _____ weeks $____

4. ANALYSES OF RESULTS

Best results will be obtained from using the ten steps if careful records are kept, both in setting up the campaign and in following through the next twelve months. Reliable records will reveal weak spots and provide an invaluable foundation for the next year's enlistment.

The minister or General chairman should ask a member who delights in statistical studies to fill in the following forms as completely as possible. When finished, these forms should be presented, with explanations, to the Finance Committee. You need be careful, however, of what figures you publish, printing nothing that would give comfort to anyone who pledges less than his share. All figures printed for broad distribution must be so presented as to encourage all to do better.

Keep full and accurate records. They will show you where you need to concentrate your efforts. Publicity given to some of these records will help your members to feel that they know what is going on. Knowledge plus concern will make them receptive to the plans the Finance Committee will present.

Analysis 1

The purpose of this analysis is to compare the potential of your church with the actual. Where are your untapped resources? How successful are you in utilizing your full strength year by year? Use the following form for your church:

Our Pledging Constituency

1. Total membership____
2. Resident membership____
3. Nonresident or inactive____
4. Total number of families____
5. Total number of resident families____
6. Number of friends (from whom some support might be expected)____

	Last year 195__	This year Goal	This year Actual
Local expense			
7. Number of pledges received	____	____	____
Renewed	____	____	____
New	____	____	____
8. Number of members represented	____	____	____
Benevolence			
9. Number of pledges received	____	____	____
Renewed	____	____	____
New	____	____	____
10. Number of members represented	____	____	____
Total			
11. Number of pledges received	____	____	____
Renewed	____	____	____
New	____	____	____
12. Number of members represented	____	____	____
13. Analysis of pledges:			
Number of adult member pledges	____	____	____
Number of nonresident member pledges	____	____	____
Number of youth member pledges	____	____	____
Number of youth nonmember pledges	____	____	____
Number of adult nonmember pledges	____	____	____
Total number of pledges	____	____	____
To be cultivated			
14. Number of families not pledging:			
Local expenses	____	____	____
Benevolences	____	____	____

Note: *Last year* represents the year you are now in. *This year* represents your next campaign.

Analysis 2

The purpose of this analysis is to see where your money comes from. Study of these categories may reveal gaps or weaknesses that could be remedied in your next enlistment.

A typical analysis is that made by the First Baptist Church of Providence, Rhode Island.

	Total Pledging		Per cent increase
	1952	1953	
Advance pledges	$4,345	$6,034	39
Workers	3,458	5,405	56
Resident members	3,943	6,440	63
Nonresident and friends	177	696	293
Total	$11,923	$18,575	56

Use the following form for your church:

Analysis of Pledges by Categories

	Last year 195__	This year		Per cent increase
		Goal	Actual	
1. Advance pledges (exclusive of 2)	$	$	$	
2. Workers in canvass	$	$	$	
3. Resident members (exclusive of 1 and 2)	$	$	$	
4. Nonresident and friends	$	$	$	
Total	$	$	$	

Analysis 3

The purpose of this analysis is to point out how many new and increased pledges may be obtained. The First Baptist Church of Providence analyzed their new and old pledges as follows:

| | Number of pledges | | | | Change in year | | |
| | Local expense | | Benevolence | | | | |
	1952	1953	1952	1953	New	Increase	Decrease
Resident members	174	223	97	119	49	181	11
Nonresident and friends	9	27	6	14	18	21	
Total	183	250	103	133	67	202	11

Harold Semple made the following analysis of the results of thirty-four churches in the 1952 United Church Canvass of Rhode Island. Especially noteworthy are the number of new and increased pledges:

| Envelope receipts | Total pledges | Number of pledges | | Number of 1953 pledges | | |
1952	1953	1952	1953	New	Increased	Decreased
$384,901	$529,724	7,603	8,192	1,310	2,650	367

Use the following forms for your church:

Pledges, Old and New

	Number of old and new pledges				
	Last year		This year		
	195__		Goal	Actual	
	Old	New	New	Old	New
Local expense					
Resident members	———	———	———	———	———
Nonresident and friends	———	———	———	———	———
Total	———	———	———	———	———
Benevolence					
Resident members	———	———	———	———	———
Nonresident and friends	———	———	———	———	———
Total	———	———	———	———	———

Analysis 3 (*Continued*)

NOTE: In the average church only two out of every three families pledge to local expenses and only one of every three to benevolences. This form will analyze your present standing and help you set a goal for your next campaign. Suggestion: Set a goal of reducing by one-half the number of families who are not today pledging.

Value of New and Increased Pledges in Next Enlistment, 19___

	Number of new pledges	Amount of new money pledged
Local expense	____	$____
Benevolence	____	____
	Total	$____

	Number of increased pledges	
Local expense	____	$____
Benevolence	____	____
	Total	$____

	Number of decreased pledges	
Local expense	____	$____
Benevolence	____	____
	Total	$____
	Net Increase	$____

Analysis 4

The purpose of this analysis is to determine the value of different types of pledges and the value of making home calls.

The thirty churches in the Boston pilot project of 1951 revealed the following facts:

Average value of each advance pledge	$176
Average value of all pledges	$ 72
Average value of each call made in home	$ 53

Use the following form for your church:

Value of Average Pledge by Categories

1. Value of average advance pledge (excluding canvass workers):
   Total pledged by advance pledgers $____
   Number of advance pledges ____
   Average value of each advance pledge $____
2. Value of average worker's pledge:
   Total pledged by workers $____
   Number of workers' pledges ____
   Average value of workers' pledges $____
3. Value of resident member's pledge (exclusive of above two groups):
   Total pledged by residents $____
   Number of resident pledges ____
   Average value of resident pledges $____
4. Value of nonresident and friend's pledge:
   Total pledged by nonresidents and friends $____
   Number of nonresident and friends' pledges ____
   Average value of nonresident and friends' pledges $____
5. Value of over-all average pledge:
   Grand total pledged by everyone $____
   Total number of pledges ____
   Average value of all pledges $____
6. Value of each home call:
   Grand total pledged by everyone $____
   Total calls made (include both pledges and refusals) ____
   Average value of each home call $____

Analysis 5

The purpose of this analysis is to discover how your people give. A study of the pledges made in five churches in Massachusetts revealed this picture. In this random sample at least two of the churches had prided themselves on their financial canvasses. Since many members did not pledge, the actual state was even worse than the following figures:

	Total pledges	Distribution of pledges		
Type of church	received	5 to 50 cents	55 cents to $1	Over $1
1. Mill town	83	55%	26%	19%
2. City (lower middle class)	92	41	34	25
3. Downtown	479	69	16	15
4. Suburban	507	44	33	23
5. City (upper middle class)	634	50	31	19
Average for the five		52	28	20

Any church that has only 20 per cent of its pledgers giving more than one dollar a week is in a poor spiritual condition. Finance committees should work on the assumption—publicly expressed—that one dollar a week per adult income is the minimum for respectable giving.

Use the following form for your church:

How Our People Pledge. The following analysis should be made for adult pledges only. All those without regular and adequate income (such as school pupils and those living on small pensions) should be eliminated for the purposes of this study.

	Number of pledges		
	Last year	This year	
Amount of weekly pledge	195__	Goal	Actual
5 to 50 cents	____	____	____
55 cents to $1.00	____	____	____
$1.10 to $4.95	____	____	____
$5.00 to $9.95	____	____	____
$10.00 and up	____	____	____

Analysis 6

The purpose of this analysis is to reveal both the number of persons who refuse to sign a pledge and the number of homes which do not receive a call during the enlistment.

The First Baptist Church of Pittsfield, Maine, reported:

"We had 154 names to call on, and since starting have added 26 more (due to great interest taken by visitors, they have increased number wanting to pledge). Of the total 180 pledge cards only 16 refused to sign, which is remarkable. Our record of $4,371 is $1,200 more than we ever pledged before. Attendance and income have already started to increase."

Leigh T. Shorey,
Twin Elms Dairy

The Pawtucket Congregational Church (Rhode Island) gave the phenomenal report that in their second year of using the ten-step program they obtained 378 pledges from 378 calls.

Fill in the following blanks for your church:

Pledges and Refusals

	Total number of calls to be made	Number of completed calls	Number of pledges	Number of refusals	Number of incompleted calls
Last year, 19—	___	___	___	___	___
This year, 19—	___	___	___	___	___

Analysis 7

This analysis is designed to aid your church in following up its enlistment. Many extra dollars for the Kingdom will be won as a careful follow-up is carried out.

Use the following form for your church:

Follow-up of Calls. The following persons stated that they might give later. They should be called on about as follows:

Name	Address	Date to be called on	Name of original visitor

4. CALENDARS

Separate calendars for each of the six chairmen are on the following pages. It is suggested that each chairman make his own notations in the calendar squares or in the margins.

1. MASTER TIME SCHEDULE

MASTER TIME SCHEDULE

Detailed information for all canvass activities is found in the chairmen's chapters of this book.

Insert the proper date in the upper right-hand corner of each calendar square.

	SUNDAY	MONDAY	TUESDAY	WEDNESDAY	THURSDAY	FRIDAY	SATURDAY
WEEK 1		MINISTER SELECTS GENERAL CHAIRMAN USE CHECK LIST 1	MINISTER AND CHAIRMAN APPROVE CALENDAR		GENERAL CHAIRMAN SELECTS COMMITTEE CHAIRMEN	FORMS B & C MIMEOGRAPHED	
WEEK 2	MINISTER GIVES NAME OF GENERAL CHAIRMAN AND STATEMENT ON ENLARGED PROGRAM FORM B DISTRIBUTED	FIRST MEETING OF GENERAL COMMITTEE. CO-CHAIRMEN SELECT COMMITTEES	ORDER CANVASS MATERIALS	PUBLICITY CHAIRMAN PREPARES APPRAISAL LIST SEE FORM D	MAKE ARRANGEMENTS FOR PRINTING PROPOSAL USE CHECK LIST 2	PUBLICITY CHAIRMAN SECURES PROFESSIONAL PHOTOGRAPHER FOR SUNDAY, WEEK 4	
WEEK 3	FIRST MEETING OF PROPOSAL COMMITTEE	MIMEOGRAPH 50 COPIES OF APPRAISAL LIST	SELECT DIVISION LEADERS MINISTER MAILS LETTER A	GENERAL CHAIRMAN MAILS LETTER B		SECOND MEETING OF PROPOSAL COMMITTEE	
WEEK 4	PHOTOGRAPHS TAKEN FOR USE IN PRINTED PROPOSAL RESOURCES COMMITTEE MEETS	RESOURCES CHAIRMAN TABULATES AVERAGES SELECT CAPTAINS	REVIEW COMMITTEE MEETS TO STUDY APPRAISAL	THIRD MEETING OF PROPOSAL COMMITTEE PUBLICITY CHAIRMAN PREPARES LEADERSHIP CARDS	BEGIN MASTER LIST GENERAL CHAIRMAN MAILS LETTER F USE CHECK LIST 3	TELEPHONE SQUAD MEETS MAIL LETTER C	PUBLICITY COMMITTEE TELEPHONES MEMBERS ABOUT CONGREGATIONAL DINNER.
WEEK 5	JOINT MEETING OF PROPOSAL COMMITTEE & RESOURCES CHAIRMAN PREPARE FORM G	PROPOSAL AND RESOURCES CHAIRMEN MEET WITH CHURCH COUNCIL CAPTAINS MEET TO SELECT WORKERS.		CONGREGATIONAL DINNER MEETING	DELIVER COPY FOR PRINTED PROPOSAL TO PRINTER, USING FORMS G AND H	DEADLINE FOR SECURING ADVANCE PLEDGE COMMITTEE	MINISTER AND GENERAL CHAIRMAN SIGN PLEDGES

WEEK							
6	MINISTER BEGINS USING STEWARDSHIP EMPHASIS IN SERVICES / ADVANCE PLEDGE COMMITTEE MEETS	GENERAL CHAIRMAN CALLS ON ALL MEMBERS OF GENERAL COMMITTEE FOR THEIR PLEDGES	ADVANCE PLEDGE CHAIRMAN CALLS ON ALL HIS COMMITTEE FOR THEIR PLEDGES		DEADLINE FOR SECURING VISITORS / USE CHECK LIST 4	PICK UP PROPOSALS AND PLEDGE CARDS BEGIN TYPING PLEDGE CARDS	PROPOSALS MAILED TO ADVANCE PLEDGE PROSPECTS WITH LETTER D
7	ADVANCE PLEDGE COMMITTEE MEETS FOR INSTRUCTION AND SELECTION OF CARDS	ADVANCE PLEDGE SOLICITATION BEGINS	MAIL LETTER E	MAIL LETTER G		FIRST ADVANCE PLEDGE REPORT	MAIL LETTERS H AND J AND PRINTED PROPOSALS TO ALL PROSPECTS
8	FIRST WORKERS' TRAINING CONFERENCE	BEGIN SOLICITATION OF WORKERS		MAIL LETTERS K AND L	USE CHECK LIST 5	SECOND WORKERS' TRAINING CONFERENCE / ADVANCE PLEDGE FINAL REPORT	PUBLICITY COMMITTEE BUILDS UP ATTENDANCE FOR DEDICATION SUNDAY / FILL IN MASTER LIST
9	11:00 SPECIAL SERMON AND DEDICATION SERVICE 12:30 WORKERS' LUNCH FIRST REPORT MEETING			SECOND REPORT MEETING		THIRD REPORT MEETING	
10	FOURTH REPORT MEETING			VICTORY REPORT MEETING / GENERAL COMMITTEE MEETS TO EVALUATE CANVASS AND PLAN FOLLOW-UP		MAIL LETTER M / PLAN COLLECTION PROGRAM	

K-89

2. TIME SCHEDULE FOR PROPOSAL CHAIRMAN

PROPOSAL CHAIRMAN

For detailed information consult the "Important Dates" for the Proposal Chairman" in this chapter.

Insert the proper date in the upper right-hand corner of each calendar square.

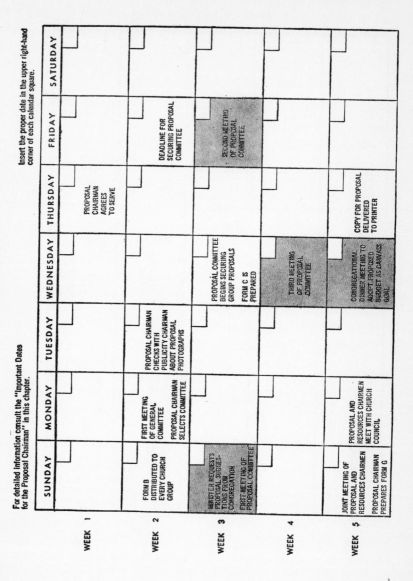

	SUNDAY	MONDAY	TUESDAY	WEDNESDAY	THURSDAY	FRIDAY	SATURDAY
WEEK 1	FORM B DISTRIBUTED TO EVERY CHURCH GROUP	FIRST MEETING OF GENERAL COMMITTEE					
WEEK 2	MINISTER REQUESTS PROPOSAL SUGGESTIONS FROM CONGREGATION	PROPOSAL CHAIRMAN SELECTS COMMITTEE	PROPOSAL CHAIRMAN CHECKS WITH PUBLICITY CHAIRMAN ABOUT PROPOSAL PHOTOGRAPHS		PROPOSAL CHAIRMAN AGREES TO SERVE		
WEEK 3	FIRST MEETING OF PROPOSAL COMMITTEE			PROPOSAL COMMITTEE BEGINS SECURING GROUP PROPOSALS FORM C IS PREPARED		DEADLINE FOR SECURING PROPOSAL COMMITTEE	
WEEK 4				THIRD MEETING OF PROPOSAL COMMITTEE		SECOND MEETING OF PROPOSAL COMMITTEE	
WEEK 5	JOINT MEETING OF PROPOSAL AND RESOURCES CHAIRMEN PROPOSAL CHAIRMAN PREPARES FORM G	PROPOSAL AND RESOURCES CHAIRMEN MEET WITH CHURCH COUNCIL		CONGREGATIONAL DINNER MEETING TO ADOPT PROPOSED BUDGET AS CANVASS GOAL	COPY FOR PROPOSAL DELIVERED TO PRINTER		

K-92

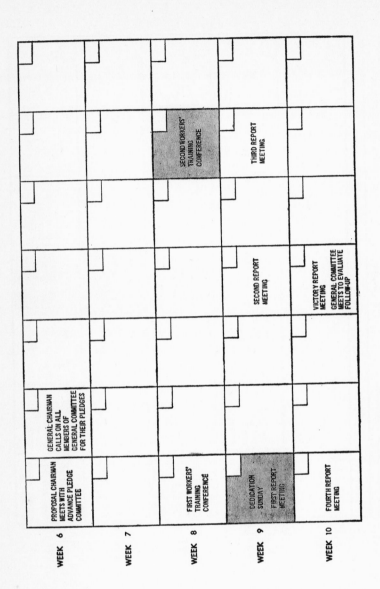

WEEK 6 — PROPOSAL CHAIRMAN MEETS WITH ADVANCE PLEDGE COMMITTEE / GENERAL CHAIRMAN CALLS ON ALL MEMBERS OF GENERAL COMMITTEE FOR THEIR PLEDGES

WEEK 7

WEEK 8 — FIRST WORKERS' TRAINING CONFERENCE / SECOND WORKERS' TRAINING CONFERENCE

WEEK 9 — DEDICATION SUNDAY / FIRST REPORT MEETING / SECOND REPORT MEETING / THIRD REPORT MEETING

WEEK 10 — FOURTH REPORT MEETING / VICTORY REPORT MEETING / GENERAL COMMITTEE MEETS TO EVALUATE FOLLOW-UP

3. TIME SCHEDULE FOR RESOURCES CHAIRMAN

For detailed information consult the "Important Dates for the Resources Chairman" in this chapter.

Insert the proper date in the upper right-hand corner of each calendar square.

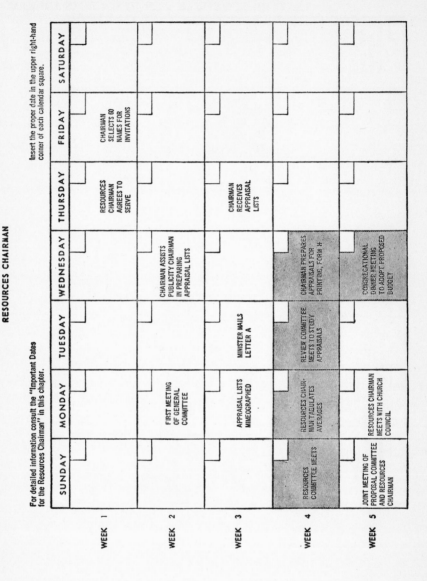

	SUNDAY	MONDAY	TUESDAY	WEDNESDAY	THURSDAY	FRIDAY	SATURDAY
WEEK 1					RESOURCES CHAIRMAN AGREES TO SERVE	CHAIRMAN SELECTS 60 NAMES FOR INVITATIONS	
WEEK 2		FIRST MEETING OF GENERAL COMMITTEE		CHAIRMAN ASSISTS PUBLICITY CHAIRMAN IN PREPARING APPRAISAL LISTS			
WEEK 3		APPRAISAL LISTS MIMEOGRAPHED	MINISTER MAILS LETTER A		CHAIRMAN RECEIVES APPRAISAL LISTS		
WEEK 4	RESOURCES COMMITTEE MEETS	RESOURCES CHAIRMAN TABULATES AVERAGES	REVIEW COMMITTEE MEETS TO STUDY APPRAISALS	CHAIRMAN PREPARES APPRAISALS FOR PRINTING, FORM H			
WEEK 5	JOINT MEETING OF PROPOSAL COMMITTEE AND RESOURCES CHAIRMAN	RESOURCES CHAIRMAN MEETS WITH CHURCH COUNCIL		CONGREGATIONAL DINNER MEETING TO ADOPT PROPOSED BUDGET			

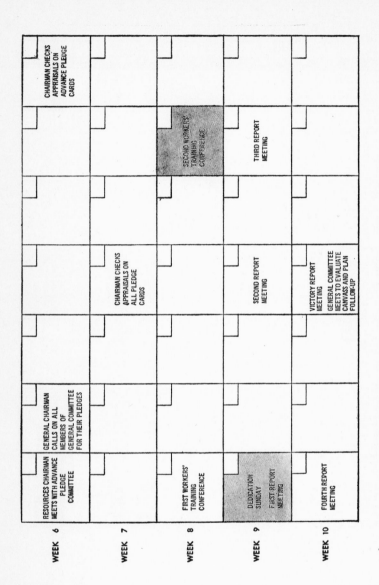

WEEK 6	RESOURCES CHAIRMAN MEETS WITH ADVANCE PLEDGE COMMITTEE	GENERAL CHAIRMAN CALLS ON ALL MEMBERS OF GENERAL COMMITTEE FOR THEIR PLEDGES					CHAIRMAN CHECKS APPRAISALS ON ADVANCE PLEDGE CARDS
WEEK 7			CHAIRMAN CHECKS APPRAISALS ON ALL PLEDGE CARDS				
WEEK 8	FIRST WORKERS' TRAINING CONFERENCE				SECOND WORKERS' TRAINING CONFERENCE		
WEEK 9	DEDICATION SUNDAY FIRST REPORT MEETING		SECOND REPORT MEETING		THIRD REPORT MEETING		
WEEK 10	FOURTH REPORT MEETING		VICTORY REPORT MEETING GENERAL COMMITTEE MEETS TO EVALUATE CANVASS AND PLAN FOLLOW-UP				

K-97

4. TIME SCHEDULE FOR PUBLICITY CHAIRMAN

TIME SCHEDULE

PUBLICITY CHAIRMAN

For detailed information consult the "Important Dates for the Publicity Chairman" in this chapter.

Insert the proper date in the upper right-hand corner of each calendar square.

	SUNDAY	MONDAY	TUESDAY	WEDNESDAY	THURSDAY	FRIDAY	SATURDAY
WEEK 1					PUBLICITY CHAIRMAN AGREES TO SERVE	FORMS B & C MIMEOGRAPHED	
WEEK 2		FIRST MEETING OF GENERAL COMMITTEE / SELECT MEMBERS OF PUBLICITY COMMITTEE	ORDER CANVASS MATERIALS	PREPARE APPRAISAL LIST SEE FORM D	MAKE ARRANGEMENTS FOR PRINTING PROPOSAL	SECURE PROFESSIONAL PHOTOGRAPHER FOR SUNDAY, WEEK 4	
WEEK 3	PLAN FOR PICTURES FOR NEXT SUNDAY	MIMEOGRAPH 50 COPIES OF APPRAISAL LIST	MAIL LETTER A	MAIL LETTER B	REMIND PHOTO-GRAPHER ABOUT SUNDAY PICTURES		
WEEK 4	PHOTOGRAPHS TAKEN	PHOTOGRAPHS RECEIVED FROM PHOTOGRAPHER		PREPARE LEADERSHIP CARDS / GIVE PHOTOGRAPHS TO PRINTER	BEGIN MASTER LIST / MAIL LETTER F	TELEPHONE SQUAD MEETS / MAIL LETTER G	TELEPHONE SQUAD CALLS ALL MEMBERS ABOUT CONGREGA-TIONAL DINNER
WEEK 5	PREPARE FORMS G & H FOR PRINTER	MEET WITH CHURCH COUNCIL		CONGREGATIONAL DINNER MEETING TO ADOPT PROPOSED BUDGET AS CANVASS GOAL	DELIVER COPY FOR PROPOSAL AND PLEDGE CARDS TO PRINTER, USING FORMS G AND H	ADDRESS PROPOSAL ENVELOPES	

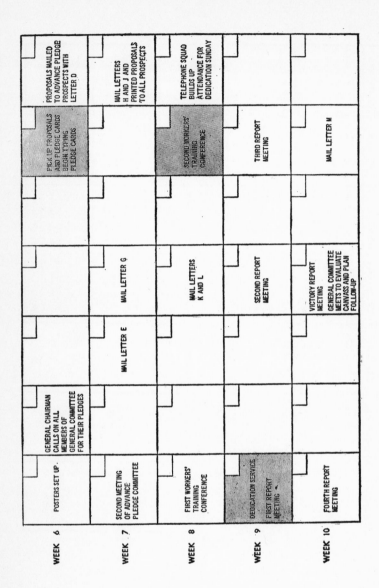

WEEK 6 POSTERS SET UP	GENERAL CHAIRMAN CALLS ON ALL MEMBERS OF GENERAL COMMITTEE FOR THEIR PLEDGES				PICK UP PROPOSALS AND PLEDGE CARDS BEGIN TYPING PLEDGE CARDS	PROPOSALS MAILED TO ADVANCE PLEDGE PROSPECTS WITH LETTER D
WEEK 7 SECOND MEETING OF ADVANCE PLEDGE COMMITTEE		MAIL LETTER E	MAIL LETTER G			MAIL LETTERS H AND J AND PRINTED PROPOSALS TO ALL PROSPECTS
WEEK 8 FIRST WORKERS' TRAINING CONFERENCE			MAIL LETTERS K AND L		SECOND WORKERS' TRAINING CONFERENCE	TELEPHONE SQUAD BUILDS UP ATTENDANCE FOR DEDICATION SUNDAY
WEEK 9 DEDICATION SERVICE FIRST REPORT MEETING			SECOND REPORT MEETING		THIRD REPORT MEETING	
WEEK 10 FOURTH REPORT MEETING		VICTORY REPORT MEETING GENERAL COMMITTEE MEETS TO EVALUATE CANVASS AND PLAN FOLLOW-UP		MAIL LETTER M		

K-101

5. TIME SCHEDULE FOR ADVANCE PLEDGE CHAIRMAN

TIME SCHEDULE

ADVANCE PLEDGE CHAIRMAN

For detailed information consult the "Important Dates for the Advance Pledge Chairman" in this chapter.

Insert the proper date in the upper right-hand corner of each calendar square.

	SUNDAY	MONDAY	TUESDAY	WEDNESDAY	THURSDAY	FRIDAY	SATURDAY
WEEK 1					ADVANCE PLEDGE CHAIRMAN AGREES TO SERVE		
WEEK 2		FIRST MEETING OF GENERAL COMMITTEE	ADVANCE PLEDGE CHAIRMAN BEGINS SECURING HIS COMMITTEE				
WEEK 3	MEETING OF RESOURCES COMMITTEE						
WEEK 4			MEETING OF REVIEW COMMITTEE		ADVANCE PLEDGE CHAIRMAN, GENERAL CHAIRMAN, RESOURCE CHAIRMAN AND PASTOR SELECT ADVANCE PLEDGE PROSPECTS		SECURE REST OF ADVANCE PLEDGE COMMITTEE
WEEK 5		CHAIRMAN MEETS WITH CHURCH COUNCIL		CONGREGATIONAL DINNER MEETING TO ADOPT PROPOSED BUDGET AS CANVASS GOAL		DEADLINE FOR SECURING ADVANCE PLEDGE COMMITTEE	REMIND COMMITTEE OF MEETING TOMORROW

K-104

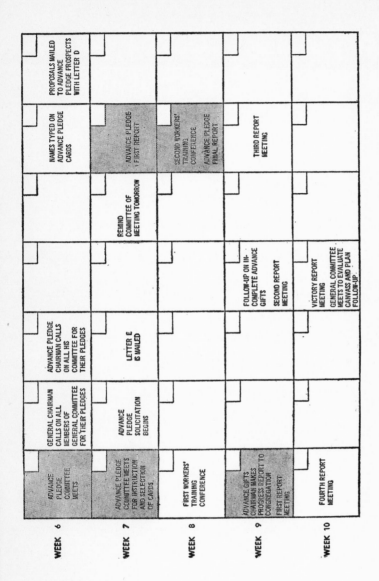

6. TIME SCHEDULE FOR ORGANIZATION CHAIRMAN

TIME SCHEDULE

ORGANIZATION CHAIRMAN

For detailed information, consult the "Important Dates for the Organization Chairman" in this and following chapters.

Insert the proper date in the upper right-hand corner of each calendar square.

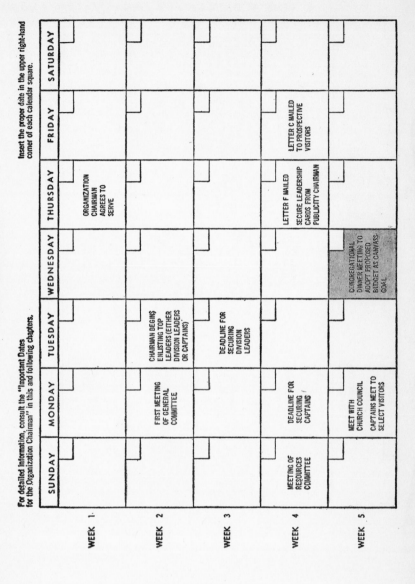

	SUNDAY	MONDAY	TUESDAY	WEDNESDAY	THURSDAY	FRIDAY	SATURDAY
WEEK 1					ORGANIZATION CHAIRMAN AGREES TO SERVE		
WEEK 2	MEETING OF RESOURCES COMMITTEE	FIRST MEETING OF GENERAL COMMITTEE	CHAIRMAN BEGINS ENLISTING TOP LEADERS (EITHER DIVISION LEADERS OR CAPTAINS)				
WEEK 3		DEADLINE FOR SECURING CAPTAINS	DEADLINE FOR SECURING DIVISION LEADERS				
WEEK 4		MEET WITH CHURCH COUNCIL			LETTER F MAILED SECURE LEADERSHIP CARDS FROM PUBLICITY CHAIRMAN		
WEEK 5		CAPTAINS MEET TO SELECT VISITORS		CONGREGATIONAL DINNER MEETING TO ADOPT PROPOSED BUDGET AS CANVASS GOAL		LETTER C MAILED TO PROSPECTIVE VISITORS	

K-108

WEEK 6		GENERAL CHAIRMAN CALLS ON ALL MEMBERS OF GENERAL COMMITTEE FOR THEIR PLEDGES		ORGANIZATION CHAIRMAN CALLS ON DIVISION LEADERS FOR THEIR PLEDGES (IN CHURCHES OF 500+ MEMBERS)	DEADLINE FOR SECURING VISITORS MEET WITH DIVISION LEADERS AND CAPTAINS		
WEEK 7		CAPTAINS CALLED ON FOR PLEDGES, EITHER BY CHAIRMAN OR BY DIVISION LEADERS		LETTER G MAILED TO ALL WORKERS		TELEPHONE CHECK FOR ATTENDANCE AT FIRST WORKERS' TRAINING CONFERENCE	
WEEK 8	FIRST WORKERS' TRAINING CONFERENCE	CAPTAINS BEGIN CALLING ON VISITORS		CHAIRMAN CHECKS PROGRESS OF CALLING ON VISITORS	DEADLINE FOR SECURING PLEDGES OF VISITORS	SECOND WORKERS' TRAINING CONFERENCE FOR ALL MEMBERS OF CANVASS ORGANIZATION	ASSIST GENERAL CHAIRMAN IN FILLING IN MASTER LIST
WEEK 9	11:00 SPECIAL SERMON & DEDICATION SERV. 12:30 WORKERS' LUNCH 2:30 SOLICITATION BEGINS 7:30 FIRST REPORT MEETING			SECOND REPORT MEETING		THIRD REPORT MEETING	
WEEK 10	FOURTH REPORT MEETING			VICTORY REPORT MEETING GENERAL COMMITTEE MEETS TO EVALUATE CANVASS AND PLAN FOLLOW-UP			